In the same series

Argentina	Denmark	Japan	South Africa
Australia	Ecuador	Korea	Spain
Austria	Egypt	Laos	Sri Lanka
Belgium	Finland	Malaysia	Sweden
Bolivia	France	Mauritius	Switzerland
Borneo	Germany	Mexico	Syria
Brazil	Greece	Morocco	Taiwan
Britain	Hong Kong	Myanmar	Thailand
California	Hungary	Nepal	Turkey
Canada	India	Netherlands	UAE
Chile	Indonesia	Norway	Ukraine
China	Iran	Pakistan	USA
Costa Rica	Ireland	Philippines	USA—The South
Cuba	Israel	Scotland	Venezuela
Czech Republic	Italy	Singapore	Vietnam

Living & Working Abroad: Barcelona	Living & Working Abroad: Moscow	A Globe-Trotter's Guide
Living & Working Abroad: Beijing	Living & Working Abroad: Munich	A Parent's Guide A Student's Guide
Living & Working Abroad: Chicago	Living & Working Abroad: New York	A Traveller's Medical Guide
Living & Working Abroad: Havana	Living & Working Abroad: Paris	A Wife's Guide Living & Working Abroad
Living & Working Abroad: Jakarta	Living & Working Abroad: Rome	Personal Protection At Home and Abroad
Living & Working in Kuala Lumpur	Living & Working Abroad: San Francisco	Working Holidays Abroad
Living & Working Abroad: London	Living & Working Abroad: Tokyo	

Illustrations by TRIGG

Published by Times Books International
an imprint of Times Media Private Limited
Times Centre, 1 New Industrial Road, Singapore 536196.
Tel: (65) 2139288 Fax: (65) 2854871 Email: te@tpl.com.sg
Online Bookstore: www.timesone.com.sg/te

Times Subang
Lot 46, Subang Hi-Tech Industrial Park, Batu Tiga, 40000 Shah Alam,
Selangor Darul Ehsan, Malaysia
Tel & Fax: (603) 56363517 Email: cchong@tpg.com.my

Printed in Singapore

ISBN 981 232 542 5

National Library Board (Singapore) Cataloguing in Publication Data

Morimoto-Yoshida, Yuko.
Living & working abroad : in Tokyo / Yuko Morimoto-Yoshida.
– Singapore : Times Books International, c2003.
p. cm. — (Culture shock!)

ISBN : 981-232-542-5
1. Tokyo (Japan) — Social life and customs.
2. Tokyo (Japan) — Guidebooks.
I. Title. II. Series: Culture shock!

DS896.38   952.135 — dc21   SLS2003004240

CONTENTS

MAP OF JAPAN

N

Hokkaido

Sea of Japan

Honshu

Tokyo

Nagoya

Osaka

Shikoku

Izu Islands

Kyushu

Pacific Ocean

Ogasawara Islands

Okinawa Islands

ACKNOWLEDGEMENTS

This book could not have been completed without the help and support of many people. Especially, I owe greatly to the following people and would like to express my sincere appreciation to them.

First and foremost, I would like to thank Lynn Witham, who was courageous enough to suggest me as an author for this book, and who supported me in every step of the creation process from drafting to editing to completion. We discussed ideas openly, and she provided continuous moral support. This would never have come to pass without her.

I received much support from Kay Jones who edited several drafts and offered valuable feedback on many topics. Together with Anthony Pan, she enhanced the focus and readability of the sections on history and religion. Tony also gave generously of his time for reviewing and editing the final drafts. Their knowledge and insights about Japanese culture were just impressive.

Other fellow interculturalists based in the San Francisco area and who have extensive experience with Japan offered ideas and insights about the unique features of Tokyo. Masahiro Shintani, a Tokyoite himself, was always gracious in answering questions about deep issues, and Chris Brannen shared thoughts and impressions. Dave Dickey and others at Meridian Resources were particularly good sports in offering their observations and intuition.

Kristy Buckingham is owed great thanks for being the first reader of the draft and for diligently editing what now seems like just a rough sketch.

As for the Japanese support crew, I am especially grateful to Masazumi Akita who kept me informed on current events and trends in Tokyo and who introduced me to a wonderful photographer, Akiko Watanabe. Watanabe-san wandered around every corner of Tokyo in search of good photo opportunities, and the results of her efforts are included in this book. Shu Ikkatai offered some photographs as well, which were much appreciated.

In addition, I wish to express gratitude to the expatriates in Tokyo who shared with me their experiences of living in the city. Their comments and stories added depth to the content of the book. Thanks are due to friends and friends of friends who referred me to these expatriates.

Hosts of other people were gracious in suggesting ideas, giving information, and encouraging me in many ways. Finally I would like to thank my family for their continuous support and encouragement during this entire adventure.

Yuko Morimoto-Yoshida

INTRODUCTION

Tokyo is a place of continuous renewal. Its landscape has been altered several times during the course of its history by fire, war, or natural disaster – but the people of Tokyo ("Tokyoites") have turned each occasion into an opportunity for rebirth, and the metropolis has bounced back bigger and better than before. Even during the two centuries when Japan was technically closed off to foreigners and travel within the country was somewhat restricted, people of the capital eagerly adopted any new trends in thought, technology, and fashion to which they were exposed. Still today Tokyoites are attentive to changing trends and eager to latch onto them. To fall behind would be unbearable. However, they are apt to grow weary of new trends quickly, and constantly seek new targets for their attention.

What are the origins of this ability to recover from adversity and this appetite and passion for things new? Perhaps they come from deep within ancient Japanese traditions. Shinto, the country's indigenous belief system, offers the idea that destruction and rebuilding are rites of purification, like a cleansing of the soul. Buddhism, a religion introduced to Japan from China, offers the idea that life is transitory, so people should not get too attached to the things of everyday life. To this day, Tokyoites appreciate traditional but fleeting seasonal events, and participate in a variety of rituals and celebrations with ancient roots – all with the latest technical gadgets tucked away in their pockets.

This contradicting, unique character of the society can be better experienced by people who live in Tokyo than by those who simply visit. Residents can easily see what is the leading trend. People dress according to the latest fashion style; "in" restaurants and entertainment spots come and go; the latest electronic gadgets rapidly sell off the shelves; popular actors and actresses appear in every magazine and television show. When one trend changes everyone shifts to the new one. At the same time, enjoyment of seasonal events gives rhythm to people's lives and participation in traditional rituals and celebrations connects them with the past. In time, newcomers learn to appreciate both the subtle and not-so-subtle contrasts of this ambivalent culture; this appreciation is a sure sign that Tokyo has become home.

Author's Notes

As you read through this book, please note the following:

- Throughout the book, Japanese words are written in *romaji* (Japanese words transcribed into the English alphabet; also known as "romanization").
- The prices mentioned in this book are estimates and are generally stated in Japanese yen.
- Many of the resources listed in this book include website addresses, all of which have English-language pages. If you go to these websites and encounter a Japanese-language home page, though, please be patient – look for a little icon that says "English" and click on it.

Every effort has been made to ascertain that the information in this book is accurate; my apologies if you find that places and websites mentioned have changed or disappeared. This is just a fact of life in this ever-changing metropolis that is at the same time very international and Japanese.

MAP OF TOKYO

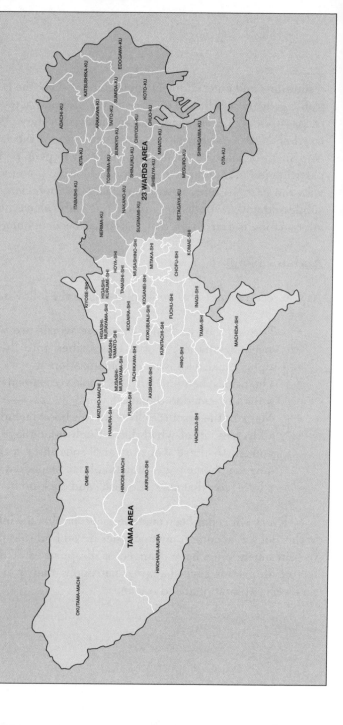

—CHAPTER ONE—

GETTING TO KNOW TOKYO

"What is Tokyo really like?" newcomers often ask. There is perhaps no one thing or place that sufficiently represents all that is Tokyo. On the surface, Tokyo is a sprawling, modern, gigantic metropolis, serving as the center of administration and commerce for most of Japan. But even visitors who spend a limited amount of time here notice that contrasting elements, such as tradition and technology, formality and informality, and symbols of East and West, co-exist. Tokyoites seem to be always on the go, rushing to catch up with life, but under the surface, people's lives follow a natural rhythm punctuated by seasonal events. Tokyo is where nature, technology, traditional and modern cultures, and people from all over the world are densely packed into a small space.

13

TOKYO IN CONTEXT

Japan is made up of four main islands: Honshu, Shikoku, Kyushu and Hokkaido. Tokyo is located near the center of Honshu, the largest island. Administratively, Japan is divided into 48 prefectures, each with its own government; these prefectures are further categorized into 10 regions without governments. Tokyo is one of the 48 prefectures, and the capital of the country.

Situated in the Kanto Plain, the Tokyo Prefecture, together with surrounding prefectures, is categorized as part of the Kanto region. The land area of Tokyo is about 2,500 square kilometers (approximately 961 square miles), and with the exception of Mount Fuji, is rather flat with no high mountains.

Tokyo metropolis is administratively divided into three main parts: 1) the 23 wards (*ku*) in the Eastern part; 2) the Tama area, consisting of 26 cities (*shi*), three towns (*machi*), and one village (*mura*), in the western part; and 3) two islands (*shima*), Izu and Ogasawara (consisting of two towns and seven villages), located south of the mainland. In this book, the name "Tokyo" mainly refers to the 23 wards, as these are the center of government, commerce, and foreign affairs. "Greater Tokyo" refers to these wards, the Tama area and the surrounding prefectures.

NEIGHBORHOODS IN TOKYO

There is no one focal point in Tokyo; rather there are several areas that serve unique functions and offer distinctive atmospheres. Six of these areas are described below.

Asakusa/Ueno (Taito-ku)

Located in Taito-ku in the eastern part of Tokyo, Asakusa is considered to be "downtown Tokyo" and is the place to experience the atmosphere of "**Old Tokyo**". The **Sensoji**, a Buddhist temple believed to have been built in the seventh century, is a famous landmark. Leading up to the temple are rows of small shops selling

Map of Major Points in the 23 Wards.

traditional Japanese crafts, and in the streets nearby rows of traditional wooden houses stand side by side. Many families residing in this neighborhood have lived here for several generations and cherish its ambiance. (*Refer to* "Old Tokyo" *in Chapter 14 for more details.*)

Just west of Asakusa, Ueno and its surrounding areas form a bustling commercial center with many wholesale shops dealing in food, clothing, and electronics. Major attractions include the food and flea market at **Ameya Yokocho (Ameyoko)** and the **Akihabara** electronic district where more than 600 shops sell elec-

15

tronic appliances at discount prices. The large **Ueno Station** used to be the junction of major train routes and served as the entrance to Tokyo for people traveling from other regions of the country. Although Ueno Station lost its former status after the introduction of bullet trains that used Tokyo Station as their hub, it continues to be one of the major transportation hubs of Tokyo. The focal point of this area is **Ueno Park**, located just across from the station. In spring, the park is crowded with people enjoying the cherry blossoms; adjacent to the park are museums and a zoo.

Marunouchi (Chiyoda-ku)

The Marunouchi area in Chiyoda-ku serves as the core of economic and political activities in Japan. The focal point in Marunouchi is **Tokyo Station**, the hub that connects all of the country's major railroad lines, including the bullet trains. As many prominent Japanese companies and banks have their headquarters located here, in the day the atmosphere buzzes with the energy of people proud to be at the center of Japan's business scene. At night, the streets are quiet and the buildings dark, save for the lights still burning in the windows of the many who are working late.

The **National Diet** building, which houses the national government of Japan, is situated in the Kasumigaseki area adjacent to the business district.

The oldest and most important landmark in the Marunouchi area is the **Imperial Palace**. At one time it was the headquarters of the Tokugawa Shogunate, which ruled Japan for more than 250 years (1603-1868). After the Shogunate lost power and was dissolved, the Emperor gained control and relocated here from his residence in Kyoto. Since then, the royal family has resided in the palace. The current Emperor and Empress, symbolic figures of the country, still reside there. The palace is surrounded by the original moat, built for protection from possible revolts. Today,

16

the sidewalk around the moat is popular with joggers, the lush trees and gardens providing a relaxing green backdrop and quiet contrast to the hustle and bustle beyond. (*Refer to* "Old Tokyo" *in Chapter 14 for details on the Imperial Palace*.)

Ginza (Chuo-ku)/Hibiya (Chiyoda-ku)

Adjacent to the financial and business district of Marunouchi is the Ginza and Hibiya area. Ginza is the most expensive and high-class shopping area in Japan and its main street, **Chuo Dori**, is to Tokyo what Fifth Avenue and the Champs-Elysées are to Manhattan and Paris. The old department stores and private shops located here have long histories and established reputations for quality and service.

These private shops specialize in items such as crafts, jewelry, *kimono*, and made-to-order suits; they have been catering to well-heeled customers for several generations. Foreigners entering these shops for the first time may be intimidated by the stores' appearance. However, perseverance will be well rewarded by a fascinating cultural experience. The displays of elegant, formal *kimono* and accessories for men, women and children are exquisite and the prices breathtaking.

In recent years, several world-famous brands such as Tiffany, Louis Vitton and Hérmes have opened branches here, adding an international flavor to the streets. (*Refer to Chapter 13 for more details on shopping.*)

In addition to up-scale shopping, Ginza offers fine dining and posh nightclubs. Most people who wine and dine here do so only on corporate expense accounts, as the costs can be exorbitant.

Several theaters are located in the Hibiya area adjacent to Ginza. Here, people can enjoy musicals, concerts and plays. Many patrons of the arts like to stop at the prestigious **Imperial Hotel** for pre- or after-theater snack or meals.

Shibuya (Shibuya-ku)/Shinjuku (Shinjuku-ku)

Shibuya and Shinjuku are popular with people who prefer more casual and less expensive shopping, dining, and entertainment options than those offered in and around Ginza. Both areas host busy railroad and subway junctions on public transportation routes connecting the inner and outer areas of the Tokyo region.

Shibuya is where the younger crowds gather. Teenagers hang out in the game centers, movie theaters, and fast-food shops, while college students congregate in the inexpensive pubs. Both frequent the department stores, many of which target young customers. The most popular meeting point in Shibuya is by the bronze statue of a dog named "**Hachiko**", located in the square in front of the station. However, the square can get so crowded, especially at rush hour, that it is almost impossible to locate anyone.

Shinjuku offers a bit more variety, with the eastern and western parts projecting entirely different images. The eastern part is as congested as Shibuya but draws a much older crowd. A few major department stores as well as discount electronic shops are located here. Shinjuku is the location of the famous **Kabuki-cho**, an area lined with small bars, strip clubs, and porno shops. As normally many drunken people roam the street, Japanese and foreign women who walk alone here are likely to be harassed. Rumor has it that the *yakuza* (the Japanese equivalent of the Mafia) is involved in many of the nocturnal activities.

Compared to the somewhat darker eastern part of Shinjuku, the western side, with its concentration of high-rise buildings, has a more modern and polished image. Prominent landmarks include the **Tokyo Metropolitan Government Office** towers, which dominate the skyline, the **Shinjuku Park Tower Building** (where the popular Hotel Park Hyatt Tokyo is located), and the **Shinjuku Sumitomo Building** which offers spectacular views of Tokyo.

Aoyama/Akasaka/Roppongi (Minato-ku)

The Aoyama, Akasaka, and Roppongi neighborhoods in Minato-ku offer trendy, fashionable neighborhoods with a cosmopolitan flavor. Unlike Shibuya or Shinjuku, these areas are quieter as there are no large department stores here to draw crowds of shoppers.

These neighborhoods host a large expatriate community, resulting in the establishment of international schools, apartments with Western-style fixtures and amenities, and grocery stores that sell international goods. More foreigners than Japanese people congregate in some of the clubs and restaurants in these areas.

Aoyama has lovely tree-lined streets where pedestrians enjoy strolling, browsing in elegant boutiques, or relaxing and people-watching from inside the many cafés with street views. Akasaka is known for its many embassies and luxury hotels. Roppongi is one of the most popular entertainment areas in Tokyo for people in their twenties.

The Waterfront

Created from landfill in the 1990s, the Waterfront is a newly developed area that is still expanding. The **Odaiba** section hosts several office buildings, upscale hotels, shopping areas, and parks that were built to satisfy the varied needs of residents and visitors. (*Refer to the* "Waterfront Area" *in Chapter 14.*)

The Suburbs

Compared to the 23 land-scarce wards of Tokyo, the suburbs in the western part of the metropolis have more space and offer more affordable housing. Many young couples with small children live here and make the daily one- to two-hour commute to their offices in central Tokyo. People living in the wards enjoy visiting the suburbs on weekends to experience a quick "nature getaway". Here they can hike, fish, enjoy the fresh air and verdant trees, and find respite from the busy and crowded city life.

THE FOUR SEASONS

Seasons are so important to Japanese people that when they write a letter, even a business letter, they customarily begin by mentioning something about the season. Tokyo has four distinct seasons that residents mark by savoring seasonal foods, attending cultural events, admiring blooming flowers, and participating in special activities. With technological advances having made most foods and flowers available throughout the year, many Japanese people are nostalgic for the days when these special foods and flowers were eagerly anticipated at particular times of the year.

Spring

With the advent of spring in March, the plum and peach trees blossom and though the average temperature is a chilly 9°C (48°F), people begin feeling the coming of spring.

On March 3, families with little girls celebrate *Hinamatsuri* (**The Doll Festival**) to wish for healthy and happy lives for their daughters. In honor of the occasion they make arrangements of peach blossoms and display *hina-ningyo*, miniature dolls in traditional *kimono* costumes.

While plum and peach blossoms hint of spring, it is the cherry blossoms that provide the definitive sign that spring has indeed arrived. In Tokyo, many parks are graced with an abundance of cherry trees. Most of the flowers are pale pink but some are almost white, and the scene with hundreds of trees in bloom at once is just stunning.

Toward the end of March, television news provide forecasts of when the cherry blossoms will be at their peak (which in Tokyo is usually around the end of March or the first week of April), and people begin planning picnics and outdoor parties. Many companies hold parties under the cherry trees in parks, and usually the first task of a newly hired university graduate is to go early and reserve a good spot for the group. The party-goers will eat

Photo by Akiko Watanabe.

Cherry blossoms in a Tokyo park herald the arrival of spring.

and drink, sing along with *karaoke* machines, and have fun under the canopy of blossoms.

April is the month when many things begin anew in Japan: the new school year starts; the new fiscal year begins; some people begin new work assignments in a different part of the country; and college graduates join the workforce, some leaving their hometowns to start new lives in Tokyo.

Spring does have one drawback. Many people will suffer hay fever and allergies to pollen, especially from Japanese cedar trees, as the levels are high at this time of year. People get itchy eyes, nasal congestion, and coughs, and no remedy has yet been found which cures the symptoms completely. Many people wear a white face mask to reduce the amount of pollen inhaled. Television weather forecasts give daily estimates of pollen levels so that allergy sufferers can prepare accordingly. The pollen counts provide good fodder for small talk.

After the brief cherry blossom period (it lasts only one week),

21

everyone's attention turns to planning for Golden Week, during which four national holidays fall in two consecutive weeks in the beginning of May. As it is not cost-effective to run manufacturing operations with so many breaks in between, sites shut down for the entire period and many factory employees can take a vacation of nearly two weeks. Some people in other industries also take time off to enjoy the long holiday.

Golden Week is a major traveling period for both the Japanese people and for foreigners living in Japan. Traffic can be heavy in resort areas and trains and flights very crowded. Consequently, some people consider this a perfect time to explore Tokyo, where the traffic is relatively light and the air refreshingly clean.

One of the holidays in Golden Week is *Kodomo no Hi* (**Children's Day**) on May 5, when families wish for their sons' happiness and health. Families with boys hang three carps (called *koinobori*) made out of cloth on a pole in the garden. The way the carps fly in the wind simulates the way real carps swim upstream, – parents hope that their sons would grow up with similar strength.

Summer

After a fresh and crisp May, the humidity starts rising at the beginning of June. Rainy fronts hover near Japan for almost the entire month, with the official announcement of the beginning of the rainy season usually occurring around June 10. During this rather depressing period, people look forward to the blooming of hydrangea flowers – the purple, blue, pink, and green blossoms look charming under gray skies and raindrops.

June is also the time for *koromogae*, which is the changing of wardrobes to that of summer. After June 1, school children and company employees replace their long-sleeved winter uniforms with their short-sleeved summer uniforms, which are worn until the next changing day on October 1, no matter how cold the weather becomes. At home, people put their cold weather gear into storage, and take out their summer attire.

The end of the rainy season, officially announced in mid-July, also marks the beginning of summer. Temperatures climb and can reach 35°C (95°F) accompanied by continuous humidity, making air-conditioning a near necessity. July is also the season for typhoons. Japan is hit by an average of 28 typhoons annually. Although Tokyo is rarely hit directly, when systems approach they bring heavy rain combined with wind and thunderstorms.

Schools begin their summer vacation around July 25, thus summer is the prime time for family travel. The heaviest traveling takes place in the week of *Obon*, which usually falls in early to mid-August. According to Buddhist teachings, this is the time when the spirits of the dead are believed to return to this life, so people gather with their families and visit their hometowns to welcome their ancestors' spirits. Although *Obon* is not a national holiday, many companies and shops close for three to four days, and trains and planes are packed to capacity.

In summer, many festivals and events are held at neighborhood parks, shrines, and school fields where stalls sell foods, crafts, and small animals such as bunnies and chicks. Some festivals include folk dances and fireworks displays. The most famous fireworks display is held at the Sumida River near Asakusa. (If you plan to attend, reserve a spot early!)

Fall

When September arrives, temperatures drop, signaling the end of summer. Children go back to school in the first week of September and adults turn their attention to enjoying books, art, museums, and concerts. Many operas, classical music concerts, and art exhibitions are held in Tokyo in the fall.

The sunny skies and crisp temperatures of fall entice many people to enjoy sports and outdoor activities. The second Monday of October is a holiday called "**Health Sports Day**". Many schools spend this as a field day where students compete in field, track, and athletic events. Many high schools plan trips out of Tokyo for their students during fall (a popular destination is Kyoto). This school trip, *shugaku-ryoko*, is one of the highlights of high school life. Fall is also a popular time for making excursions to the mountains and countryside to see the colorful fall foliage.

Food is a common topic of conversation in the fall. Fall is the best season for seafood such as saury, sardines, and mackerel, and for several fruits including pears, grapes, and persimmons. All mushrooms taste specially good in fall, and one type – *matsutake* – are sold only at this time of the year. It is renowned for its aroma, which is comparable to that of French truffles. However, the domestic variety costs more than 10,000 yen for a large stem, so few people have the opportunity to savor it.

Winter

In December, the wind turns cold and winter clothes are taken out of storage and parties called *bonenkai*, which loosely means "forget what has happened during the year" are held. Colleagues and friends get together to thank each other for their support and to wish each other a happy new year; clients are invited out to restaurants; and colleagues and friends wine and dine.

Although Japan is not a Christian country, streets and shops in Tokyo are decorated for **Christmas**, and celebrating Christmas is popular among young people and families. Parents buy Christmas presents for their children, and young men crowd the Tiffany jewelry store in Ginza to buy gifts for their girlfriends. On Christmas Eve, many restaurants and hotels are packed with young couples spending a romantic night together. At home, special Christmas cakes are served to families and friends. As the cakes are decorated with strawberries, the price of the berries always rises sharply just before the holiday. To most Japanese, Christmas offers a festive atmosphere and a reason to shop; few attach religious sentiments to the occasion.

The **New Year** is the most important holiday for Japanese people. Many companies close their businesses from around December 28 until around January 4. Schools finish the semester around December 25. At the end of December, many people clean their houses from top to bottom to greet the New Year with a fresh mind and spirit. They also place special decorations inside and outside their homes, and prepare special foods to be eaten over the course of the holiday period, although fewer and fewer younger people are observing this custom. Everyone writes *nengajo* (postcards) to thank others for their support over the last year.

People who have families in other parts of Japan usually return to their hometowns for the New Year holidays. On January 1, almost every business is closed, as this is a day to spend time with the family. Some people, especially males, also visit their manager's house to exchange New Year's greetings, and in return, are treated with *sake* (Japanese rice wine) and traditional New Year meals. Many people also visit temples or shrines, regardless of their religious beliefs, to pray for a healthy and happy new year. On New Year's Day you can see many people wearing the *kimono* (Japanese traditional costume). The New Year holidays last until January 3, but the holiday mood continues until mid-January with people still holding parties to celebrate the New Year.

Another holiday in January is **Coming of Age Day** (*Seijin no Hi*) which celebrates young people having reached the age of 20, when they are officially regarded as adults – they can vote, drink and smoke. On this day on the second Monday of the month, many young people wear *kimono* and attend ceremonies or parties.

Mid-January to February is the coldest time of the year and in some years Tokyo receives occasional snowstorms. As the metropolis is not equipped to handle snow, a heavy deluge can result in long delays in public transportation and severe traffic jams on the roads. Generally, winter in Tokyo remains very dry, with crisp temperatures and clear skies.

Photo by Akiko Watanabe.

Young people in their best kimono attend a Coming of Age Day ceremony.

Because of the dryness, winter is the season for fires. As houses are built very close to each other, fire in one house spreads quickly to other houses. In Old Tokyo, men would alert residents to the dangers of fire by walking through the neighborhoods, beating wooden clappers calling out "Look out for fire!" Even today, you can still hear the call in some neighborhoods.

Winter is also flu season. Flu viruses affect many people each year and sometimes cause serious symptoms such as high fever. To protect against flu, people are encouraged to gargle well, wash their hands often, and eat warm and nutritious foods such as hot-pots, which is the most popular winter dish.

While early February often has the coldest temperatures, this is also the time when plum blossoms start appearing and people appreciate this as the very first sign of spring.

Average Monthly Temperatures in Tokyo

	Jan	Feb	Mar	Apr	May	Jun
°C	5	6	9	14	19	22
°F	41	43	48	57	66	72
	Jul	Aug	Sep	Oct	Nov	Dec
°C	25	27	24	18	13	8
°F	77	81	75	64	55	46

PEOPLE IN TOKYO

Tokyo is a crowded metropolis with a population of just over 12 million, which is about 10 per cent of the total population of Japan.

Stereotypes

As in other big cities in the world, Tokyo residents are not necessarily people who were born and raised in the metropolitan area. Many moved here from other parts of Japan when they were young, when they entered college, or when they joined a company. Yet, people in other parts of Japan attach certain labels or traits to Tokyoites, most common of which are: "snob", "elite", "cold", "fast-paced", and "busy". These labels may be somewhat accurate. Tokyoites must function in this crowded metropolis, interacting daily with people from diverse regions and backgrounds. Consequently, they tend to ignore what others are doing and approach strangers with a reserve that may be interpreted as coldness or snobbishness.

The inhabitants of Tokyo and those of Osaka (the second largest city in Japan, located in the western part of the country) have a kind of rivalry. People from Osaka tend to think that Tokyoites are rather obnoxious, while Tokyoites regard the people of Osaka as being rather vulgar, given that they tend to be more direct and to talk more openly about money than do the people of

27

Tokyo. These contrasting perceptions might be caused by the historically different functions these cities served. Since the Tokugawa Period (1603-1868), Tokyo, which was then called Edo, has been the center of politics in which bureaucrats play a major role. Osaka, in contrast, has long been known for its commercial endeavors in which merchants play the primary role in society.

Within Tokyo, people who live in the downtown area claim themselves to be *edokko* (natives of Edo) and display traits distinct from those of the previously mentioned stereotypical Tokyoites; they are generally more open, sentimental, short-tempered and caring. *Edoko* is a title conferred only on those who are at least third-generation born in Tokyo and residents of the downtown area. The term was created during the Tokugawa Period when *samurai* (warriors) held all the power in society. Civilians (such as merchants, artisans, and craftsmen) flourished as a separate and somewhat extravagant culture, distinct from the disciplined *samurai* culture. The civilians proudly called themselves *edoko* and tried to enjoy life, resisting the heavy regulations imposed by the authorities. But as Tokyo was transformed into a cosmopolitan society and the mobility of its residents increased, the number of *edokko* declined.

Among foreigners, common first impressions of Tokyoites are that they are polite, organized, and hard working. These impressions may change over time as they get to know them better.

A Tokyo Family

What is life like then for a typical Japanese family in Tokyo? The life of the fictional **Yamada family** provides some insight.

To reduce confusion, in this description family members are referred to by their given (first) names. In Japan, however, first names are used only among family members and close friends. (*Refer to* "Getting to Know People" *in Chapter 8 for more details about Japanese names.*)

The head of the family is 43-year-old **Takeshi Yamada**. He was born in Sendai, in the northern part of Japan, and moved to Tokyo when he entered university. After graduation he was hired by the headquarters of a bank in Tokyo and has been working there ever since. He is now the manager of the accounting department and has an annual income of 7 million yen.

Takeshi is married to 38-year-old **Hiroko Yamada**. Her parents moved to Tokyo when they were young and Hiroko was born and raised in the city. She met her husband at the bank, where she was also an employee. Like many Japanese women of her generation, she quit her job after getting married. Hiroko's parents built a house for the newlyweds in Toshima-ku, in eastern Tokyo, on land they had owned for many years.

Takeshi and his wife feel very fortunate to own a home so near the center of Tokyo, as doing so is just a dream for many people. Most of Takeshi's colleagues live outside of Tokyo and commute more than one hour to work, but Takeshi's commute is only half an hour.

Takeshi wakes up at 7am in the morning. He eats a traditional Japanese breakfast consisting of rice, *miso* soup, and a slice of fish fillet or some leftovers, prepared by Hiroko, and leaves home around 8am. He walks to the station to take the subway, which is tightly packed with people. When he arrives at his office, most of his colleagues are already there. They chat about the weather, last night's baseball game, and exchange information about ongoing projects. At noon, Takeshi and his colleagues usually lunch at the company cafeteria which has a reasonably priced set menu. Some of Takeshi's colleagues, mostly those who are single women, lunch at restaurants, but as Takeshi has two children to support, he does not have the luxury of splurging on lunch.

Takeshi and his department colleagues have been working on a quarterly financial report, so he has worked until 11pm every day for the past week. The bank recently restructured to cut expenses and some employees were laid off, thus Takeshi feels great pressure to work hard and perform well. He now feels insecure about his own position. He has been working for this bank for 20 years and does not know what he would do if he lost his job.

When Takeshi and other men of his generation started working, they believed that once they had a job at a major bank or manufacturing company, stable incomes and lifetime employment would be guaranteed. But economic changes are forcing companies to change their employment policies, and typical Japanese families to restructure their expectations and lifestyles.

Concerned about Takeshi's job security, Hiroko has started working part-time at a small company, helping with the accounting. She did not delay looking for a job as her best friend's husband, who used to work for a big manufacturing company, was recently laid off during a corporate restructuring exercise. A couple of her friends have also taken part-time jobs to help cover rising expenses. Hiroko feels it is useful to have a second source of income in case Takeshi loses his job, and as the costs of their children's education are also likely to increase. While Hiroko enjoys working again after spending more than 10 years taking care of her family, if the situation had not required it, she would not have thought about re-entering the workforce. She feels lucky to have her current job as it is generally difficult for women to re-enter the work force once they have quit.

Kanami, age 14, is the oldest child in the family. She is in the second year of a public middle school located in her neighborhood. She and many of her classmates are from the same primary school. Since joining middle school their interests have changed to fashion and make-up. Some of Kanami's friends have dyed their hair and she wants to dye her hair too, but she knows her parents will disapprove. She always feels that she does not have enough money for socializing and shopping, so she wishes she could have a part-time job, but her school does not allow students to work.

Her school requires all students to engage in some kind of extra-curricular activity. Kanami is a member of the tennis club and practices three times a week. She enjoys going to fast-food joints and family-type restaurants with her club mates after practice. On days when she does not have tennis practice, she attends tutoring sessions to prepare for senior high school entrance exams.

The youngest member of the family, **Yuji**, is 10 years old and goes to the same public primary school Kanami attended when she was younger. Yuji does not like studying, but his parents send him to a tutoring class after school because they want him to go to a private middle school. They believe that he will have a better chance of getting into a good university if he goes to a particular private school. He enjoys playing computer games with his friends, and has recently been trying to convince his parents to buy him new game software if he gets good grades on his next report card.

The **maternal grandparents** (Hiroko's parents) live with Hiroko's younger sister, **Kyoko,** in the same neighborhood. Kyoko is 35 years old and works in the marketing department of an apparel company. As she lives with her parents, she does not have to pay rent and can spend all the money she makes. She dines in trendy restaurants, purchases luxury goods and travels overseas at least once a year. Although her parents pressure her to get married, she prefers the single life. She does not envy her sister Hiroko, whose only concern is her children's education.

Societal Changes

The lifestyle of the Yamada family is quite typical of the average family in Tokyo today. Their lives have been greatly affected by the recession that started in the early 1990s, by women's role in the society, and by the ever-increasing costs of education.

Many middle-class males in Tokyo work for relatively large companies and are called *sarari-man* (salary man) because they spend their lives working for a salaried wage. Lifetime employment, promotion based on seniority, and long working hours described the life of these employees until recently. With the economic downturn, lifetime employment is no longer guaranteed in many companies, and a greater number of people now change jobs mid-career. Some younger people now prefer to work as part-timers or as contractors. They have learned that even if they worked full time for a large company, their future is not guaranteed.

Women's lifestyles have changed dramatically in the past 20 years in Japan, especially in Tokyo. More women remain single by choice, and both the average age of marriage as well as divorce rates have risen. Some women who do marry decide not to have children; recent research indicates that the average number of children per household is less than two.

There has also been an increase in women who choose to continue to work after marriage, although many of them still quit once they become mothers. It is extremely hard for women to rejoin the work force and rebuild their careers after spending several years taking care of their family. On the other hand, the number of married women who engage in part-time jobs is increasing, although these jobs may not lead to serious careers. Some work simply to supplement their overall family incomes or to seek a degree of financial freedom. Others work outside their homes in search of "self-realization".

Despite these changes in women's lifestyles, there are still differences in the roles of men and women in Japanese society. In the corporate world, the number of women in managerial positions is still limited and women tend to engage in administrative or support work. (*Refer to the* "Employment of Women" *Chapter 9.*) In families, women assume most of the responsibility for housework and managing the education of children. Most male employees work long hours and it is virtually impossible for them to do anything at home but sleep.

Children in Tokyo

Raising children in Tokyo is an increasingly daunting task due to the escalating costs of education and a rise in crime among youths.

The cost of supporting a child from birth through university is now 10 million yen. Parents work hard and sacrifice much to send their children to tutoring classes or to hire private tutors to prepare their children for school exams. In order to be hired by the best companies, students must attend the best universities. To enter good universities, students must attend good senior high schools and to enter good senior high schools, they must go to good junior high schools. Stringent entrance exams must be passed at each step in order to enter good schools. The only way parents can help children avoid the stress of this series of exams is to enrol them in one of the elite primary schools, which offers the potential for continuous education all the way through to university. Children need only take an exam to enter the primary school, after which they can enjoy the rest of their school life. Competition to enter such primary schools is extremely stiff, however.

Another factor adding to the challenge of child raising is that the crime rate among young people has increased dramatically in recent years; these crimes include robbery, assault, and homicide. Of great concern to society is the fact that some students in Japanese schools tease and bully classmates for no obvious reason, with the bullying sometimes leading to actual assault. Occasionally, some youngsters who are the targets of persistent bullying even commit suicide.

Observers attribute the rise in youth crime to several factors. One is the stress from continuous educational pressure. Another is the sense of insecurity that young people feel regarding work, as during times of economic slowdown graduating from a good university does not guarantee lifetime employment or career success. Still another possible factor is that many children spend more time on their computers than with their friends or parents.

Their inner worlds are greatly affected by the stories and characters that appear in computer games, some of which are extremely violent. It is suspected that children accustomed to seeing simulations of crimes in games have thus become desensitized to the seriousness of the crimes, and to the probable consequences to themselves and their families.

Elderly People in the Society

Japan is rapidly becoming an elderly society. It is expected that in the year 2015 the percentage of people older than 65 will account for 25 per cent of the entire population. With many older people collecting social security each month, reserving adequate funds for future payments is of great concern for the Japanese government. As interest rates in Japan have been kept low in recent years, older people who expected additional income from interest on savings are having a hard time.

For centuries, Japanese people, influenced by Confucian teachings, have believed that adult children are supposed to take care of their parents both physically and financially. But nowadays, many parents and children prefer to live separately even when the parents have grown old, partly because rents are so expensive in Tokyo it is difficult to find an adequately large yet affordable place to live with one's parents. In addition, the lifestyles of parents and adult children are generally so different that an unreasonable amount of tension can be expected if they live together. Finally, younger generations have been influenced by a more Western, independent mindset, with priorities shifting to the pursuit of individual rather than family goals.

Despite changes in people's mindsets and lifestyles, the belief that adult children are responsible for taking care of their parents is still strong, and most children feel hesitant to put their parents into external facilities such as nursing homes. Consequently, few of such facilities have been built.

Many Japanese people are still physically sound and energetic even after retirement (generally at age 60). Having a fulfilling life after retirement is a challenge for them, and creating stimulating opportunities for these valuable members of society is a challenge for the country.

Foreigners in Tokyo

Today, more than 300,000 foreigners are registered to live in Tokyo. Among them, the largest numbers are from Korea (both North and South) and China. Many are descendants of people who moved to Japan before World War II; but the number of recent immigrants from China is also increasing. Newcomers from the Philippines, Thailand, and other nations in Southeast Asia also account for a large percentage of the foreign population; many came to Tokyo in search of jobs. Employment opportunities have also led to an increase in the number of Brazilians living in Tokyo.

In addition, there are a number of people from Western nations such as the United States, the United Kingdom, Australia, and France, most of whom have been posted there to work for their employers in the Japanese subsidiaries of foreign firms.

People from the same countries or similar cultural backgrounds tend to live together in certain neighborhoods. As a result, a few distinct foreign communities have developed in Tokyo. Many people from the Philippines live in Shinjuku-ku, for example; those from China live in Toshima-ku; and many Westerners reside in Minato-ku. In some of these places it is possible to see more foreigners than Japanese people.

Tokyoites are generally gracious hosts, willing to help foreigners. When asked for directions, Japanese people not only suggest the best route but sometimes accompany foreigners to their destinations. However, some Japanese people seem hesitant to interact with foreigners; in many cases, it is because they lack confidence speaking in English. Although everyone studies the

English language in high school, emphasis is placed on grammar and vocabulary rather than on practical conversation, thus many people are better at understanding written English than spoken English. Foreigners who feel that their spoken English is not being understood by Japanese people can often communicate successfully by writing down their requests or main points.

Japanese people have a tendency to prize and value anything from the West (including food, clothes, and pop culture). This can be attributed to the nature of Japan's historical relationship with Western nations. Extensive contact with Westerners began in the middle of the 19th century when Japan opened its doors to foreign countries after more than 200 years of insularity. Japanese people were shocked to see the advanced technologies, wealth and different customs of these Westerners, and an attitude of "learn from the West" emerged. This same pattern was repeated after World War II when Japan rebuilt under the leadership of the United States. During both periods, Tokyo was the locus of interaction with Westerners. Even today, after becoming one of the world's most advanced nations, Japan still tends to follow trends initiated in Western cultures.

Because of this strong preference for things Western, Japan is sometimes accused by other Asian nations of neglecting the fact that it is part of the Asian community. In addition, because during World War II Japan pursued a cruel military strategy of expanding its territory into other Asian countries, tensions remain. However, in recent years exchanges between Japan and other Asian cultures have increased. For example, popular music has been exported from Japan to other Asian countries and vice versa. In future, more understanding and collaboration can be expected between the Japanese and the inhabitants of other Asian nations.

Foreigners who have lived in Tokyo for long periods of time comment that the metropolis has become more friendly to foreigners. There has been an increase in the number of instructions and signs in foreign languages (mainly in English, but also in Chinese and Korean). Foreign products are more readily available in local supermarkets and at lower prices. Japanese people seem more open and willing to speak in English although their abilities may be limited.

❀ ❀ ❀

While to some observers Tokyo seems like a huge, modern metropolis with little natural beauty, Tokyoites appreciate the many little charms that can be glimpsed in daily life: a view of Mt. Fuji from a home or office building window; cherry blossom trees lining the way to a train station; plush greenery surrounding the Imperial Palace; and seasonal festivals at neighborhood shrines.

—CHAPTER TWO—

EXPLORING TOKYO'S PAST AND PRESENT

Today Tokyo is the center of economic and political activity in Japan, but this has not always been the case. This chapter traces the development of Tokyo by looking at the country's history, economy, government and political system, as well as the belief systems that have influenced the Japanese people.

TOKYO IN JAPANESE HISTORY

Japan, sometimes referred to as *Nippon*, has a long and colorful history. Most historians divide this history into periods based on a variety of names relevant to the times, such as those of ruling families, political or military leaders, significant symbols and events, or locations of activity. This section offers a glimpse of the history of Tokyo within the context of the country's development and traces its rise to its current status as the country's center of government and commerce.

Early History (Prior to 1185AD)

The earliest written accounts of Japan are found in Chinese chronicles that had references to inhabitants of Japan visiting China as early as 57AD. But archeologists have found pottery and other evidence confirming human activity took place in Japan during the Jomon Period (11,000BC to 300BC), and recent findings suggest the possibility of even earlier activity.

The next segment of early Japanese history is known as the Yayoi Period (300BC to 300AD), named after an area near Tokyo University where a second distinctive type of pottery was reportedly found. Around this time, metal working and rice cultivation were introduced to Japan, probably through contact with people on the Korean peninsula and the Asian continent.

During the Kofun Period (300 to 593AD), so named because of the existence of many large tombs (*kofun*) built for the leaders, most human activity in Japan seems to have been centered in the Yamato Plain. It was on this plain, located in the mid-western part of Honshu Island (in the general area of today's Nara Prefecture), that a clan of people known as Yamato gained power over other clans in the region and established a court.

The rulers of this clan claimed to be direct descendants of the Sun Goddess (called Amaterasu), and are believed to be ancestors to the imperial family of modern Japan. By the middle of the 6th century, the Chinese writing system and Buddhism had been introduced to the Yamato rulers via China and Korea. These were important developments as, subsequently, scholars began using the Chinese writing system and Buddhist teachings began influencing the political structure and values of the Yamato court.

In the Asuka Period (593 to 710AD), Prince Shotoku, serving

39

as regent of the Empress Suiko, sent several diplomatic missions to China. He also issued the "Seventeen Article Constitution", a document that emphasized the importance of reverence for Buddhism, ethical behavior among people, and loyalty to imperial rulers. It is significant in that it established a political and religious foundation for early Japan. Also during this period, Japan began to be known by a pair of Chinese characters pronounced *Nihon* or *Nippon* in Japanese (literally "sun origin", and often more loosely translated as "Rising Sun"). Westerners developed the word "japan" in their attempts to simulate the Chinese pronunciation of these same characters.

At the time of the Nara Period (710AD to 784AD), a capital called *Heijokyo* was founded in Nara; and during the Heian Period (794AD to 1185AD), *Heiankyo* in Kyoto was established as the capital. The plans for both cities were modeled after the Chinese capital Chang-an (now called Xi'an), which was then the ruling center of the Tang Dynasty. This was just one reflection of the extent to which early Japanese society was influenced by China.

Though close contact with China continued during the Heian Period, the Japanese began to develop their own distinct culture, including the development of the arts. The origins of some forms of Japanese literature, art, and architecture still enjoyed today can be traced to this period of time in the country's history.

Another focal point at this time was the development of a writing system that, unlike Chinese characters alone, could reflect the language spoken in Japan. Scholars set about modifying and simplifying Chinese characters and eventually created the *hiragana* and *katakana* writing scripts. These new phonetic scripts combined with Chinese characters resulted in a more useful writing system. This facilitated the expression of thoughts and emotions as well as the proliferation of literature and poetry. The famous Japanese classic, *The Tale of Genji*, written by Lady Murasaki Shikibu, is a hallmark achievement of this period.

This was a time of prosperity during which the aristocracy devoted themselves to indulging in cultural pursuits, rather than to governing their territory. Within the aristocracy, rivalries developed and the power of the Heian court diminished. The lack of governance resulted in significant unrest and lawlessness, especially in rural areas, amongst the populace. In an attempt to maintain order in their individual territories, local leaders created small groups of armed guards known as *samurai* (warriors). The *samurai* from different areas began to form alliances based on financial and military might, and over time, a *samurai* class (that later became based on heredity) emerged.

The Feudal Period (1185~1602)

Two of the most prominent clans at the time were the Taira and the Minamoto. Their rivalry culminated in a decisive war in 1185, in which the Minamoto clan emerged victorious. Interestingly, a powerful member of the Taira clan who had established a home in the Tokyo region was said to have aided the Minamoto clan members in achieving victory. The residence of this Taira clan member was called Edo, a centuries-old name for Tokyo.

In 1192, the reigning court appointed the head of the Minamoto clan, Minamoto Yoritomo, as the first *shogun* (general) of Japan. Minamoto's shogunate (a military government headed by the *shogun*) was based in Kamakura, just west of Tokyo. His appointment signaled a shift eastward in control and political power, and set the stage for the development of the Kanto region.

The *samurai* were attracted to several geograophical features of the Kanto Plain: natural ridges surrounding the plain offered protection from invaders; the broad, flat lands were perfect for exercising horses; and a confluence of rivers and tributaries provided irrigation as well as means of transportation. As the might of the Minamoto Shogunate grew, the position of the Kanto Plain, where modern Tokyo is located, shifted from the periphery to the

41

center of political and cultural activity in Japan.

The emperor and the *shogun* began to share authority in governing the country, although the emperor and aristocracy remained in Kyoto. This dual power structure would continue for several hundred years, during which time the authority of the *shogun* – as well as military and political activity in the Kanto region – would grow steadily, while the emperor's position became largely symbolic. The *samurai* class eventually became the dominant social class in the country, and each shogunate, with a few exceptions, was headed by the most powerful *samurai* clan of its period. Some positions of power in the shogunate were given to members of other clans that pledged their allegiance to the ruling *shogun*.

This period of Japanese history is usually called "feudal", as subordinates were expected to demonstrate loyalty to their military leaders (*samurai* and/or the *shogun*) in exchange for societal privileges or rights to land.

In 1338, the Muromachi Shogunate, ruled by the Ashikaga clan, succeeded the deposed Minamoto (Kamakura) Shogunate. This military regime was based in Kyoto, giving rise to a resurgence of emphasis on aristocracy and culture. Many aspects of traditional Japanese culture, such as Noh theater, flower arrangement and the tea ceremony, had their origins in this period.

Gradually, the Muromachi Shogunate also declined and the country was ravaged by civil strife as regional warlords (*daimyo*) vied with each other and with the Shogunate for power. In 1573, a *daimyo* named Oda Nobunaga brought down the Muromachi Shogunate. He is best known for laying the groundwork for the unification of Japan, although he did not succeed in his quest. His successor, Toyotomi Hideyoshi, completed the process and gained the title of regent to the emperor. Known for his extravagant tastes, Hideyoshi built elaborate and imposing castles. Born a commoner, Hideyoshi's "rags to riches" success story makes him one of Japan's favorite historical heroes.

After Hideyoshi died in 1598, his successor, Tokugawa Ieyasu, persuaded the emperor to confer on him the title of *shogun*.

The Tokugawa Period (1603~1868)

The Tokugawa Shogunate formally began in 1603 and retained power until 1868. Tokugawa chose his own territory of Edo as the seat of government. From this point on, the city (now called Tokyo) would remain the political and cultural center of Japan.

According to legend, Edo was founded by the previously mentioned Taira clan member who established his home there. The name "Edo", literally meaning "door to the bay", was supposedly derived from the location of his home. Edo took on added significance when Ota Dokan, a powerful resident of the Kanto region, built a fortress there in 1457. It is said that Tokugawa Ieyasu built his castle on the remains of the fortress. This castle – the remnants can still be seen on the grounds of the Imperial Palace of Tokyo – became the seat of the Tokugawa Shogunate.

Historians have offered a number of reasons why Tokugawa Ieyasu chose Edo as his seat of power. It was located in the Kanto Plain, the largest bed of fertile soil in the country. Its strategic location allowed it to serve as both a port city and as a nexus between western and northern Japan, with natural barriers that made it relatively easy to defend. Some historians also believe that Tokugawa wanted his base to be located away from Kyoto, the seat of imperial power and a frequent source of political struggles and intrigue. Edo eventually became so closely identified with the Tokugawa regime that the terms "Tokugawa" and "Edo" are used almost interchangeably to characterize this era and its culture.

After the Tokugawa Shogunate was established, it instituted a number of measures to ensure its strength and longevity. These measures not only transformed the entire society, they also had a major impact on Edo, the political capital. Suspecting that free trade with foreign countries might allow the *daimyo* to build wealth, foreign trade was restricted to two ports in Kyushu. Christianity, introduced in 1549 by Jesuit missionaries, was suppressed for fear of undermining loyalty to the *shogun*. Afraid that social mobility might cause political disorder, the Tokugawa regime established a clear hierarchy among the social classes (warriors, peasants, artisans, and merchants, in descending order), which were made hereditary and marriage across class lines was prohibited.

The Tokugawa policy that had the most dramatic impact on life in Edo involved the system of *sankin kotai* (alternating obligatory visits). Under this system, almost all *daimyo* were required to maintain at least one residence in Edo where their wives and children would live permanently, while they themselves were required to divide their time equally between their residences in Edo and their home domains. The system was a huge financial burden on the *daimyo* but, with their families held hostage in Edo, it also reduced the potential for revolts. A by-product of this system was the improvement and expansion of the transportation network between Edo and regional towns, completely transforming Edo.

In order for Edo to function as the country's political center, the Tokugawa Shogunate built a castle, numerous bridges and waterways. Moreover, once Edo became a place of residence for all *daimyo* and their entourages, the city had to support a huge concentration of *samurai*. A flourishing community of merchants, craftsmen, artisans, and other workers developed.

The *daimyo* and their followers lived in the castle's vicinity, generally to the west and south. This hilly part of the city was commonly known as *Yamanote* (literally, "hand of the mountain"; commonly translated as "High City"). The *daimyo* residences reflected its owners' power and status, and some were truly elaborate estates. Commoners, including merchants, craftsmen, artisans, and workers, lived east of the castle in the flat area known as *Shitamachi* (literally, "bottom town"; usually translated as "Low City"). Their activities centered around Nihombashi and Asakusa. In the early years of the Tokugawa Period, rows of small wooden houses were built to accommodate the burgeoning population. Residences of both commoners and *daimyo* were periodically destroyed in the fires that swept the city. In the destructive Great Fire of Meireki (1657), even part of Edo Castle was severely damaged.

The Tokugawa Period lasted over 250 years and was generally peaceful; by the 18th century, it had also become quite prosperous. As a result, many *samurai* did not have occasion to engage in battle, even though they cherished their reputations as warriors. Although merchants held the lowest rank in society, in time many became rich and an earthy, hedonistic culture catering to the tastes of commoners developed in Shitamachi. Kabuki theater became a popular form of entertainment as did the elegant pleasure quarters where courtesans plied their trade. The demimonde pleasures of urban commoners, as well as landscape scenes (such as views of Mount Fuji), were captured in a new art form – prints created from woodblocks, called *ukiyo-e* ('pictures of the floating world').

The relative stability of the Tokugawa Period was dramatically interrupted in 1853 when Commodore Matthew Perry of the United States sailed into Japan with four huge warships, demanding that the country open its doors to foreign trade. Having been isolated from much of the outside world for over 200 years, the Tokugawa Shogunate felt threatened by the display of advanced weaponry and acquiesced to Perry's demands. This submission to foreigners fueled the social discontent that was simmering due to a declining economy and a weakened social hierarchy. Among the *samurai*, anti-Tokugawa forces rallied around the symbol of the emperor. After a series of battles between supporters of the emperor and those of the Tokugawa regime, the Shogunate collapsed in 1868 and Japan was jolted out of isolation.

The Meiji Period (1868~1912)
The beginning of the Meiji Period saw the restoration of the

45

authority of the emperor. The imperial capital was officially relocated from Kyoto to Edo and renamed "Tokyo", meaning "Eastern Capital". The imperial family moved into Tokugawa Castle, which became known as *kokyo*, meaning "imperial residence" (better known today as the Imperial Palace). Policies of the new government were formulated and implemented by a handful of relatively young supporters of the emperor.

In the early years of the Meiji Period, the government felt an urgency to modernize, and especially to learn from the West. Japanese scholars and others were sent abroad to learn science, technology, and foreign languages, and the government hired foreigners to assist in the development of banking, education, transportation and other infrastructure systems.

By 1872, technological progress was clearly visible. A British-built railway connected Tokyo with Yokohama; buildings in Ginza sported gas-lit lamps and fire-resistant red brick construction; pedestrian and boat traffic were supplemented by horse-drawn carriage and buses, and later the electric trolley.

Social changes during the Meiji Period were no less momentous. The former social hierarchy was banned and *daimyo* were forced to surrender their land. A national military was formed and the *samurai* class was summarily abolished. Marriage between people of different classes was permitted and commoners were allowed to change jobs. Freedom of religion was proclaimed and compulsory education instituted.

The Meiji leadership wanted to turn the country's capital into a cosmopolitan city worthy of international respect. Tokyo became the cultural center of Japan – the place that set the standards in, among other things, fashion and food. Japanese people began wearing Western clothes instead of *kimono*. Dairy products and meat were introduced to the Japanese diet, and *sukiyaki* (sliced beef cooked with vegetables) became a favorite dish.

Admiration of Western culture was exemplified with the

building of the *Rokumeikan* (Deer Cry Pavilion) in Hibiya. Here high-ranking government officials and others from the Japanese social elite entertained Westerners with ballroom dancing, music recitals, and elaborate dinners. Designed by a British architect, the Rokumeikan was where Japanese people, dressed in tuxedos and ballroom gowns, could show the world how advanced and civilized they had become.

Artists portrayed the changes. Woodblock prints, which during the Tokugawa Period had depicted the world of the Edo commoner, now displayed symbols of modernity: trains; red brick buildings; men and women in Western dress; and the Meiji Emperor and Empress attending ceremonial events in Western garb.

After a couple of decades, this emulation for all things Western was more than the conservatives could bear. A return to traditional values was promoted and, although this movement eventually lost steam, practices such as ballroom dancing all but disappeared.

Japan's modernization movement originated from its ambition to gain the respect of the Western powers and membership in the elite world community. As Japan's economy and military grew stronger, the self-confidence of the Japanese people grew as did their desire to emulate Western powers by building an empire.

This was enhanced when victory over China in 1895 resulted in the acquisition of Taiwan. In 1905, the Japanese took special pride in defeating Russia, a European power, over issues concerning Manchuria and Korea. By 1910, Japan had annexed Korea. When the Meiji Emperor died in 1912, the curtain was drawn over a remarkable period in Japanese history. Japan had transformed itself from a feudal country cut off from the outside world to an industrialized nation and a burgeoning world power.

The Taisho Years and the Great Earthquake (1912~1925)
The Emperor Meiji was succeeded by his son, the Emperor Taisho.

47

In poor health for most of his reign, Taisho had little say in governing the country; his son (who would later become Emperor Hirohito) began serving as regent in 1921.

When the First World War broke out in 1914, Japan sided with the Allied Powers of Britain, France, and Russia. Japan continued its policy of territorial expansion after the war by seizing and occupying German territories in China. During the conflict, Japan received massive orders for military goods from its European allies, turning a trade deficit into a trade surplus. The country experienced an unprecedented economic boom, and Tokyo was one of the primary beneficiaries. This was most evident in the growth of the Marunouchi area, where the headquarters of many Japanese conglomerates were located.

The economic boom accelerated a process that began during the Meiji Period – the development of an urban working-class culture distinct from that of the Edo commoners and that of the high culture of the wealthy in Yamanote. Since the Meiji Period, Tokyo's population had grown substantially and large numbers of women entered the work force, especially in light industry and services. Universal education ensured most Japanese were literate. By the late Meiji and Taisho eras, Tokyoites were enjoying newspapers, magazines, photographs, records and movies – all products of the new industrial age. In sports, baseball began to surpass *sumo* (a form of Japanese wrestling) in popularity.

Tragedy struck on September 1, 1923, when Tokyo was jolted by a huge earthquake. The Great Kanto Earthquake destroyed much of Tokyo as well as Yokohama. Estimates vary, but most researchers concur that well over 100,000 people died and more than 50,000 injured. It was a traumatic event in Tokyo's history and reconstruction took years. Avenues were widened and many buildings replaced with Western-style structures. A celebration was held in 1930 to mark the completion of the reconstruction, though the actual work continued for several more years.

The Rise of Militarism and World War II (1926~1945)

When Emperor Hirohito ascended to the throne in 1926, Japan was facing a time of challenge. Efforts at reconstruction and recovery from the earthquake drained the economy. A few years later, the worldwide depression that started in New York in 1929 wreaked further havoc on Japan. While the government grappled with the economic situation, the military gained power.

By 1931, the Japanese military had occupied the whole of Manchuria and in 1937, Japan invaded China proper. Subsequently, during the early 1940s, Japan provoked Western nations by attempting to gain control over Southeast Asia. To stop the expansion of Japanese control in Asia, the United States, Britain and other world powers imposed an embargo on exports to Japan. In December 1941, panic over dwindling oil supplies led Japan to attack the United States at Pearl Harbor in Hawaii – Japan had officially entered World War II.

From 1942 to 1945, the United States carried out air raids on the city of Tokyo. These had a devastating effect; estimates of the number of casualties run as high as a quarter of a million people. The most intense bombing occurred in March 1945 when an estimated 80,000 to 100,000 people lost their lives. By the end of the war, much of the city lay in ruins. In August 1945, in an attempt to defeat Japan and end the war, the United States dropped atomic bombs on Hiroshima and on Nagasaki. It is estimated that over 200,000 people died; countless numbers were injured and large areas of both cities were destroyed.

The Post-War Years: Recovery and Reconstruction (1945~1970s)

At the conclusion of World War II, Japan was devastated and Tokyo was in ruins. Air raids had destroyed much of the city and more than a million people were left homeless; disease among residents was rampant. There was an acute shortage of food and other necessities. Conditions were miserable for everyone in Tokyo.

September 1945 saw the occupation of Japan by the Allied powers, but in many ways it was an American occupation under the command of General Douglas MacArthur. He projected self-confidence, and under his command the occupation was more benevolent than many had expected. Given the demoralized state of the Japanese people and the loss of confidence in their militarist leaders, MacArthur was able to command respect. Some people referred to him as "the last *shogun*."

While there were incidents of tension between the Americans and the local populace, on the whole there was relatively good cooperation between the two sides. In part, this was due to the fact that the Americans appeared to be making a concerted effort to help rebuild the Japanese economy. The American presence was most evident in Tokyo where MacArthur and the American forces were based – many buildings in the Marunouchi area and others were requisitioned for use by the occupying forces.

From his headquarters in Tokyo, MacArthur oversaw the process of remolding Japan into a democratic society, stripping the emperor of divine status, and disassembling commercial conglomerates. Occupation forces drafted a new constitution, which came into effect in 1947, as a foundation for the post-war society. To prevent further attempts at territorial expansion fueled by militarism, Japan relinquished its right to maintain military forces or to engage in war. Equal rights for men and women were granted. The formation of a two-house legislature called the Diet (*Kokkai*) was mandated, and every citizen age 20 or older was given the right to vote.

The occupation was formally concluded with the ratification of a peace treaty between the United States and Japan in 1952. Japan was now on the way to rebuilding its economy and society.

The event that signaled Japan's full recovery and return to the limelight in the world stage was the 1964 Tokyo Olympics.

Japan engaged in an earnest endeavor to showcase itself to the world, building a cluster of remarkable sporting venues for the games. A network of highways improved the flow of traffic in the city. The year also marked the debut of the high-speed bullet train, or *shinkansen*, linking Tokyo and Osaka. By all measures, the Olympic Games was a resounding success; a milestone in the history of Japan as well as that of Tokyo.

Industrialization and urbanization continued apace as the 1960s and 1970s marked an age of steady economic growth for Japan. The country became a major producer of world-class goods for both the domestic and international markets. As Japan prospered, the standard of living improved; many households could afford electrical appliances such as televisions and washing machines, and private ownership of automobiles increased.

MODERN JAPAN (1980S ~ PRESENT DAY)
The Economic Scene

In the 1980s, continued growth and low interest rates enticed Japanese companies and individuals to invest in real estate and the stock market. As a result, both markets skyrocketed and Japan experienced a "bubble" in its economy. Large companies used their profits from investments to purchase properties in other countries. Individual investors spent their gains on luxury goods, overseas travel, and expensive restaurants and entertainment. The booming economy attracted foreign investors and many foreign companies established subsidiaries or regional headquarters in Tokyo; the metropolis soon became known as a center of international business.

In the early 1990s, the "bubble" burst and Japan paid a high price for having partied hard. The stock and real estate markets tumbled and the economy fell into a serious recession. Many companies could not sustain their competitiveness in the world market, as they had insufficient funds to continue developing new products and services. Some went bankrupt because they could no longer repay their debts to the financial institutions from which they had borrowed. Left with a heavy burden of bad debt, many financial institutions followed suit.

Job security became a significant concern for Japanese workers, as many companies that had previously practiced lifetime employment were forced to implement restructuring plans that included employee layoffs. These layoffs, combined with hiring freezes in struggling companies, resulted in a significant increase in the unemployment rate. All of this led to a drop in consumer spending which further drained the economy. Tokyo was also hit hard by the recession. In the last decade of the century, real estate values declined substantially, corporate revenues dropped and consumer spending slowed.

The future of the national economy is difficult to predict, yet it is clear that Tokyo is well positioned to continue leading Japan's economy. The metropolis is the home of major Japanese corporations and foreign subsidiaries, it is the center for the information technology industry, and it offers access to a highly skilled labor force.

Marunouchi continues to be Tokyo's main business and financial district and the site of the headquarters of major corporations and banks – the Bank of Japan and the Tokyo Stock Exchange are conveniently located nearby. Nearly all foreign embassies and the subsidiaries of many foreign companies are located in Minato-ku (which includes Akasaka and Azabu). Other business districts include Shinjuku and the newly developed Odaiba area.

Prominent industries in Tokyo include financial services, real estate, retail, and other services. The Tokyo Metropolitan Government Office predicts that future growth of the local economy is likely to be concentrated in the service sector, especially in information technology and corporate support services, as well as in the entertainment, restaurant, and hotel industries.

The Political Scene

For administrative purposes, Japan is divided into 48 prefectures, each with its own local government (a single-house legislature) and a governor who is elected by public vote. Local governments manage their own budgets and fund part of their revenues through local taxes paid by corporations and residents. Each of the prefectures elects representatives to the national government.

In accordance with the constitution implemented after World War II, the Japanese national government consists of a two-house legislature called the Diet (*Kokkai*). The upper house, or House of Councillors, currently has 252 members who are elected every six years. The lower house, or House of Representatives, has 500 members elected every four years. Political power resides primarily with the House of Representatives. The Prime Minister is chosen by the Diet and generally is the leader of the majority party or of the coalition of parties that make up a majority. The Diet building, as well as other government buildings are concentrated in the Kasumigaseki area.

Photo by Haga Library Japan.

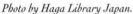

The National Diet building in Kasumigaseki.

For several decades after the war, the Liberal Democratic Party (LDP) dominated Japanese politics. That dominance diminished after 1993 when a series of political scandals involving the party occured – for the first time since 1955, a coalition of other parties gained the majority. Although the LDP is still the largest and most influential party, it is less powerful now as compared to the 1990s. Public interest in politics has declined in recent years, however. This may be due to a relative absence of charismatic leadership in the government and slowness in implementing strategies to stimulate the economy.

RELIGION AND BELIEFS

Japanese people have a relatively pragmatic attitude towards religion and spiritual life. Although most people do not consider themselves devout followers of any particular faith or belief system, elements of Confucianism, Buddhism, and Shinto have become integrated into the cultural fabric of their lives and permeate their world outlook if only at a subconscious level.

Confucianism

Although it is not considered a religion, Confucianism has had great influence on the Japanese people. The teachings of Confucius were brought to Japan in the third century AD, promoting social order and the observance of hierarchy. In particular, the *samurai* found the emphasis on hierarchical relationships appealing, as they could use it to foster loyalty from subordinates. Likewise, the Tokugawa Shogunate strongly promoted Confucianism to create social order and strengthen loyalty to the regime. Throughout Japanese history, Confucianism has also been used to reinforce an indigenous tendency towards subordinating or even sacrificing oneself for the good of the group. This tendency remains a strong component of Japanese morality.

Buddhism

Buddhism, which originated in India, was introduced to Japan in the sixth century AD via China and Korea. By the turn of the seventh century, it had been promoted heavily by the ruling elite and made into the state religion; numerous temples were built.

The central belief of Buddhism is that everything in this world is transient, and that life produces suffering due to attachment to material things; one can achieve nirvana only by freeing oneself from the self and its desires. Concepts rooted in Buddhist thinking can be found in various aspects of Japanese culture, including the arts, architecture, and even gardening. One of the reasons Japanese people love cherry blossoms may be that they cherish things that last for a short period of time, savoring every moment.

Shinto

Shinto is the indigenous religion of Japan. It spread among the people long before Confucianism and Buddhism were introduced. It is animistic and based on the belief that *kami* (sacred spirits) reside in natural elements such as mountains, rivers, and forests. These *kami* must be honored if humans want to comfortably share their environment with them. Shinto priests perform purification rituals in the presence of the *kami* to promote harmony between human beings and nature, and when people visit Shinto shrines, they typically cleanse their hands and mouths with water. An associated purification ritual is the annual cleaning of homes in preparation for the new year.

According to the Japanese creation myth, the first emperor was a descendant of the Sun Goddess, Amaterasu. This myth has been used by Japanese leaders to their advantage throughout the nation's history. In the late Tokugawa Period, it was used to enhance the status of the emperor and to emphasize the unique character and superiority of Japan, the country, and its people.

At the end of the Tokugawa Period, regional leaders used the myth to rally people around the emperor in order to overthrow the Tokugawa Shogunate, and subsequently Meiji leaders infused politics and education with Shinto precepts. In the 1930s and 1940s, during Japan's war efforts in Asia and the Pacific, these same beliefs were articulated to stir up nationalism and militarism. After the World War II, the Allied occupation forces strongly encouraged the adoption of democracy and other Western ideals. Henceforth, the emperor was no longer considered divine and Shinto was separated from politics.

Today Japanese people go to Shinto shrines to mark milestones and turning points in their lives and to celebrate seasonal events. After the birth of their children and when they have reached the ages of three, five and seven, parents visit shrines to pray for a happy life for their offspring. Before school entrance examinations, students and their parents often go to shrines to pray for good luck. And people of all ages go to Shinto shrines on New Year's Day to pray for health and happiness throughout the year.

During some Shinto festivals, people carry around *mikoshi* (portable shrines) in the belief that this will exorcise evil spirits in

Photo by Akiko Watanabe.

Meiji Shrine crowded with people on New Year's Day.

the neighborhood. Participation in Shinto ceremonies and rituals is open to all, regardless of religious beliefs or affiliation. (*Refer to* "Old Tokyo" *in Chapter 14.*)

While Buddhism teaches that people can achieve enlightenment in the next world, Shinto guides life in this world. Buddhism offers a more positive perspective on life after death than does Shinto. That may be one reason why there is a saying that Japanese people are "born Shinto and die Buddhist"; they go to Shinto shrines when babies are born, and have Buddhist funerals whether or not they ever went to a temple when they were alive.

Christianity

Christianity accounts for only about one percent of the Japanese population today, yet various customs and practices of Christianity have become popular, more as social customs than as religious practices. Christian wedding ceremonies with brides wearing white wedding gowns are considered more fashionable than traditional Shinto weddings with couples dressed in kimono. Many Tokyoites, especially young people, enjoy the festive atmosphere of Christmas, holding parties to celebrate the occasion.

In modern Japan, people have the tendency to adopt whichever practices of Confucianism, Buddhism, Shinto, and Christianity they think are most suitable to any given situation or time of year. Adherence to any doctrinal truths or ideals assumes relatively low priority in the lives of most Japanese people, who tend to be more concerned about leading a good moral life in harmony with nature and other human beings.

✿ ✿ ✿

During the course of Japan's history, Tokyo achieved the status of a modern capital city. Natural and man-made catastrophes destroyed much of the city. Yet the fact that Tokyo has recovered and continues to prosper is a testament to the energy and perseverance of its people.

—CHAPTER THREE—

ARRIVING IN TOKYO

An international move requires much preparation. Applications for travel documents must be completed, belongings packed and arrangements made for the importation of certain items, including pets. This chapter offers some guidelines to help you prepare before departure, and provides some information to familiarize you with Tokyo's airport procedures and transportation options.

VISA REQUIREMENTS
Foreigners of every nationality need a valid passport (with no less than 90 days validity remaining) to enter Japan, and most also require a visa. To determine if you need a visa to enter Japan, contact the Japanese embassy or consulate in your home country.

Generally, foreigners do not need a visa if they meet the following criteria: 1) they are citizens of a country that has a reciprocal visa exemption arrangement with Japan; 2) they will not be earning money in Japan; and 3) they do not intend to stay in Japan beyond the period of time allowed under the visa exemption arrangement, which varies according to the country of origin. This exemption also applies to people who are visiting Japan for business purposes, such as attending business meetings, as long as they do not receive payment from any entity in Japan.

Immigration officials stamp the passports of arriving foreigners with the date until which they are allowed to stay in Japan. Occasionally officials will ask to see proof that visitors have a confirmed ticket to leave Japan.

Visas must be obtained by foreigners who plan to stay in Japan for a period of time longer than that granted upon entry, and by those who plan to work in Japan. The type of visa, application form and required supporting documents vary according to the purpose of the stay. A Japanese embassy or consulate can provide further details.

In general, a visa applicant must obtain a Certificate of Eligibility issued by the Ministry of Justice in Japan. However, visa applicants cannot apply directly for the Certificate of Eligibility. A sponsor in Japan, such as an employer, school, or spouse, must apply for the document on behalf of the visa applicant. (Sponsors can call the Immigration Office in Tokyo at 03-3213-8111 for more information.) After obtaining the Certificate of Eligibility, the sponsor sends it to the applicant, who must then complete the visa application procedures specified by the Japanese embassy or consulate in the applicant's home country.

Regardless of the type of visa, staying beyond the date of expiration is against the law, and those who do so can be fined or imprisoned.

THINGS TO TAKE AND NOT TO TAKE

The length and purpose of your stay, budget and lifestyle will determine what to take and what to leave behind. Some people prefer to live surrounded by familiar belongings, while others prefer to take as little as possible and buy whatever is needed in Tokyo.

Many expatriates recommend that newcomers leave large pieces of furniture and appliances back home, as most neither fit nor function well in Tokyo. Instead, they suggest bringing personal items such as family photographs and favorite books or videos – in other words, things that cannot be purchased in Tokyo.

Men's Items

In Tokyo, good quality men's clothes of both domestic and imported brands are available. However, if you are tall or larger than an American size 40, an English size 40, or a European size 50, you should bring an adequate supply as large sizes are hard to find in Tokyo. (*Refer to the size comparison chart in Chapter 13.*)

Tokyo has four distinct seasons and most people prefer to wear different sets of clothes for each season. Winter can be cold and windy with occasional snow, so you will need long-sleeved shirts, woolen sweaters, a rather heavy coat, a scarf or muffler, and a pair of gloves. Spring and fall are more moderate, so you will need both short- and long-sleeved shirts, cotton sweaters and a light coat. Summer can be hot and humid and you are likely to perspire a lot, so bring plenty of T-shirts and cotton short-sleeved shirts. Most Tokyoites carry a handkerchief at all times, which can come in handy for wiping a sweaty brow.

Due to seasonal temperature changes, most Japanese businessmen have an array of business suits in heavy-, moderate-, and light-weight fabrics. Foreign executives working in Japan may wish to dress as Japanese businessmen do for the sake of comfort and image. (*Refer to* "What to Wear" *in Chapter 9 for suggestions.*)

Some foreign businessmen living in Tokyo order tailor-made suits from Hong Kong, as these are much less expensive and the service fast. As Hong Kong is only a six-hour flight from Tokyo, it is possible to have suits made while there for business or over a long weekend. (Be sure to allow time for at least two fittings.) Also, several tailors from Hong Kong come to Tokyo regularly to take orders, mainly from foreigners. To find a good tailor, ask other expatriates for recommendations.

Shoes wear out quickly in Tokyo, as most people walk a lot getting to and from public transportation stops. If you wear shoes larger than an American size 9.5, an English size 9, or a European size 42.5, you will find only a limited selection for sale in Tokyo. Shoes that are easy to slip on and off are more convenient than shoes that must be laced, as it is a Japanese custom to take shoes off in homes, and before entering the restaurants and inns that have *tatami* (straw mat) floor coverings.

Women's Items

Many of the same guidelines on packing that apply to men apply to women as well. Japanese women tend to spend a lot of money on clothing, and there is a wide selection of fine apparel (both domestic and imported) available in Tokyo. Sizes, however, may pose a problem if you are tall or larger than an American size 10,

61

an English size 12, or a European size 42, so bring along plenty. *(Refer to the size comparison chart in Chapter 13.)*

For the cold winter weather, you will need a heavy coat, warm sweaters, a muffler or scarf, and warm gloves. For the hot and humid summer weather, take shirts and dresses made of fabrics that absorb perspiration and are easy to wash. As the temperatures in air-conditioned buildings can be low, light sweaters, jackets and scarves are useful. For the more moderate but variable weather of spring and fall, take clothes that can be worn in layers (sweater sets, comfortable suits, and dresses with jackets, for example). Those who anticipate size problems should also pack sufficient quantities of lingerie and hosiery.

Women who wear shoes larger than an American size 7, an English size 5.5, or a European size 38, are likely to have difficulty buying shoes in Japan.

In general, Japanese women dress very neatly, conservatively, and in most Westerners' eyes, rather formally. To make a good impression, foreign businesswomen may want to do the same. *(Refer to* "What to Wear" *in Chapter 9 for suggestions.)*

A variety of imported cosmetics are sold in Japan, but some of them are produced specifically to suit Japanese preferences as well as skin types and tones. Consequently, if you are partial to a particular brand or type of cosmetic, bring along a supply that will last until you can find a suitable substitute in Tokyo. Also worth noting is that feminine hygiene products available in Japan tend to be smaller in size than those made for Western women, so some foreign women prefer to take a supply from home.

Children's Items

Buying clothing and shoes for children in Tokyo may be much easier than for adults. Goods for children are available in a great variety of sizes, designs, and colors. As children grow fast, you might want to take only the essentials with you and then shop in

Tokyo as your children need them. Although some expatriates find children's clothing rather expensive in Tokyo, it is possible to save money by shopping during seasonal sales or by buying used clothes. For children who are on the larger side, however, it is a good idea to take sufficient clothes from home, as it is not easy to find apparel for big-sized children in Tokyo.

High-quality toys are abundant in Tokyo, although they tend to be more expensive than in other countries. Some parents have also noted the preponderance (to the exclusion of other types, in many stores) of "character" toys, such as Hello Kitty or Anpan-Man. (*Refer to* "Toys" *in Chapter 13.*)

Foreign books and videos are also expensive, so you may want to take a good supply. They can be great for consoling homesick children. Be sure to bring several copies of your children's school transcripts, as they will be required for admittance into schools in Japan.

General Household Items
Furniture
Whether you take large household items such as furniture may depend largely on the transportation costs and whether the items will fit into your new home. In general, homes in Tokyo are smaller than those in many countries (especially the United States, Canada, and Australia). Therefore, unless you know the size of your new living area and that your furniture will fit, it may be safer to leave it behind. If you are taking your beds, pack also the bed linens as it may be difficult to find items in Tokyo that fit your bed size – Japanese beds are shorter than those found in many other countries. (*Refer to* "Furniture" *in Chapter 13 for stores.*)

Electrical Appliances
The electric power in Tokyo is 100 volts and 50 cycles (hertz). (Electricity in eastern Japan is 50 cycles, but in western Japan it is 60 cycles.) Small appliances such as radios and hair dryers that

are 110 volts and 60 cycles (the standard in the United States and Canada) can be used in Tokyo, but might run a little hot. Most portable computers are equipped with internal converters and should run with no problems, although some very early models might not have this capability. Electric clocks and other sensitive appliances may not work properly. It is generally better to buy large appliances, such as televisions and refrigerators, in Tokyo.

Not all foreign-made videos will work in Japan. Japan uses the NTSC video format, as do the United States and Canada, so videos made in those countries can be played on Japanese VCRs. However, the PAL video format used in most of Europe and Australia is not compatible with the majority of Japanese VCRs. In Tokyo it is possible to buy VCRs that can handle multiple formats, but they are more expensive than single-format VCRs.

As for DVDs, regional codes are generally programmed into them in the countries in which they are released. The regional code for DVDs released in Japan and many European countries, for example, is "two", whereas it is "one" for DVDs in the United States and Canada. Most DVD players sold in Japan accept only DVDs with the regional code "two". Thus, if you want to watch DVDs with other regional codes you will need a player that accepts multiple regional codes. Such players can be found in some shops in Akihabara.

The electrical plugs in Japan are flat two-pronged plugs, similar to the two-pronged plugs used in the U.S. and Canada. Three-pronged grounded plugs will not fit into Japanese sockets. If necessary, take a supply of converter plugs or buy them after you arrive.

Medication
You can bring up to a month's supply of prescription drugs and up to a two-month's supply of non-prescription medications into Japan. If you are taking prescribed medication, you should bring a copy of the prescription and/or a letter from the prescribing

physician explaining the nature of the medication. Most prescription drugs can be taken into Japan, including drugs that may not be available there.

Drugs that contain narcotic, psychotropic, and/or hallucinogenic components will be confiscated unless pre-approval has been obtained. Also, some over-the-counter medications that are sold overseas are prohibited for sale in Japan because they contain some of the components mentioned above, for instance Tylenol Cold, Nyquil and Sudafed.

Birth control pills can be prescribed by doctors in Japan, but to obtain refills, a doctor's visit is required. Therefore, many foreign women who use birth control pills take ample supplies with them. (*Refer to* "Having a Baby in Tokyo" *in Chapter 11.*)

Foodstuff

Japanese Customs regulations do not allow people to carry most fresh fruits, vegetables and meat products into Japan. However, canned fruits, vegetables, and prepared meat products are generally allowed. Dried meat, such as beef jerky, may be taken into Japan if it has been commercially prepared and packaged. Other dry products such as cookies, crackers, candies, and cereals, as well as dried noodles, may be taken into Japan. Most types of nuts can also be imported if they are salted, dried, or roasted, but walnuts are prohibited.

Pets

Upon arrival, all imported animals are subject to inspection by the Japanese Animal Quarantine Service. The time required for the inspection depends on the type of animal and the health condition of the pets. Health certificates are required for several types of animals.

For dogs and cats, the inspection period will be up to 12 hours if the animals enter from countries that are known as "rabies-free", and if they are accompanied by a certificate issued by the government authorities of such a country. These countries include Taiwan, Australia, New Zealand, Singapore and Britain. The certificate should state that: 1) the pet is free from rabies and leptospirosis (for dogs only) and any infectious diseases; 2) the pet was kept for six months or since its birth in one of these countries prior to transport; and 3) there has been no outbreak of rabies for six months in the country prior to shipment.

The quarantine period for dogs and cats from other countries (such as the United States) generally ranges from 14 to 180 days, depending on the condition of the animal. In order to qualify for the 14-day quarantine period, dogs and cats must be accompanied by rabies vaccination certificates (proving that the pets were inoculated for rabies more than 30 days prior to the date of entry into Japan) and with health certificates from veterinarians.

For rabbits, as long as no abnormalities are found, the inspection will take only one day (not including the arrival day and the day of release). In addition, a health certificate issued by a government agency in the country of export must accompany this type of pet.

For small birds, inspection will be completed within one day of the pet's arrival as long as no abnormalities are found; no additional documents are required.

IMMIGRATION AND CUSTOMS

By air, the international gateway to Tokyo from most countries is Narita New Tokyo International Airport. Built in the 1970s and known simply as "Narita", the airport is located in the city of the same name, a relatively distant 60 kilometers (about 37 miles) from the center of Tokyo.

International passengers arrive at either Terminal 1 or Terminal 2; both have similar facilities and immigration procedures. After deplaning, passengers will pass Quarantine Station booths on their way toward the Immigration Counter. Passengers from countries in which epidemic diseases such as cholera or typhus are prevalent, such as Africa, Southeast Asia, or Central and South America, and those who are experiencing any symptoms of these diseases should stop at one of these booths and complete a yellow questionnaire (usually distributed on incoming flights) regarding their health condition. Quarantine officials might immediately conduct an examination or arrange to contact them later.

The immigration process is quite simple. Fill out an embarkation/disembarkation card and present it with a valid passport and visa, if required. This card is provided during the flight and along the walk toward the Immigration Counter. Foreigners should go to the Immigration Counter labeled "Foreigners". Residents of Japan who have a Foreign Registration Card and a re-entry permit (*See* "Obtaining Necessary Documents" *in Chapter 4*) can go to the counter labeled "Japanese". If you are entering the country without a visa (for short-term visitors), the Immigration officer might ask to see a confirmed ticket for transportation to your next destination outside of Japan. The officer will then stamp your passport, indicating the length of stay permitted.

After completing the immigration process, collect your luggage and go through Customs. If you have something to declare, you must fill out the Customs Declaration form provided to passengers on incoming flights and give it to a Customs officer, who might ask to inspect your luggage. Customs' duties can be paid at the special office located just past the Customs inspection point.

Airport Facilities

Several money exchange counters are conveniently located in the arrival area. Some of them are open from 7am to 10pm and others from 6.30 am to 11 pm. The Bank of Tokyo-Mitsubishi offers full-service banking and is open from 9am to 3pm. If you are not carrying any Japanese currency (yen), it might be a good idea to get some here, as cash is often the only type of payment accepted

Photo by Akiko Watanabe.

Kaminarimon gate at Sensoji Temple in Asakusa.

by taxis and other forms of public transportation. Also, exchange rates posted at the airport are generally better than those at hotels. There are also medical clinics located in the basements of both Terminal 1 and Terminal 2.

It can be a hassle to get around Tokyo while carrying heavy luggage. In the arrival area you will find several companies (GPA, ABC, Kamataki, and NPS) that offer a wonderful service; for a reasonable fee they will deliver your luggage anywhere in the Tokyo area on the day following your arrival.

Transportation to the Metropolis
Several options for transportation into Tokyo are available and all take nearly two hours.

Taxi
If money is not an issue, taking a taxi may be the easiest, although not necessarily the fastest, way to get to your destination. The ride to the center of Tokyo can cost about 20,000 yen and will

take close to two hours, longer if traffic is congested on the highway or in central areas. Wagon taxis can be convenient for passengers carrying more than one large suitcase as regular taxis have limited trunk space. The price is the same for either type of taxi.

Taxi drivers in Tokyo generally do not speak English, so if your destination is not one of the major hotels and requires some explanation, you might want to write down the address and directions and hand them to the driver. It is much preferable to ask someone to write the directions in Japanese, but if that is not possible, do write them in English as many Japanese people can read English better than they can understand it.

Limousine Bus

A limousine bus is not as luxurious as you might imagine its name; it is more like a sightseeing bus. But at 3,000 yen or so to most points in central Tokyo, it is less expensive than a taxi.

These buses cover several routes around Tokyo, stopping at major hotels and train stations, as well as at major spots such as Tokyo Disneyland, Haneda Airport, and the Yokohama area. If none of the bus routes passes by your specific destination, you can get off at the closest scheduled stop and take a taxi from there. Taxis are available at most bus stops.

Buses depart every 10 to 15 minutes and the ride takes between one and two hours, depending on your destination and traffic conditions. You can take up to two suitcases with you. (If you have more suitcases, use the delivery service previously mentioned.) Tickets can be purchased at the limousine counter located in the arrival area of the airport.

Train

An express train, called the Narita Express, connects Narita with major stations in Tokyo (including Tokyo, Shinagawa, Shinjuku, Ikebukuro, and Yokohama Station). Depending on the final destination, the trip will take an hour or more. Prices range from

69

3,000 to 4,000 yen for regular seats, and 5,000 to 7,000 yen for deluxe seats. Tickets can be purchased at Narita Airport Station, located on the lower level of the airport building of both terminals.

There is also a regular train (JR Line) that connects Narita Airport with some of the major stations previously mentioned. The ticket costs only about half the price of the Narita Express, but as this is a local train the trip takes longer.

Still another express train, the Keisei Railway Skyliner, runs from Narita Airport to the eastern part of Tokyo, stopping at Nippori and Ueno Station. It is possible to transfer to other major train lines at these two stations and then travel to other parts of Tokyo. The ride takes approximately one hour and costs about 2,000 yen. Keisei Railway also has a regular ("limited") express train service to Nippori and the Ueno terminal. This trip takes about an hour and a half, but costs only 1,000 yen.

The greatest drawback to taking the train is carrying luggage up and down escalators before and after the trip. However, you can avoid this by using the delivery service mentioned earlier. Another drawback is that trains run less frequently than do limousine buses, so if you have to wait for more than half-an-hour for the next train to Tokyo Station, it would probably be faster to take a limousine bus.

❈ ❈ ❈

Welcome to Tokyo! You will find the city's transportation system is efficient and well organized, and the Japanese people with whom you interact at the airport and on public transport, such as Customs officers, bank tellers and taxi drivers, polite and efficient (even though they may not be fluent in English).

—CHAPTER FOUR—

STARTING YOUR LIFE IN TOKYO

Setting up a new household and starting a new life can be exciting but also overwhelming, especially in unfamiliar surroundings. This chapter familiarizes you with procedures to obtaining necessary documents, finding housing, and arranging for utilities and services.

OBTAINING NECESSARY DOCUMENTS

All foreign residents must obtain Foreign Resident Registration Cards which serve as identification within Japan. Re-entry permits are also required if you wish to travel outside Japan during your stay in Tokyo. In addition, Seal Registration Certificates are sometimes required when signing important documents.

71

Foreign Resident Registration

All foreigners who plan to stay in Japan longer than 90 days are required to register at the ward or municipal office of the area in which they live. If this requirement applies to you, be sure to register before the 90 days have passed. You will need your passport and two photographs (4.5 cm by 3.5 cm, that have been taken within the last six months); photographs are not required for children under 16. Anyone age 16 or older must apply in person; parents can apply for children younger than 16.

If you do not read or speak Japanese, it is best to go to the ward or municipal office with someone who does, as many application forms are in Japanese and office personnel are not always fluent in English. After your application is processed, you will receive a Foreign Registration Card valid for five years. This card will serve as identification and, within Japan, is almost as important as a passport. All foreigner residents aged 16 or over are required to carry their card at all times.

Foreigners are also required to report to the ward or municipal office closest to their residence within 14 days if changes are made to any of the following: name, nationality, occupation, status of residence, period of stay, name of employer, work address, or home address. Foreigners who move to a new location during their stay in Tokyo are required to report to the ward or municipal office closest to their new address.

Re-entry Permit

Foreign residents who want to travel overseas must obtain a re-entry permit prior to departure from Japan. A single permit allows the holder to make one trip out of Japan and to return with no change in visa status. A multiple re-entry permit allows the holder to make unlimited trips abroad until the date of expiration of the permit. To obtain a permit, apply in person with your passport and Foreign Registration Card at one of the following

Immigration Bureaus in Tokyo:

>   **Tokyo Regional Immigration Bureau**
>   1-3-1 Otemachi, Chiyoda-ku,
>   Tokyo 100-0004
>   Tel: 03-3286-5241
>   **Shibuya Regional Immigration Office**
>   1-3-5 Jinnan, Shibuya-ku,
>   Tokyo 150-0041
>   Tel: 03-5458-0370

Seal Registration

In Japan, people use seals (*hanko*) instead of written signatures when signing contracts or documentations. They usually have family names in Chinese characters on their seals. Written signatures are accepted from foreigners in most cases, but some expatriates make their own seals for convenience and as a memory of their stay in Japan. Seals with family names, given names, or full names are considered valid stamps and can be ordered at stationary stores or stamp shops.

In particular, seals that are registered with ward or municipal office are required when signing important documents (for example, when renting or purchasing a house, or purchasing a car). If you need to register your seal, take it and your Foreign Registration Card to the ward or municipal office of your residence. You will receive a Seal Registration Certificate that proves that your seal is registered. Seals with names that are not recorded on the Foreign Registration Card cannot be registered.

ARRANGING HOUSING
Choosing a Neighborhood

When choosing a place in which to live, two important factors most expatriates consider are the location of their workplace and, if they have children, the location of their children's schools. People who will use public transportation to get to work generally prefer to live near public transportation stations. Families with children who will attend an international school generally prefer to live near a bus stop for the school's bus service. (Japanese private and public schools do not offer school bus services.)

In addition to the practical considerations mentioned above, many foreign residents consider the type of neighborhood in which they would prefer to live: international, old-style Tokyo, quiet residential, or suburban greenery.

International Neighborhoods

Foreign residents who want to be immersed in an international environment often choose to live in one of the large expatriate communities that have developed in Minato-ku (areas such as Azabu, Aoyama, Roppongi, and Akasaka), and in Shibuya-ku (areas such as Hiroo, Jingumae, and Ebisu). Many embassies, foreign clubs, international schools and international supermarkets are located in these areas. Be forewarned that rent here can be very high.

Old-style Neighborhoods

For those wanting to experience the flavor of old-style Tokyo, neighborhoods such as Bunkyo-ku, Taito-ku, and Toshima-ku in the eastern part of the city are ideal. They each have a small-town feel created by the many small wooden houses standing next to each other and the mom-and-pop shops that have been doing business in the same location for generations. Housing here is reasonably priced compared to those in other areas of the city.

Quiet Residential Neighborhoods

Foreigners seeking quiet neighborhoods that are somewhat distant from expatriate communities often settle in the residential areas of western Tokyo, including Meguro-ku (Jiyugaoka, for example),

Ota-ku (Den-enchofu, for example), and Setagaya-ku (Yoga, Komazawa, and Seijo, for example). The rents in these areas tend to be high, especially for larger homes.

Suburban Neighborhoods

Finally, foreigners who prefer to live in a suburban environment with attractive greenery often enjoy the neighborhoods located further west. These include Musashino-shi, Mitaka-shi, Chofu-shi, and some areas in Kanagawa Prefecture such as Kawasaki-shi and Yokohama-shi. Rents for apartments and houses are generally lower in these areas, allowing residents to lease larger places than they could in central Tokyo. One drawback, however, is the long commute into the city on crowded trains.

Choosing Accommodation

Three main types of accommodation are found in Tokyo: apartments, *manshon* ("mansion") units, and houses. While these differ in terms of size and amenities, all three types are described using a similar "code" – 1K, 2LDK, or 3DK, for example. "K" stands for kitchen, "L" for living room and "D" for dining room; the number indicates the number of bedrooms. Therefore, a 2LDK house or apartment has two bedrooms, a living room, a dining room and a kitchen.

The overall sizes of apartments, *manshon* units, and houses are indicated using square meters. However, the size of an individual room is usually indicated by the number of *tatami* (straw) mats that will cover the floor – *tatami* mats were, at one time, found in most rooms of Japanese houses. The size of one *tatami* is about 90 cm by 180 cm (3 feet by 6 feet) and a space equivalent to one *tatami* mat (about 1.60 square meters/18 square feet) is called a *jo*. *Tatami* sizes can vary; often one finds widths of 80 cm. Even though many modern Japanese houses are designed in a more Western style and some rooms do not have *tatami* mats, the same

75

measurement system is used. The size of a room might be indicated, for example, as 8 *jo*, which means that the size is equivalent to eight *tatami* mats.

Apartments

Apartments are generally the smallest and least expensive housing option. Most apartment buildings are two stories tall and made of wood, although some have exterior walls made of mortar. The most common floor plan for apartments is 2LDK (two bedrooms, a living room, a dining room and a kitchen). Bedrooms range from 4.5 *jo* (about 7 square meters/80 square feet) to 6 *jo* (about 10 square meters/110 square feet), and usually at least one bedroom is a *tatami* room. Very old apartments do not have showers or baths, so residents use public baths nearby. Renters may be required to pay monthly management fees for the maintenance of public spaces in the apartment buildings; these fees vary from building to building.

Manshon Units

The term *manshon* is used to refer to newer apartment buildings that are made of reinforced concrete; most are higher than three stories and some are taller than 10 stories. These buildings started appearing in the late 1960s and were called *manshon* (meaning "mansions") because they looked so luxurious compared to the old-style wooden apartment buildings. They are more durable than wooden apartment buildings, and as they generally have better facilities, such as elevators and garages, are more expensive than apartments. *Manshon* come in three types: regular, those catering to foreigners, and those in which units can be rented by the week.

The smallest *manshon* unit is called a "one-room *manshon*", which is basically a studio apartment with a small kitchenette attached to it. The largest *manshon* units are 4LDK or 5LDK (four or five bedrooms, a living space, a dining area, and a kitchen). The sizes and the types of rooms vary; the average bedroom size ranges from 6 *jo* (about 10 square meters/110 square feet) to 8 *jo* (about 13 square meters/144 square feet). The entire area of a typical *manshon* unit ranges from 30 square meters (about 330 square feet) to more than 100 square meters (about 1,100 square feet). Most have at least one *tatami* room; some have balconies or patios. Like the apartment buildings, most *manshon* require payment of monthly management fees.

In areas with high expatriate populations there are many *gaikokujin-yo manshon* (meaning foreigner-style *manshon*). These *manshon* usually do not have *tatami* rooms and have an average bedroom size of 8 *jo* (about 13 square meters/144 square feet) to 10 *jo* (about 16 square meters/180 square feet). Appliances such as clothes washers and dryers, dishwashers, and gas ovens are often already built in. Some buildings have separate living quarters attached for tenants' domestic helpers. Because these types of *manshon* are larger than the average apartments and *manshon* in Tokyo, they are one of the most expensive housing options. The majority of tenants in such apartments are foreigners, but some are Japanese people who prefer a Western-type lifestyle and can afford the rent.

For temporary housing, there are also "weekly *manshon*". As the name indicates, units can be rented on a weekly basis. They are furnished and usually include basic items such as cookware and linens. Although rents are high, staying in a weekly *manshon* is generally much cheaper than staying in a hotel.

Single-Family Houses

A single-family house is the third option for foreigners, although the selection in central Tokyo is limited. Some houses are built completely in Western style, similar to the foreigners' *manshon*, with large rooms and no *tatami* room. Rents for large houses can be very high.

Photo by Akiko Watanabe.

A home in suburban Tokyo displays New Year's decoration at the front gate.

Design Features

In all these types of housing, foreigners may notice some unique features unique in Japanese-style bathrooms. Most have a deep, square bathtub, though Western-style oblong bathtubs are increasingly the norm in new apartment buildings, and a separate adjacent area for washing; some have a showerhead on the wall outside of the bathtub. (Japanese people only soak in bathtubs – they do not wash their bodies or shampoo their hair in them.) While some residences have a bathtub that fills with hot water from the tap, others have bathtubs where cold water from the tap is heated by a gas heater attached to the tub.

Another design feature of Japanese bathroom facilities is the squat toilet, instead of the ceramic "chair" on which people sit. This is most common in some older apartments, as well as in some public restrooms. Also, either type of toilet may have a water tank attached above or adjacent to it (in place of the toilet tank) in which one can wash one's hands; water automatically comes out of a spigot after the toilet has been flushed.

Finding a Home

The easiest way to find accommodation may be to work with a relocation company with offices in both your home country and in Tokyo. The Tokyo staff of the relocation company will pre-select a couple of places for you to view when you arrive in Tokyo. The staff will probably be fluent in English, so you will not have to worry about language issues.

In order to find a home without the services of a relocation company, you can work with a real estate agency. There are several such agencies in Tokyo that cater mainly to foreigners. They have English-speaking staff and understand foreigners' needs. Because they target expatriates, the places they show you will be mainly those built for foreigners, and thus, can be expensive. Real estate agencies servicing foreigners include the following:

KEN Corporation
1-2-7 Nishi Azabu
Minato-ku, Tokyo 106-0031
Tel: 03-5413-5666
http://www.kencorp.com

Kimi Information Center
2-42-3 Ikebukuro
Toshima-ku, Tokyo 171-0014
Tel: 03-3986-1604
http://www.kimiwillbe.com

Liberty Corporation (Jiyusha Co. Ltd.)
Nihonbashi D.M. 6F, 1-6-3 Nihonbashi Honcho
Chuo-ku, Tokyo 103-0023
Tel: 03-3517-1866
http://www.jiyusha.com

Nord House
Masuya Bldg. 6F, 3-21-24 Nishi Azabu
Minato-ku, Tokyo 106-0031
Tel: 03-5474-7412
http://www.nord.co.jp

Plaza Homes
1-9-12 Azabudai
Minato-ku, Tokyo 106-0041
Tel: 03-3583-6941
http://www.plazahomes.co.jp

If you do not want to live in housing built for foreigners, you can work with a local real estate agency. Several agency offices are located near major train and subway stations. If you plan to visit these agencies, ask a Japanese friend or colleague to accompany you. People at local agencies generally do not speak English, and some may not feel comfortable communicating with foreigners, even if you do speak some Japanese. Also, you may discover that some landlords are hesitant to rent to foreigners because of limited experience in interacting with them. The Japanese person who accompanies you can help build your credibility and reduce the anxiety of the agent and potential landlord.

Another approach to gauging prices and finding housing is to check rental listings in housing magazines and to contact the designated real estate agencies for details. This approach has a couple of drawbacks, however. First, almost all of these magazines are written entirely in Japanese. Second, because the magazines are published weekly instead of daily, they seldom contain the most up-to-date listings. In most cases, by the time you contact the agencies, the properties listed are no longer available.

Finally, information available through informal networks may be a valuable source for finding a place to live. You can also check bulletin boards in places where foreigners are likely to gather (for example, international clubs, supermarkets, and organizations), or the housing advertisement columns in English-language newspapers such as *The Japan Times*, magazines such as *Metropolis*, and the *Tokyo Notice Board*.

Signing the Contract

Once you have chosen a place to live, a formal contract must be signed with the landlord. The contract period is generally two years, although for some properties it is one year. Most contracts are renewable; however, the rent might change and tenants could be asked to pay a renewal fee equivalent to approximately one month's rent. Before signing a contract, check to see if it includes any penalties for early termination. The following are required to finalize a rental contract:

1. Foreign Resident Registration Card
2. Income Statement

   You may be asked to show documentation that proves your income. Most employers in Japan are accustomed to issuing such documents.
3. Guarantor (*Hoshonin*)

   In Japan, it is common practice to have a surety's (guarantor) signature to finalize a rental contract. The guarantor should be someone who has income and who can pay the rent in case the tenant is unable to. Ask your manager, a colleague, or a friend to act as your guarantor.
4. Seal Registration Certificate

   Japanese people usually use seals when signing contracts. Signatures are often acceptable for foreigners. Ask your landlord what is required.

   Initial rental payments usually include the first month's rent, a *shikikin* (deposit), and a *reikin* (monetary reward). The *shikikin* is a deposit that is equivalent to two- to three-months' rent and is generally refunded when you move out. However, if there is any damage to the residence, the landlord will subtract from the *shikikin* the amount required to repair the damage. The *reikin* is a payment of one- or two-months' rent made to acknowledge the landlord for accepting the tenant. It is neither optional nor refundable.

In addition, real estate agencies usually charge one-month's rent as their commission. Relocation companies often combine all such fees into a package.

ARRANGING UTILITIES AND SERVICES
Gas

Many homes have gas ovens, stoves, water heaters, and room heaters. Gas distributed in the Tokyo area is primarily natural gas provided by the Tokyo Gas Company.

When tenants move out, gas service is discontinued. Therefore, prior to moving into a new home, you must call the nearest Tokyo Gas office and notify the staff of your moving date. Usually, instructions for new tenants (including the telephone number to call) are hung on the front door of the apartment or house. The instructions are in Japanese, however, and operators may not speak English, so it might be a good idea to ask your landlord or the real estate agent for assistance. After you make the call, a representative from Tokyo Gas will visit your home and make the necessary arrangements.

The gas meter will be checked once a month and you will receive a monthly bill. Most people pay their gas bills using the automatic transfer system at the bank with which they have a general deposit account. Payments for the monthly bills are then automatically deducted. Applications for enrollment in this system are available at all banks that offer the service. If you choose to enroll, make sure that your account contains sufficient funds on the monthly payment date. (*Refer to* "Payment of Bills" *in Chapter 7* .) If you prefer not to use automatic debit, you can pay your bill in cash at a bank, post office, or convenience store such as 7-11 (Seven Eleven), Lawson, or AmPm. These places serve as clearing agents for Tokyo Gas and no additional fees are charged.

Electricity

Electricity in the Tokyo area is provided by the Tokyo Electric Power Company. When you move into a new place, you will generally find a circuit-breaker box near the entrance to your home. Lift the circuit breaker (usually the biggest switch on the board) as well as the other small switches on the board, and you should begin to receive electricity. If there is no electricity, call the nearest TEPCO office. You should also send an application postcard to the company to notify them of your billing information. You will generally find the postcard on the circuit-breaker box or hanging on the front door of your residence. If you require assistance in calling the company or reading the postcard, ask your landlord or real estate agent.

A person from the Tokyo Electric Power Company will check the electric meter monthly, and you will receive a monthly bill. Payment of bills is similar to that for gas – by automatic debit, or by cash at a bank, post office, or convenience store.

Water

Water is supplied by the Tokyo Metropolitan Bureau of Waterworks. To get water running, prior to moving into your new residence, contact the Tokyo Metropolitan Bureau of Waterworks Service Station or the Waterworks Section of your area's ward or municipal office. You should also send an application postcard to notify them of your billing information. Ask the landlord or real estate agency for the appropriate number to call and where to find the postcard, if it is not hanging on the main door. You will receive a bill once every two months. The payment methods are the same as those for gas and electricity. Tap water in Tokyo is safe to drink but does not taste very good, so many people use water filters or buy bottled water.

Garbage Collection

If you live in an apartment, there will usually be a garbage disposal area in your building. If you live in a house, there will be places every few blocks to put garbage on the day of pick-up. Garbage should be separated into combustible materials and noncombustible materials and these should be disposed of separately. In most of Tokyo, combustible materials are picked up twice a week; they should be placed in paper bags or specially-marked plastic bags (sold at supermarkets). Noncombustible garbage is picked up once weekly.

Recyclable materials such as glass, aluminum and steel cans, newspapers, and magazines should be gathered separately and are picked up once a week.

To arrange for disposal of larger materials such as furniture and electrical appliances, call the ward or municipal office in your area. Special arrangements must also be made to dispose of air conditioners, televisions, refrigerators, or clothes washers. Shops from which new appliances are purchased are responsible for recycling old items. If you do not know where to take old appliances, ask your ward or municipal office for recommendations. You will have to pay a fee to recycle or dispose of appliances (even if you are buying a new one from the shop).

Telephone

In addition to private home telephones, cellular phones are very popular in Tokyo; because of the increase in cellular phone usage, the number of public telephones has decreased. Details about each type of telephones follow.

Private Telephone Service

Most rental units already have a telephone line installed. If you have to arrange for installment of a telephone line, you must submit an application to your area's Nippon Telephone and Telegraph (NTT) Corporation East branch office. When applying, you will need your passport or Foreign Resident Registration Card as well as documentation to confirm your address. You must pay the following: a contract fee, a telephone ownership fee, and an installation fee. Call the NTT Information Service (in English; Tel: 0120-364463) for more information.

Telephone Numbers

Telephone numbers in Tokyo consist of an area code followed by an exchange number and the subscriber's number. Telephone numbers within the 23 wards are indicated by the area code "03", followed by eight-digit numbers (03-1111-1111). In several areas (including Koganei-shi and Kokubunji-shi), the area code is "042" followed by seven-digit numbers (042-111-1111). In other areas (such as Chofu-shi, Hachioji-shi, and Ome-shi), telephone numbers are prefixed with a variety of area codes including "0424", "0426" and "0428", followed by six-digit numbers (for example, 0424-11-1111). Area codes are not necessary when placing a call within the same area code. Area codes are also unnecessary when calling emergency numbers (such as "110" for police or "119" for fire-fighting and ambulance services). Telephone numbers starting with "0120" are toll-free numbers.

Telephone Carriers

A new system called MYLINE lets customers use different telephone carriers for different distances without dialing each telephone carrier's access code. Before the system was implemented, all local calls and long distance calls (except international calls) automatically went through NTT, and people who wanted to use different carriers had to dial prefixes such as "0055" before dialing the individual telephone numbers. Now, by pre-selecting and registering your preferences with various telephone carriers, calls can be connected through those designated carriers each time you make calls. You can select a telephone carrier for each of the following four categories of calls: 1) local; 2) in-prefecture long distance; 3) out-of-prefecture long distance; and 4) international.

Each carrier offers a unique pricing structure. Application forms are available directly from each carrier or at the MYLINE Center. For further information, contact MYLINE Center Phone-in customer service (Tel: 0120-000-406 in English, Chinese, Spanish and Portuguese, or log onto **http://www.myline.org**).

You can also make telephone calls without registering with MYLINE. Simply dial the area code (for a call outside your own area) followed by the number, and the call will automatically go through NTT. To use different telephone carriers, simply dial the prefix numbers designated for those carriers before dialing the area codes.

International Calls
Since April 2003, you need to dial "010" to make an international call. The procedure for making an international call is as follows:
• If you have registered with the MYLINE system and have
    pre-selected an international carrier, dial:
        010 + country code + your counterpart's number
• If you have not registered with MYLINE, dial:
    the prefix of the carrier of your choice + 010 + country code
    + your counterpart's number

Telephone Bills
You will receive telephone bills monthly – one bill for dialing charges from each of the telephone carriers through which you made calls, and a separate bill from NTT for basic charges for domestic calls (because all telephone carriers are required to use the network installed by NTT). The payment methods available for telephone bills are the same as for other utilities.

86

Cellular Phone

More than 50 percent of Japanese people now use cellular phones. The major carriers for cellular phone service are NTT DoCoMo, J-Phone, and *au*. You can buy cellular phones at retail shops operated by these cellular phone service companies or at large electronic shops.

Using cellular phone service for Internet access is very popular in Japan. In addition to exchanging e-mail through cell phones, people can receive information such as weather forecasts, stock quotes, and train schedules, and can also complete transactions such as making reservations, purchasing tickets, and transferring money from their bank accounts. The most popular Internet service on cellular phones is "**i-mode**" provided by NTT DoCoMo.

Public Telephone

As the number of cellular phone users has increased, the number of public telephones in Tokyo has decreased – but you still can find pay phones in retails shops, department stores, train and subway stations, and some other public places. The minimum charge for using a pay phone is 10 yen.

Photo by Akiko Watanabe .

Cellular phones are everywhere in Tokyo.

87

The most common type of public telephone in Tokyo is either green or grey in color. Some of them accept 10 and 100 yen coins, but no change will be provided even if your actual charge was under 100 yen; and prepaid telephone cards – the number of public phones that accept only telephone cards is increasing. Telephone cards can be purchased at kiosks and from the vending machines that are often located near public phones. International calls can be placed from some public telephones. Look for telephones with signs saying "International Calls". Most have instructions in English; some accept credit cards.

Internet Access

Internet usage in Japan is growing rapidly. Now around 30 per cent of the population has access to the Internet and, as mentioned earlier, a large portion of that access is through cellular phones. For computer access, modem connection is the most popular method, followed by ADSL (Asymmetric Digital Subscriber Line – broadband connection using the telephone line) as the pricing of the latter becomes more competitive. Cable connection is also available. Popular Internet providers include Nifty, So-net, Yahoo, and Biglobe. The TELL Calendar (*See the* "English-Language Information Resources" *in the* Resource Guide.) has a list of Internet providers that offer services in English.

❋ ❋ ❋

While obtaining documents, finding a home, and arranging various services take time and patience, once these tasks are finally completed, you can breathe a sigh of relief and start settling into what will become your everyday life in Tokyo.

—CHAPTER FIVE—

ORGANIZING EVERYDAY LIFE

As a resident of Tokyo, you may depend on a variety of services to keep in touch with the world and to meet your personal needs. This chapter provides information on communication services, personal services and other topics related to everyday life necessities in Tokyo, including emergency procedures.

MAIL
Writing Addresses
The format used in Japan to address letters and parcels is different from that used in many countries. In Japan, addresses are written from general to specific, beginning with the postal code, administrative region, numbers, building name, company and

department name, and finally the intended recipient. The following is an example of how an address in the Tokyo metropolitan area is written and a brief description of its components:

00777-8888
Tokyo-to, Minato-ku, Akasaka, 10-20-30
General Office Building 3rd Floor
Service Company Accounting Department
Mr. Ichiro Suzuki

Line 1: Postal code. The "0" before the number indicates that the numbers following are the postal code.
Line 2: The first item on this line is the largest administrative region contained in the address; "-*to*" indicates the capital. The second-largest area is usually indicated by either "-*ku*" (ward) or "-*shi*" (city). Next is the neighborhood, followed by three numbers separated by hyphens. The first number is the "*chome*" (block), the second the "*ban*" (lot number), and the third the "*go*" (building number).
Line 3: Building name and floor number.
Line 4: Company and department names, sometimes written at the end of Line 3.
Line 5: Name of the intended recipient.

If the correct seven-digit postal code is clearly marked on the envelope or package, then you may omit the first and second large areas contained in the address, that is, up to "Akasaka" in the example above. Of course, if the postal code is incorrect your mail may be misdirected, so it is safest to write the full address.

When Japanese people write addresses in other languages or in *romaji* (Romanized Japanese words), especially when sending mail overseas, they usually switch the sequence (writing from the recipient's name or smaller entity first) to match other systems.

When you write addresses in Japan using *romaji*, you can use either system; if you write them in Japanese, it is better to follow the Japanese way. Please note that when Japanese people write their names in Japanese they usually write the family name first followed by the given name. (*See* "Japanese Names" *in Chapter 8*.)

Postal Services

The business hours of local post office branches vary. Large branches are open from 9am to 7pm Monday through Friday, and from 9:am to 3pm on Saturday; some branches are also open on Sunday, generally from 9 am to 12pm. Small branches are usually open from 9am to 5pm Monday through Friday and are closed on Saturday and Sunday. Mail is delivered to homes and offices once a day from Monday through Saturday.

Domestic letters can be sent using either *futsu yubin* (regular mail which usually takes two to three days) or *sokutatsubin* (express mail which usually takes one day or less). Important documents can be sent using *kakitome* service (registered mail), which ensures compensation for lost items. Cash, in particular, must be sent using this type of service and must be enclosed in a specially designated envelope; sending cash in a regular envelope is not allowed. Packages are best sent using the *Yu-pack* service; packages generally reach any domestic destination in one to two days. Fresh foods can be sent using the postal *chirudo Yu-pack* (chilled *Yu-pack*) service; they are carried in refrigerated cars to keep foods fresh.

Overseas letters or packages can be sent by three different types of services: air mail (about one week to Europe and the U.S.); SAL (Surface Air Lifted) mail (about three weeks to Europe and the U.S.); or sea mail (five to six weeks to Europe and the U.S.). For packages lighter than thirty kilograms (about 66 pounds), International Express service is available; it takes only two to three days to Europe and the U.S.

In addition to mail services, post offices also offer an array of financial services. (*Refer to* "Financial Services at Post Office" *in Chapter 7.*)

Delivery Services

Domestic package delivery service is provided by several private companies. This service, called *takuhaibin*, is convenient because packages can be dropped off at many places including grocery shops, supermarkets, and convenience stores that contract with the delivery service companies. Also, some delivery service companies will send representatives to your home to pick up packages you want to send. Some companies offer *kuru bin* (cool delivery) services by which you can send fresh foods. Packages usually reach most domestic destinations within one day. Companies that offer *takuhaibin* delivery services include Yamato, Nittsu, and Sagawa.

International delivery service for packages and documents is provided by Japanese companies (such as Yamato, Nittsu, and Sagawa), and foreign companies including the following:

FEDEX
Tel: 0120-003200, 043-298-1919
http://www.fedex.co.jp
DHL
Tel: 0120-39-2580, 03-5479-2580
http://www.dhl.co.jp
UPS
Tel: 0120-27-1040, 03-3520-0082
http://www.ups.com

MEDIA

Foreign residents can access world and local entertainment and news through English-language media such as newspapers, magazines, television and radio programming. The availability of media in languages other than Japanese and English is limited.

Newspapers

Home delivery is available for both English- and Japanese-language newspapers.

English-Language Newspapers

The following English-language newspapers are published in Tokyo and sold in bookstores that have foreign book sections, as well as at the kiosks in most major train and subway stations. (Refer to "Foreign Reading Materials" in Chapter 13.) Their websites also contain snapshots of current news and events. Newcomers can arrange for home delivery by calling the telephone numbers provided below:

International Herald Tribune/Asahi Shinbun
Tel: 0120-456-371
http://asahi.com
This paper contains news and articles from both the *International Herald Tribune* and the *Asahi Shinbun*, while the website offers news tidbits from *Asahi Shinbun*.

Mainichi Daily News
Tel: 03-3212-3266
http://mdn.mainichi.co.jp

The Daily Yomiuri
Tel: 0120-43-1159
http://www.yomiuri.co.jp/daily

The Japan Times
Tel: 0120-03-6242, 03-3453-4350
http://www.japantimes.co.jp

The Nikkei Weekly
Tel: 0120-00-9907
http://www.nni.nikkei.co.jp
This is primarily a business newspaper.

Major international newspapers such as the *Financial Times*, the *Asian Wall Street Journal*, and *USA Today* can be purchased at major bookstores and large kiosks around Tokyo. Subscriptions are also available.

Newspapers in Other Languages

Foreign newspapers in languages such as Chinese and French, are available in the foreign book sections of some major bookstores.

Japanese-Language Newspapers

The major Japanese-language newspapers, sold at most kiosks, are: *Asahi*, *Mainichi*, *Nikkei*, *Tokyo*, and *Yomiuri*. To arrange for home delivery, visit one of their representative offices located throughout Tokyo.

Television and Radio

There are seven television broadcasting channels available in Tokyo (Channels 1, 3, 4, 6, 8, 10, and 12). You can watch certain programs with English subtitles if you buy a television that supports the bilingual function.

Channels 1 and 3 are national public channels hosted by Nippon Hoso Kyokai, commonly known as NHK or the Japan Broadcasting Corporation. Viewers must pay monthly subscription fees, as these channels do not broadcast commercials and therefore do not receive funding from sponsors. When you move into a new home in Tokyo, an agent from NHK will come to your home and ask for the subscription fee. Some people claim that they should not have to pay because they do not watch Channels 1 and 3, but usually the agent is quite persistent. You can arrange for automatic debit of the subscription fee from your bank account. (Refer to "Payment of Bills" in Chapter 7)

Satellite channels are also available at an extra charge. Popular channels are NHK Satellite 1 (BS1), NHK Satellite 2 (BS2), and WOWOW. These Satellite channels offer bilingual (Japanese and English) broadcasts of news, movies, and some international sports events (including American baseball games involving teams on which Japanese players play). SKY PerfecTV offers foreign channels such as BBC, CNN, and the Discovery Channel. For detailed information, visit their website (**http:// www.skyperfectv.co.jp**) or call the SKY PerfecTV customer service center at (0570) 039-888 or (045) 339-0202. (Be patient - an announcement in English will follow the Japanese announcement.)

A few **radio stations** also offer programs in English. The AFN (American Forces Network; formerly known as FEN and found at 810 AM) broadcasts news and a variety of programs in English. InterFM (76.1 FM) also broadcasts programs in English. J-Wave (81.3 FM) is a music station that broadcasts in both English and Japanese.

VARIOUS SERVICES

The best way to find good service providers is to ask people you know for recommendations. To find English-speaking providers, check advertisements in English-language newspapers, magazines, and phone directories. (*Refer to the* "English-Language Information Resources" *in the* Resource Guide.)

Household Repairs

If appliances or the interior or exterior of your home need repairs, ask the landlord for the repair service person's contact number. If you need to find a repair service person on your own, or if you need repairs made on your own belongings, ask neighbors to refer you to someone they know. If there is a concierge in your apartment building, he or she may be able to offer some suggestions. If small electrical appliances need repairs, sometimes a person from a small electronics shop will come to your home to fix them, even if you did not buy the items from that shop.

Domestic Help

Because typical Japanese houses are small, and many Japanese women used to (and still do) stay at home and take care of housework, hiring domestic help has not been a common practice in Japan. As a result, finding reasonably priced domestic helpers can be a challenge. In the past decade as the number of Japanese women who work has increased, families find it convenient to have some help from time to time. Thus, a number of cleaning companies have begun doing business in Tokyo. If you want someone to clean your house periodically, you can contract a cleaning company such as Duskin to have someone come to your home according to a pre-arranged schedule. The company has franchises throughout Tokyo; they are listed in the English-language directory NTT TOWNPAGE. (*Refer to the* "English-Language Information Resources" *in the* Resource Guide.)

On the other hand, you may want to hire a full-time, live-in domestic helper to assist you with child care and/or with a variety of household chores. If so, there are numerous issues to consider.

Many expatriates choose to hire foreign domestic helpers, usually from the Philippines or Thailand, as this is less expensive than hiring a Japanese domestic helper. Employers are normally required to sponsor employment visas for their foreign domestic helpers if the helpers do not have valid Japanese work visas. If you intend to employ a foreign domestic helper, consult the Tokyo Immigration Office, as well as the embassy or consulate of the country of your potential employee, for details regarding employment visas and other required documentation.

Photo by Yuko Morimoto-Yoshida

Bulletin board with English-language notices at an international supermarket.

The best way to find a good domestic helper is through word-of-mouth. If you can "inherit" a foreign domestic helper from an expatriate family who is leaving Japan, then you will have a helper who comes to you with references and you will have some idea about her skills, reliability, and personality. Alternatively, check advertisements tacked onto bulletin boards at international clubs or at international supermarkets such as National Azabu. Finding, interviewing and supervising a full-time, live-in domestic helper involves many issues. First-time expatriate employers are advised to discuss the matter with those who have experience.

Child Care

Leaving children in the care of others is not as common in Japan as in some Western countries. Therefore, it is difficult to find Japanese teenagers who want to do baby-sitting as a part-time job. However, you might be able to find foreign teenagers who want to earn some spending money. Locate them by asking other expats, by contacting the international schools, or by putting up bulletin board ads in places frequented by expats. An online source with a listing of babysitters along with recommendations from actual users is Tokyo with Kids (**www.tokyowithkids.com**). As mentioned earlier, some expatriates hire live-in domestic helpers who are responsible for child care as well as other household duties. As the number of Japanese mothers who work increases, however, so will the number of child-care facilities.

Dry Cleaning
There is no shortage of dry cleaners in Tokyo, but prices and quality of service vary from shop to shop. Some offer express service for men's business shirts. Others offer pick-up and delivery service. One well-known dry cleaning chain store, Hakuyosha, offers the service of keeping coats and heavy jackets in cold storage during the hot and humid summer season.

Hairdressing and Other Treatments
There are two types of hairdressing shops in Japan: barbershops (*tokoya*) and hair salons (*biyoin*). Barbershops are allowed to perform shaving in addition to hair cutting, and are mainly for men. Barbershops are easy to identify – look for the red, blue, and white pole just outside the front door. Hair salons perform hairdressing only, and are frequented by both men and women. Usually hair salons are more fashionable and the services are much more expensive than those at barbershops. People generally make appointments for hair salons. No tipping is required in either barbershops or hair salons.

Some foreigners (especially women) prefer to go to hair salons that have many foreign clients for several reasons. First, the hair texture of Japanese people tends to be coarser than that of most foreigners, so many stylists are not used to cutting, perming, and styling finer hair. Second, the hair color of Japanese people tends to be quite dark, so ordinary salons may not carry a wide variety of coloring suitable for lighter hair. Finally, in ordinary salons, language can be an obstacle in communicating preferences. Ask your friends for recommendations. If that approach does not yield results, check the English-language telephone directory or magazines for advertisements of hairdressers who speak English.

For beauty treatments other than hairdressing, women generally go to "aesthetic salons". Aesthetic salons offer facials, waxing, nail care, and body treatments; some salons offer all of these services, while others specialize in certain ones.

RULES AND REGULATIONS

There are a few rules and regulations concerning pets and smoking which newcomers should be aware of.

Pets

Having pets (especially dogs and cats) is very popular in Tokyo, and many people consider their pets to be part of their family. Not all landlords will allow pets, however, so be sure to check in advance.

All pets entering Japan must go through certain quarantine procedures. (*Refer to* "Pets" *in Chapter 3.*) Any dog that is 91 days or older must be registered at the local ward or municipal office, after which the owner will receive a "dog license". Also, all dogs must be given an annual vaccination against rabies. The "dog license" and the tag indicating the receipt of the annual rabies vaccination must be attached to the dog's collar, which the dog must wear at all times. If a dog dies or disappears, the owner must notify the ward or

When walking a dog, you should keep it on a leash, clean up its mess, and avoid letting it enter public buildings or go on other people's property. (Pets, except guide dogs for the blind, are generally not allowed in shops and restaurants.) If you want your dog to learn commands and proper etiquette, take it to one of the several dog training schools in Tokyo.

Smoking Policy

Many public places in Tokyo have adopted a non-smoking policy. For example, at most train stations, smoking is permitted only in designated areas. In certain central Tokyo districts, smoking on the street is prohibited. Many offices only allow employees to smoke in designated rooms. Restaurants that offer non-smoking seats are increasing, but smoking is still allowed in many places where food and drinks are served.

EMERGENCIES
Fire, Ambulance, and Police

To report a fire, ask for rescue, or request an ambulance, call **119**. An English-speaking operator is on duty 24-hours a day. If you place a call to 119, state the type of emergency, your address, and your name. Firefighters and/or an ambulance will be dispatched and will usually reach you in a short time. This service is free of charge. (*Refer to* "Calling an Ambulance" *in Chapter 11*).

To report a burglary or any incidents that require the help of police officers, call **110**. An English-speaking operator is on duty around the clock. For non-urgent matters, go to one of the police boxes located throughout Tokyo; they can be recognized by the sign KOBAN. A few police officers are stationed at each KOBAN to assist people with matters such as lost and found items, as well as bicycle theft . You can also ask directions at a KOBAN.

Traffic Accidents

In case of a traffic accident, call the police at **110**; for an ambulance, call **119**. If you and another person are involved in an accident, exchange names, addresses, telephone numbers, driver's license numbers, and license plate numbers, as well as insurance company names and policy types. If there are any witnesses, ask for their names and telephone numbers, as the police may wish to contact them later.

Earthquakes

Earthquakes are one of the natural disasters Tokyo is prone to and its residents have become accustomed to feeling periodic tremors. The most recent disastrous earthquake to hit the Tokyo area was in 1923; more than 100,000 people lost their lives during the initial quake and in subsequent aftershocks and fires. In 1995, Tokyo residents were reminded of how vulnerable a large modern city can be when the Great Hanshin Earthquake hit the city of Kobe in western Japan, killing more than 6,000 people.

As a new resident of Tokyo, you should familiarize yourself and your family members with the procedures to follow in case of an earthquake, some of which are outlined here.

In case evacuation is necessary, there are areas throughout Tokyo designated to accommodate refugees. These places are usually large open spaces such as parks or fields. Ask neighbors to show you the designated area nearest your home. Then visit the area with your family and identify a point where you will all meet in case you are separated. If you have young children, test them to make sure they know where to go.

Prepare an earthquake kit that includes a minimum supply of items necessary for the first few days after an evacuation. Place the kit in a location in your home that allows easy access, and

101

make sure everyone knows where it is. Suggested items include:

- First-aid supplies and any prescription medicine you may need;
- Enough bottles of water to last for two or three days;
- Instant and dried foods such as crackers, chocolate, and noodles;
- A portable, battery-operated radio and light;
- Copies of the Foreign Registration Cards and the main identification page(s) of the passports of all family members.

In the event of a major earthquake, NHK (Channel 1) will broadcast information and instructions in English. Tune your radio to NHK at 594 AM or the English-language channels AFN (810 AM) or InterFM (76.1 FM).

The Tokyo Metropolitan Government suggests residents take the following 10 steps in case of an earthquake:

1. Secure your safety as well as that of your family. During a major tremor, hide under a solid table so that your head is protected from falling objects.
2. Turn off all sources of heat. If a fire breaks out, extinguish it immediately.
3. Do not panic and do not rush outside. Leaving a room or building is not necessarily safer than staying inside. Check the situation first and act calmly.
4. Secure an exit. Tremors may warp doors and you could be trapped inside, especially in concrete buildings. Keep at least one door open by putting something (a shoe, for example) between the door and the door frame.
5. If you are outside, watch out for falling objects and loose electric wires. Stay away from buildings and evacuate to an open space.
6. If you are in a department store or theater, follow the instructions of the personnel in charge.

7. Park your car on the left-hand side of the road if you are driving when an earthquake occurs.
8. Move away from cliffs and the seashore, as landslides and tidal waves may occur.
9. Evacuate on foot, and keep the belongings you bring with you to a minimum.
10. Never be influenced by rumors. Act on accurate information only.

ENGLISH-LANGUAGE INFORMATION RESOURCES

Foreign residents of Tokyo rely to a great extent on information available in English. Fortunately, there are many convenient resources, such as directories, magazines, and telephone counseling. The magazines are published in Tokyo and sold in major bookstores that have foreign book sections. (*Refer to* "Foreign Reading Materials" *in Chapter 13.*) These magazines provide classified ads, restaurant recommendations, interesting interviews with local residents, and information about Japanese society and current events. Websites sponsored by these magazines also contain information on a wide variety of topics about life in Tokyo. (Refer to the *Resource Guide* for a list of these resources; additional English-language resources for specific subjects are introduced throughout this book.)

***

Expatriates living in Tokyo generally find that most of the services they need are available and efficient. Communication can sometimes be difficult, however, as not many Japanese service people are fluent in English or other foreign languages.

—Chapter Six—

GETTING AROUND IN TOKYO

The public transportation system in Tokyo covers the metropolis like a spider web and may be one of the most extensive and efficient urban systems in the world. Residents use a variety of modes of transport, including train, subway, bus, taxi, automobiles and walking. While the system may seem rather daunting initially, once you are familiar with the major transportation routes and ticketing methods, you will find that getting around Tokyo is easy. This chapter provides information about each mode of transport as well as about the address system in Tokyo.

THE ADDRESS SYSTEM

Some streets in Tokyo are very narrow and many do not have

names; instead, addresses are indicated by area and block numbers rather than by street names and building numbers. (*Refer to* "Writing Addresses" *in Chapter 5*.)

As block numbers are not always indicated on the front of buildings, to find specific locations people rely on peripheral information such as the closest landmark, public transportation station, or other distinguishing features of the area. When you are given directions, Japanese people might describe a location by saying, for example, "next to the drug store", "the second building from the corner", or "the tallest building in the block".

People also look for metal plates that are posted every few blocks on walls, buildings, or telegraph poles indicating the name of the area and the block number. Some plates are spelled out in *romaji* (Romanized Japanese words) as well as in Japanese writing. However, it is best to have clear and specific directions when going to a place that is new to you, as blocks and their numbers are not always logically arranged.

TRAIN AND SUBWAY LINES

Most people in Tokyo take trains or the subway to work; they avoid driving because of traffic congestion and high parking fees in business areas. As a result, the distance from a residence to the nearest station is a key factor in determining property value; the shorter the distance, the greater the value. Real estate advertisements commonly show the number of minutes it will take residents to walk from a home to the closest station.

Train Lines

Several different train lines cover Tokyo and also extend out to greater Tokyo. Major train lines in Tokyo are categorized into two main groups: those operated by the East Japan Railway Company (JR), including the Yamanote, Chuo, and Keihin-Tohoku Lines; and those operated by private companies such as the Odakyu, Keio, Seibu, and Tokyu Lines. All lines intersect with other lines at major junction stations such as Shinjuku, Shibuya, Tokyo, and Ikebukuro. Railway maps (sometimes in *romaji*) are available free of charge at major train stations, and major hotels often carry railway and subway maps in *romaji*.

Tickets, Passes and Prepaid Cards

To enter the boarding platforms, passengers must present either tickets, passes, or prepaid rail cards to be examined by automated machines or by station officials. It is important to always keep tickets, passes, or cards with you after presenting them, as they will be examined again when you exit the train.

You can buy tickets at the automatic vending machines located in all stations. Above the machines, there is usually a large board that shows the train system and the fare to each station; at many stations, names are written in both Japanese and *romaji*. You can buy your ticket using coins or bills, but not credit cards.

If you commute to the same destination regularly, purchasing a pass may be more convenient and less expensive than buying single tickets. The pass shows your original station and the destination, and allows you to get on and off at any station in between without buying additional tickets. Monthly, quarterly, and semi-annual passes are usually available, and are sold at most large stations. Ask station officials for more detailed information.

It is also possible to buy prepaid rail cards. JR Lines issue prepaid cards called "IO" (In-Out) and "Suica" (Super Urban Intelligent Card) which can be used on JR lines. Private lines issue a common prepaid card called "Passnet" which can be used for all of the various private train and subway lines. "IO" "Suica" and "Passnet" cards can be purchased at train stations or kiosks. When using the "IO" or "Passnet" card, insert the prepaid card into the automatic checking machine before and after boarding the train, and the machine will deduct the appropriate fare from

Photo by Yuko Morimoto-Yoshida.

Thousands of people ride the trains into Tokyo every day.

your card. To use the "Suica" card and a few other train passes, just tap on a readout surface on the checking machine, indicated by the "Suica" logo. The convenience of using cards is that you do not have to check fares or wait in line to purchase tickets.

Most lines offer both regular (local) trains that stop at each station, and express trains that stop only at major stations. Announcement boards indicate the service each train provides, and there is usually an audio announcement as to which type of train is approaching the platform. Be careful to check the train service before jumping onboard, or you may end up on an express train that does not stop at your desired destination! If you cannot figure out whether a particular train stops at the station you want to go, you can ask other passengers for assistance by stating the name of the station, pointing to the train and raising your eyebrows. People may nod (indicating "yes"), or wave one hand side to side in front of their faces (indicating "no") to let you know whether the train stops at the station mentioned.

While on the train, prior to arrival at each station you will

107

hear an announcement stating the name of the station. Even if you miss the announcement, when the train arrives at the station you will see the name of the station on the platform signs in both Japanese and *romaji*.

Train Schedules

Trains covering the central part of Tokyo are generally scheduled to arrive at each station every five to ten minutes and are very punctual. Station officials will make an announcement of apology if a train is to be delayed even by a minute or two. Service begins as early as five in the morning and stops around midnight.

Rush hours are from 7.30 to 9 in the morning and from 5 to 6.30 in the evening. Surviving crowded stations and trains at these hours requires determination and certain skills. People normally wait in lines at platforms, but at rush hour the lines merge into a stream of people. When the train comes, just swim with the stream and jump into the train; otherwise you will never be able to board.

It is when boarding trains that some Tokyoites, normally polite and considerate, seem to take on a different persona as they push and shove to squeeze themselves in. The busiest stations even have railway officials who help to push in extra people, much like packing sardines into a can. Be careful when carrying purses or briefcases with thin straps or delicate handles, as they may break in the squeeze. After riding the same train several times, you will learn which section of the train is less packed, and board that section from the appropriate location on the platform. If you are traveling with small children or are not feeling well, it may be best to avoid riding on trains during the intensity of rush hour.

Another busy hour occurs around midnight, when trains can be crowded with people who have worked late or enjoyed dinner and drinks. It is quite safe to ride the trains at this time, even if you are alone. The only hassle you may encounter is someone who has had too much to drink and wants to practice his English.

In that case, walk away from him (it is usually a "him") and go to another section of the train. Usually he will not follow you, but in case he does, you can complain to the conductor when the train arrives at the next station.

Subway Lines

Subway lines are concentrated in central Tokyo. Main lines include the Ginza, Hibiya, Chiyoda, Hanzomon, and Marunouchi Lines (all under the Eidan Group), as well as the Toei Lines (including the Toei Mita, Toei Oedo, Toei Shinjuku and Toei Asakusa Lines) operated by the Metropolitan Transit Bureau. The ticketing system for subways is the same as that for trains. Unlike trains though, most subways offer only regular, local service (no express service), so there is less risk of missing your station.

Amazingly, the number of subway lines continues to increase in already crowded Tokyo. Each new line is built deeper underground, necessitating the use of long escalators to transport passengers to the surface or to other subway platforms. Foreigners not used to riding on subways have claimed that they sometimes feel claustrophobic in subway stations. However, most foreigners find the subways convenient, especially when it is raining or cold, because it is possible to get to so many points in Tokyo without having to step outside. Some subway stations are even located in the basements of large buildings or shopping complexes.

Buses

Riding buses may be a little more intimidating than using trains and subways until you become familiar with the bus routes and the neighborhoods they cover. It can be difficult to tell where bus stops are located and to decipher the names of the stops as they are seldom written in *romaji*. Still, buses offer convenient transportation to points not covered by trains or subways. Bus services are operated by the Metropolitan Transit Bureau and other private companies. They cover separate routes and fares vary slightly, but other than that, there are no major differences.

Between many points in central Tokyo, the fare is a fixed rate regardless of the distance traveled. Generally you enter the bus by the front door, and pay the fare by putting coins or inserting a bill into a machine located beside the driver. Alternatively, you can pay the fare with a prepaid card (which you can buy on the bus) or by showing a pass (sold at major bus terminals). When the bus approaches a stop, you will hear the driver or an automated tape announce the name of the stop. To get off, alert the driver by pushing one of the buttons located beside the windows.

In suburban areas, the fare is based on the distance traveled. Generally you enter the bus through the back door and take a numbered ticket from a machine located near the door. The number indicates the zone in which you entered the bus. When the bus approaches a stop, you will hear the driver or an automated tape announce the name of the stop. If you want to get off, alert the driver by pushing one of the buttons located beside the windows, make your way to the front door and put your fare into the machine next to the driver. In most buses there is a board posted in the front indicating the fare from each zone; find your zone number on the board and pay the amount indicated under it.

Taxis

Getting around Tokyo by taxi can be rather expensive, so it is not recommended for traveling long distances. However, taxis can be convenient and economical for short distances, especially when traveling with a few friends; if you travel only a few blocks, the taxi fare will be comparable to the total amount of the bus fare for the same number of people. Every taxi has a meter with a minimum charge and the fare increases by distance and time. Taxis also charge extra fees for reservations and for rides between 11pm and 5am. The number of taxis that accept credit cards is increasing, but many still do not.

In most locations taxis stop when you wave your hand, but in some locations (in Ginza, for example) taxis stop only at taxi stands. Taxi stands are also located at large train and subway stations. At midnight, the lines at the taxi stands at train stations can be long as bus services usually end at that hour.

You will arrive at destinations more quickly if you can provide taxi drivers with exact addresses, as well as with information such as major cross streets, well-known landmarks, or nearby train stations. It is highly recommended you have a map in Japanese showing this information and your destination. As mentioned earlier, many streets in Tokyo do not have names, so drivers may need to consult maps to go to places unfamiliar to them. As most taxi drivers do not speak English well, be sure to have addresses, directions and landmarks written down (preferably in Japanese).

AUTOMOBILES

Convenient and efficient public transportation makes owning a private car unnecessary, especially for people living in the central part of Tokyo. Many Tokyo residents with cars use them mainly for out-of-town trips, for moving heavy items, or, in the case of mothers with small children, for carrying grocery shopping bags.

Traffic Rules

Driving in Tokyo requires some preparation and caution. Japan uses the international traffic sign system, so foreigners understand most signs without extensive study. However, as not all traffic signs are written in English, important Japanese signs must be memorized. The Japan Automobile Federation (JAF) issues a booklet called "Rules of the Road" that explains traffic rules in Japan in six languages: English, Spanish, Chinese, Persian, Korean, and Portuguese (Tel: 03-5976-9777, **http://www.jaf.or.jp**).

Drivers from countries in which vehicular traffic flows on the right-hand side of the road (the United States, for example) should drive with extra caution because in Japan (as in Britain), traffic flows on the left-hand side of the road. People from these countries are advised to practice in areas in which there is little traffic and to use extreme caution when making turns (as the opposite lanes must be checked for cars and pedestrians).

In principle, bicycles are supposed to travel on the left-hand side of roads designated for cars. As roads in Tokyo can be narrow, bicycles travel in close proximity to cars, so drivers must watch carefully for bicycles, particularly when turning.

Seat belts must be worn by drivers and front seat passengers. If either drivers or front seat passengers do not wear their seat belts and are caught by the police, the drivers will be fined and penalty points recorded on their driving records. Drivers who accumulate excessive penalty points must surrender their licenses. While it is not mandatory for back-seat passengers to wear seat-belts, child car seats are mandatory for children under 6; violation of the latter will result in penalty points for the driver.

Using a cellular phone while driving is also banned by law; using a cellular phone with a hands-free device is permitted. Violation of this law will result in either a fine or a sentence (less than three months), as well as penalty points on the driver's record.

Drivers' Licenses

You may be able to obtain an international driver's license in your home country that will allow you to drive in Japan for up to one year. As an international driver's license cannot be renewed in Japan, many foreigners acquire Japanese drivers' licenses. Those who have a driver's license from a foreign country can usually convert it to a Japanese license. This type of conversion will exempt foreigners from having to take intensive written and driving exams, but sometimes short tests will be conducted to confirm driving skills and knowledge.

Foreign driver's license can be converted to a Japanese one

at any of the following Driver's License Testing and Issuing Centers of the Metropolitan Police Department:

Samezu Driver's License Testing and Issuing Center
(Samezu Jidosha Shikenjo)
1-12-5 Higashi-Oi, Shinagawa-ku, Tokyo 140-0011
Tel: 03-3474-1374

Fuchu Driver's License Testing and Issuing Center
(Fuchu Jidosha Shikenjo)
3-1-1 Tama-Cho, Fuchu-shi, Tokyo 183-0002
Tel: 042-362-3591

Koto Driver's License Testing and Issuing Center *(Koto Jidosha Shikenjo)*
1-7-24 Shinsuna, Koto-ku, Tokyo 136-0075
Tel: 03-3699-1151

The following documents are required to obtain a license:
1. Your Foreign Resident Registration Card (See "Foreign Resident Registration" in Chapter 4.)
2. A photograph (3 cm by 2.4 cm)
3. A certified translation of your driver's license into Japanese from your embassy, consulate or the JAF
4. Your passport

For additional information in English regarding the application process call either 03-5463-6000 or 042-334-6000. Automated information is available 24 hours a day.

If you do not have a driver's license from your country and want to acquire one in Japan, you must pass two written tests and two driving tests conducted at any of the Driver's License Testing and Issuing Centers mentioned earlier. As tests are stringent and thorough preparation necessary, most Japanese people attend driving schools to acquire driving skills and knowledge of both driving rules and automobile mechanics. In addition, graduates of certified driving school are exempted from having to take the driving tests at a License Testing and Issuing Center. Not many driving schools in Tokyo conduct lessons in English or other languages, though, so first-time foreign drivers often find it difficult to obtain a Japanese driver's license.

The minimum age for obtaining a driver's license is 18 (16 for a motorcycle license). A Japanese driver's license is valid until the driver's third birthday after its issue.

Purchasing a Car

Many expatriates decide to buy cars in Japan, as importing cars into Japan can be expensive and time-consuming. Car dealers sell both new and used models of Japanese- and foreign-made cars. In general, the price of Japanese-made cars is about the same in Japan as in Europe or the United States, while new European or American cars cost much more in Japan than in the country of manufacture. Before visiting a car dealer, check the Internet and car magazines for typical prices of the models you like. Car dealers may offer discounts if you can negotiate skillfully.

Used cars can be purchased from departing expatriates. Advertisements for such cars appear regularly in English-language newspapers or magazines, newsletters of foreign social organizations, and on the bulletin boards of international supermarkets.

After purchasing a car, you must register your car at one of the following locations: 1) ordinary cars at the District Land Transportation Office, or automobile inspection and registration office administering the area you reside in; 2) light three-or four-wheeled cars at the Light Car Inspection Association or branch office administering the area you reside in; and 3) motor scooters at the ward or municipal office nearest your residence.

To register, you will need a Parking Space Certificate issued by a police superintendent, providing evidence that a parking space has been secured; in other words, you should secure a parking lot before buying a car. If your apartment or house does not have parking space, you can rent one near your home. You will also need your Seal Registration Certificate and Foreign Registration Card. (*See* "Obtaining Necessary Documents" *in Chapter 4.*)

Maintaining a Car

In order to maintain your car, you will need car insurance, check-ups, and perhaps roadside assistance.

Car Insurance

Car owners are required to buy compulsory insurance when they buy a car. The application can be handled at insurance companies, car dealerships, and repair shops. Compulsory insurance provides compensation for bodily injury only to victims and passengers and not for drivers, and the amount covered is quite low.

As the coverage of compulsory insurance is limited, buying supplementary insurance is strongly recommended. Supplementary coverage typically includes additional amounts for victim and passenger bodily injury liability, bodily injury to the driver, as well as collision coverage, property damage liability and other expenses such as medical payments. Such additional insurance coverage is offered by Japanese insurance companies, as well as several American and European insurance companies with operations in Japan. Contact information for these companies are available in the English-language directory, NTT TOWNPAGE.

Regular Checkup

Private passenger cars registered in Japan must undergo an inspection in the third year after the purchase of a new car, and once every two years for a used car. The inspection can be done by the dealer from whom the car was purchased or at certified repair shops or garages. On the windshield of used cars, there is generally an inspection sticker printed with the next inspection date. To receive an inspection, the owner must show proof of payment for automobile tax. Tonnage tax and compulsory insurance must also be paid to the inspector at the time of inspection. After a car is inspected, the owner receives a new inspection sticker to place on the windshield of the car.

Roadside Assistance

If you drive in Japan, you might want to join the **Japan Automobile Federation** (JAF; Tel: 03-5976-9777, **http://www.jaf.or.jp**). You will pay an annual membership fee and receive roadside assistance in case of emergency.

Parking

Finding a parking spot in Tokyo is extremely difficult and parking fees are high. As streets are narrow, most cars parallel park. Many large buildings, such as hotels and department stores, offer space for parking, and hourly parking spots are sometimes available on the street. But finding a spot is such a nightmare that many people just give up and park illegally.

The fines for illegal parking are quite high, however, and illegally parked cars may be towed. If you find a parking ticket on your windshield, take it to the police station specified on the ticket for payment instructions, and pay the fine at a designated bank or post office branch. If your car is towed, go to the police station specified at the place you parked your car, pay the fine and the towing expense, and pick up your car from where it has been towed (usually a different spot from where the police station is located). In addition to the fine, illegal parking also results in penalty points on drivers' records.

Highways

The highway that connects key points in Tokyo is called the Shuto

Expressway; this highway makes several loops within Tokyo. Highways in Japan are not free, and the charge to use the Shuto Expressway is 700 yen regardless of the distance driven. Drivers usually avoid getting on the highway during rush hour, as it can be very congested. Highways that go to other parts of Japan (including the Tomei, Chuo, and Kan-etsu Expressways) can be accessed from several locations in Tokyo.

WALKING

As residents of Tokyo use public transportation often, they spend a lot of time walking to and from train, subway, and bus stops. And as not all train and subway stations are equipped with elevators or escalators, residents also climb a lot of stairs. People used to getting around by car may initially feel fatigued by the incessant walking, but most will eventually get used to the change and value the opportunity for exercise; some are also pleased to find that they have lost weight!

Where in "car societies" people go straight to their destina-

117

tions, by walking, Tokyo residents discover the intricacies of various neighborhoods. Busy side streets have developed around most train and subway stations, and here one can find major supermarkets and grocery stores, coffee shops, bookstores, and other small shops carrying a variety of goods. These shopping streets are usually narrow and parking places rare, so the best way to explore them is on foot.

One potential hazard is that bicyclists often use the same sidewalks as do pedestrians. While they are supposed to use throughfares designated for cars, they are allowed to walk their bicycles on sidewalks when riding on the roads may seem dangerous. The problem is that instead of walking, many bicyclists run. In addition, some sidewalks are designated for use by both pedestrians and bicyclists. The fact is, bicyclists are likely to use virtually any sidewalk, whether "designated" or not, to ride their bikes on, and there is virtually no police enforcement on bicycle laws. As speeding bicycles can be hazardous to pedestrians, espe-

Photo by Akiko Watanabe

An average afternoon crowd crosses the road at Shibuya Intersection.

cially on narrow streets, both bicyclists and pedestrians should be careful before changing course.

Foreigners from countries in which vehicle traffic flows on the right-hand side of the street should be careful when crossing, because in Japan, traffic flows on the left-hand side. When crossing the street, be sure to look first to the right, then left. Tokyo streets can be narrow and winding, so in many places, especially around corners, drivers have difficulty seeing pedestrians. If you have small children, you must remind them repeatedly to watch for cars and to never rush out onto the street.

From the perspective of personal safety, walking around Tokyo is generally safe. However, as the capital is large, not all areas are equally safe, so unfortunate incidents do happen from time to time. It is generally advisable to avoid walking alone in parks or other quiet places after dark, especially for women and children. Late night encounters with drunken men are not unheard of, but usually no harm will come to innocent bystanders. Walking on busy streets should be fine both day and night.

❀ ❀ ❀

Most foreigners are impressed with Tokyo's public transportation system, as it is convenient and efficient (although they admit that it can be very complicated and overwhelming initially). If you choose to drive in Tokyo, you should take into consideration traffic congestion and the time required to search for parking space.

Chapter Seven

HANDLING FINANCES

TRIGG.

The options for handling finances in Japan may be different from those in your country. This chapter will familiarize you with the various options.

BANKING SERVICES

Several types of banks and financial institutions operate in Japan, including Japanese city banks, regional banks, trust banks, credit associations and foreign banks. They are categorized based on their size and range of services provided.

Most expatriates will need to open at least one account with a Japanese bank, as salaries are usually deposited directly into employees' bank accounts, and various bill payments are often made through domestic bank accounts. Most foreign residents choose to open an account with a Japanese city bank (such as Tokyo-Mitsubishi Bank, Sumitomo Mitsui Bank, or UFJ Bank), as these banks hold large assets, have branches all over Japan (even though they are called "city banks"), and offer a wide range of services to retail customers. Services include deposit accounts, savings accounts, automatic teller machine (ATM) cards, and foreign currency exchange.

Employees at large branches are likely to be more familiar with the kinds of services foreigners often need, such as overseas remittance and foreign exchange transactions.

Types of Accounts

For regular transactions, such as paying bills or receiving salary and other payments, foreign residents generally find it most convenient to open a general deposit account (*futsu yokin*). Money can be deposited and withdrawn from this type of account at any time. The interest rate on general deposit accounts, however, is the lowest among the several different types of accounts.

Checking accounts, which bear no interest, are not popular in Japan as personal checks are generally not accepted for commercial transactions, and because payment via transfer of funds between bank accounts has been common practice for some time.

For savings purposes, most banks offer various types of accounts, including time deposit accounts and long-term deposit accounts.

Opening an Account

In order to open a bank account, you must complete an application form (available at the counter of the bank of your choice) and show proof of identification such as your Foreign Resident Registration Card, passport, or driver's license. Seals are required for Japanese people but written signatures are usually accepted from foreigners. (*Refer to* "Obtaining Necessary Documents" *in Chapter 4.*)

121

ATM Cards

City banks have ATM machines located in many places through-out Tokyo. When opening a general deposit account, you will receive an ATM card. You will also receive a deposit notebook in which you are supposed to record the transactions for your account. It is easiest to record transactions by inserting the deposit notebook into the ATM machine at the time of each transaction.

The hours during which ATM machines operate vary. Many of them close around 9pm on weekdays and around 5pm on weekends; some locations are closed on Sundays. The number of ATM machines in operation 24 hours a day is increasing, but most still operate a limited number of hours per day. Recently, several large convenience store chains have begun installing ATMs in their outlets, offering round-the-clock withdrawal, remittance and deposit services for many major city banks.

As all city banks are part of a coordinated network, for a small fee you can withdraw cash from an ATM of any city bank in the network. You will find English-language instructions posted on the ATM machines at most major banks.

Payment of Bills

The most convenient way to pay utility bills is by automatic de-duction through the bank with which you have an account. Each bank has specific application forms to initiate automatic payment for utilities such as gas, water, and electricity. Automatic payment is also commonly used for other services such as telephone, news-paper delivery and credit cards; application forms are available from these service providers. It is important to make sure that you have ample money in your account by payment due dates. If you have insufficient funds, service providers will not be able to debit your account, and your bills will be overdue. Service pro-viders may charge interest for any overdue amounts, and if the overdue status continues, service may be terminated. (*See*

"Arranging Utilities and Services" *in Chapter 4.*)

For one-time transactions, it is possible to make payment by transferring money to a bank account specified by the potential recipient. You can make such transfers through bank tellers by depositing cash, or debit directly from your bank account at ATMs with a transfer function.

Sending Money Overseas

Money can be sent overseas by making a direct withdrawal from a bank account or by presenting cash at a major bank. Some form of personal identification, such as a Foreign Resident Registration Card, passport, or driver's license, will be required. Post offices also provide overseas money remittance services.

Popular international remittance methods are:

1. Telegraphic Transfers
   Money is wired to the recipient's bank account and is available within two to three days.
2. Demand Drafts
   The bank issues a draft based on payment by the customer, and the customer sends the draft to the recipient. The recipient then brings the draft to a bank and exchanges it for cash.

Currency Exchange

In Japan, only banks that are authorized to handle foreign exchange transactions can buy and sell foreign currencies. All city banks are so authorized, but it is best to visit large branches for such services, as smaller branches might not carry large amounts of cash in foreign currencies.

Internet Banking

Major banks offer some services over the Internet. Popular services include the transfer of funds, verification of balances and transaction records, and postings of current market rates (such as foreign exchange and interest rates). However, as instructions are provided almost entirely in Japanese, foreigners may not find Internet banking particularly useful. Citibank Tokyo offers Internet banking in English as well as Japanese.

Foreign Banks

Several foreign banks operate in Japan, including Australia and New Zealand Banking Group, Barclays Bank, Citibank, Deutsche Bank, J.P. Morgan Chase and Lloyds TSB Bank. Citibank (**http://www.citibank.co.jp**) is probably the most popular among foreign residents as it offers a wide variety of retail banking services and has branches in all major Japanese cities. Customers can withdraw money from their local Citibank accounts by using Citibank ATMs or the ATMs of any of the Japanese city banks, as Citibank participates in the network of Japanese city banks. In addition, Lloyds TSB Bank offers overseas remittance services at a reasonable rate, while the Australia and New Zealand Banking Group also offers some retail services.

FINANCIAL SERVICES AT POST OFFICES

Financial services are also provided by large post office branches in Japan. Here you can open a variety of accounts including ordinary saving accounts, fixed-period saving accounts, and long-term saving accounts.

Post offices generally offer slightly higher interest rates than do banks for equivalent accounts, but limit the total amount of deposits per customer to 10 million yen. Customers can withdraw money from ordinary deposit accounts using ATM machines located at post offices. However, a disadvantage of using these ATMs is that they only operate during office hours, which are generally from 9am to 5pm. People can also arrange automatic deduction of utility payments through ordinary deposit accounts.

Post offices also handle two types of overseas remittances:

1. Remittance to the recipient's address

   Post offices will issue a money order equivalent to the amount you want to remit and will send the money order to the recipient's address. The recipient then takes the money order to a local post office and exchanges it for cash. The fee for this form of remittance varies based on the urgency of the delivery and the amount.

2. Remittance to the recipient's bank or post office account

   Fees for this type of remittance also vary based on the urgency of the delivery and the value of the remittance. More information is available on the Japan Post Office website (**http://www.yu-cho.yusei.go.jp**).

CASH

Japanese people prefer to use cash for many daily transactions. This preference for cash in Tokyo and throughout Japan stems perhaps from the relatively low crime rate – people can still carry relatively large amounts of cash without worrying about theft. In Tokyo, cash is easy to obtain as ATMs are everywhere.

Many shops and service providers now accept credit cards and their use has increased dramatically in recent years. However, foreigners in Tokyo are advised to always carry a certain amount of cash as some services (including doctors, small shops and public transportation) generally accept only cash for payment.

CREDIT CARDS

As Japanese people prefer cash transactions, the use of credit cards has lagged behind that in some countries. However, people now enjoy the convenience of credit cards and their use is likely to increase, accompanying an increase in Internet shopping and other forms of electronic commerce.

Nowadays, a great number of stores, restaurants, and other service establishments in Tokyo and other cities accept credit cards. However, you may not be able to use credit cards for public transportation or for some taxis, or in small shops, restaurants, hospitals, or public offices. Also, some shops set a minimum charge for credit card use.

Major credit cards such as VISA, MasterCard, and American Express are the most widely accepted. If you use a credit card issued from your home country in Tokyo, the credit card company will convert any charges from Japanese yen to your home country's currency, and bill you in that currency. Thus you will face the risk of foreign exchange fluctuations. In addition, most card companies charge a small fee for the conversion. You may want to get details from your credit card company and make sure that your card can be used overseas. For security purposes some credit card companies ask customers to notify them before using their cards outside their home countries; others require a special personal identification number for withdrawing money from foreign ATMs.

As most foreigners in Japan have not established credit histories there, obtaining a credit card may take some time. The easiest approach is to apply for a card with a bank or credit card company with which your employer has some kind of relationship.

Credit card bills are usually paid once a month by automatic debit from customers' bank accounts. Customers generally can choose to pay the amount in full or in installments. You should ensure your account has sufficient balance by the payment due date or else you may be charged penalties for the overdue bill; if the overdue status continues, the card may be canceled.

TAXES

Tax requirements in Japan are probably different from those in your country. You should contact a professional tax advisor for detailed information.

Consumption Tax

Consumption tax is imposed on most products and services in Japan. Usually, this tax is added to the advertised prices of products or services. The current consumption tax rate is 5 per cent.

Income and Resident Taxes

All residents in Japan, regardless of their nationalities, are required to pay both national personal income taxes (levied by the national government) and local resident taxes (levied by the governments of municipalities and prefectures). Both types of taxes are calculated based on annual personal income earned between January 1 and December 31.

For salaried employees, employers withhold and deduct estimated personal income tax from monthly salaries. Near the end of the calendar year, employers calculate any excesses or shortfalls in taxes deducted during the year and make corresponding adjustments to the December salary amount.

Employees do not have to file personal income tax reports unless they fall into one of the following categories:

1. Salaried employees with an annual income of more than 20 million yen.
2. Salaried employees with extra annual income amounting to more than 200,000 yen.
3. Salaried employees with incomes from two or more employers.

Local resident taxes are computed by the ward or municipal office of the area of residence of each employee on the basis of the income reported by the employer. These taxes are also deducted from monthly salaries in 12 installments from June through May of the following year.

Non-salaried workers (such as the self-employed and part-time workers) must calculate personal income tax based on income during the year, submitting tax reports and making payments at local tax offices. Tax reports should be filed between February 16 and March 15 of each year. Non-salaried workers must also pay local resident taxes in four separate installments in June, August, October and January. The ward or municipal office will send out notifications, and payments can be made through banks, post offices, or other financial institutions.

You may consult English-speaking representatives at the Tokyo Regional Tax Bureau for details (Tel: 03-3821-9070).

❀ ❀ ❀

While getting used to the Japanese financial system may take some time, it is a relief that banks and post offices employees are generally very polite and helpful toward customers' queries.

—CHAPTER EIGHT—

INTERACTING WITH JAPANESE PEOPLE

The unwritten rules of a new culture are rarely immediately apparent to newcomers. Rather, they are slowly revealed in the course of daily life. It can be helpful to know in advance about some of these unwritten rules, as well as about the deeper values that serve as their foundation. To give you some insights into ways of interacting with Japanese people, this chapter discusses the cultural values and the communication styles of the Japanese, as well as tips for communicating effectively with them.

JAPANESE CULTURAL PATTERNS

Japanese culture emphasizes some traditional values and beliefs that may seem different or unusual to foreign visitors (especially to Westerners). These values derive from historical, political, and religious influences. For foreigners, understanding these values and beliefs is often the key to successful interaction with Japanese people, although the degree to which individual Tokyoites adhere to these traditional values varies. Acceptance of diversified values and beliefs are gradually increasing. In general, younger people fit less closely to the stereotyped view of Japanese people.

Group Orientation

The most prominent feature of Japanese culture is its group orientation; group goals, achievements and interests are emphasized in social and business situations. It is important for Japanese people to have a sense of affiliation with a group (such as a school, company, or interest group) and they value collaboration and teamwork.

One reason for this focus on groups may partially be attributed to the country's geography and history. Japan is a small, mountainous country surrounded by water. As a result, mobility was low and many people remained in the same community throughout their lives. In addition, rice cultivation was historically an important industry in Japan; successful rice cultivation required extensive, continuous care of the rice fields – the more effectively people worked together in groups, the more efficiently they could work the fields and achieve good annual harvests.

The importance of teamwork is taught to Japanese children from a young age. School children are encouraged to play and study in groups with other children, and to accomplish tasks together with other group members. Most junior and senior high schools require students to participate in group extracurricular activities (such as tennis, volleyball and theater), so that they will learn how to organize and participate in group events. Teachers and parents believe that the students can nurture team spirit by working together towards a team goal, and that this team spirit will strengthen each individual's mental state.

Group lessons and activities are common in Japan, even among adults. Instructions in tennis, foreign languages, and flower arrangement are often provided to groups of people, and groups of friends, especially women, tend to do many things together, for example, shopping, eating out, and going to movies. By doing things jointly, there is an increased sense of bonding; on the negative side, there is sometimes hidden pressure for continual group participation in order to maintain friendships.

At companies, projects and tasks are often assigned to groups rather than to individuals, and group members help each other complete the task. Thus, it is difficult to distinguish individual performance, and both rewards and punishment are typically given to a group rather than to an individual. Also, much of personal identity is derived from the groups one belongs to; people tend to be more concerned about the company they join than about the actual job itself. Because of this emphasis on the group, when introducing themselves, people often mention the name of the company they work for first, followed by their own name.

Harmony

Japanese people believe that in order for a group to function optimally, the maintenance of harmony and good relationships among members is crucial. Japanese people take great care to avoid hurting other people's feelings and, consequently, use a communication style that is indirect and relatively tentative.

Group members are connected to each other through a sense of interdependence and responsibility. They constantly monitor each other's well-being and try to offer help before others ask for it. Those who receive favors show appreciation by returning favors. In other words, people practice reciprocity in many aspects of life. For example, people usually return from vacation with souvenirs for neighbors and colleagues to show appreciation for work done during their absence and on their behalf. Japanese people usually bring gifts when visiting – even for very brief visits – to show appreciation for being hosted.

Japanese people also maintain group harmony by following protocol or rules. There are many formal as well as informal rules in Japan, and people generally follow them. For example, most people wait for the traffic signal to turn green before they cross the street, even when there are no cars coming. The Japanese feel most comfortable when everybody follows the same rules, and harmony and conformity are maintained.

Another example of this preference for conformity can be observed in the Japanese tendency to follow what others do. As a result, when a particular style of clothing comes into fashion, everybody wears it, and Tokyoites often form long lines to buy a popular type of food, or to get seats in trendy new restaurants.

Hierarchy

Hierarchical differences are observed and respected in Japan because doing so keeps order. To show respect, Japanese people

Photo by Akiko Watanabe.

Japanese people form a line to buy a popular snack.

use special phrases and verb forms when interacting with people higher than themselves in the hierarchy.

In organizations, work titles are a reflection of the hierarchy; employees in Japanese companies often call their superiors by title instead of by name, and are reluctant to take on new responsibilities unless they have been officially given an appropriate title. As Japanese people tend to work for the same company for a long time and are generally promoted on the basis of seniority, title and age often go hand-in-hand.

In social interactions, age determines one's place in the hierarchy. As people are expected to show respect to their elders, they want to know the ages of their acquaintances or neighbors so that they can use the appropriate language and behavior.

Insider/Outsider (*Uchi/Soto*)

Because the sense of affiliation to a particular group is important to Japanese people, they tend to differentiate between members of their own group (insiders – *uchi*; literally, "within" or "home") and those outside of their group (outsiders – *soto*; literally "outside") based on several factors, including the specific group people belong to (such as company or school), background (such as age or place of origin), and common interests. Different sets of behavioral and communication styles are applied depending on whether the person with whom one is interacting is considered *uchi* or *soto*.

With insiders, the Japanese discuss things relatively openly and share their true feelings directly. They believe that insider group members are mutually dependent, caring, and supportive. In contrast, they often keep a certain distance from outsiders, treating them with what can seem like excessive politeness, but not openly disclosing their true feelings.

A significant insider-outsider differentiation frequently made is between Japanese and non-Japanese. Generally speaking, foreigners are considered outsiders. As a matter of fact, a popular, and often objected to word for "foreigner" literally means "outside people" (*gaijin*). Keep in mind that this word does offend many foreigners. This differentiation is applied more strongly to Westerners and other foreigners whose cultural backgrounds are distinct from the Japanese, than to other Asians. Some expatriates feel that, even after having lived in Tokyo for a long time, the Japanese people have yet to fully accept them.

To add to the confusion, Japanese people sometimes adjust their attitudes towards insiders or outsiders according to the context. Because of the emphasis on group harmony and hierarchy, Japanese people are attentive to figuring out and engaging in the behavior and communication style that is most appropriate in a given situation. And because what is appropriate depends on the context, such as the occasion and people involved, their perceptions of who is an insider and outsider are affected by who else is present.

For example, when alone, a Japanese person may treat a foreign friend as an insider and share confidential information; however, when other Japanese people are present, he or she may treat the foreign friend in a more formal and distant manner. When alone with the foreign friend, the Japanese feels it is appropriate to be open and casual, in other words to behave like insiders, as no one else is present. But when other Japanese people are present, the Japanese person may be more concerned about showing culturally appropriate behavior, such as respecting hierarchy and maintaining harmony among those present. Out of such concern for others, the Japanese person now considers the foreign friend to be an outsider and treats him or her likewise.

This modification in behavior and communication style often confuses foreigners and gives the impression that Japanese people are insincere or even dishonest. While it may sometimes be difficult to judge what factor caused the shift in attitude, it might be comforting to know that the behavioral changes were based on context, and not on how they actually feel about the foreign friend. It may also be comforting to know that this shift also applies to interactions with other Japanese people.

One way to reduce this gap between insider and outsider is to establish something in common with Japanese people. Having similar interests, sharing common experiences and spending time together can all serve to create more open and personal relationships with Tokyoites.

Changing Trends

Many young Japanese people identify more with the individualistic values of some Western cultures than with traditional Asian ways of thinking. For example, their individual goals and interests take priority over those of others, and they tend to assert their uniqueness and differences of opinion more openly in public than do older people. As a result, particularly in Tokyo, there is increasing acceptance of a diversity and variety in people's tastes, lifestyles and working habits.

As young people become more focused on personal interests, they seem to care less about other people's feelings and about following rules and social etiquette. This shift is particularly prominent in Tokyo where people are busy taking care of their individual lives. For example, some young people speak loudly on their cellular phones in public, and do not use the appropriate language to show respect when speaking to older people.

JAPANESE COMMUNICATION STYLES

People tend to attribute miscommunication between Japanese people and foreigners to a lack of proficiency in each other's languages. However, the cause is more frequently due to differences in communication styles, which reflect differences in cultural values. Even when speaking in English, many Japanese people tend to use elements of their own communication style.

Indirectness

Japanese people tend to avoid saying things directly, preferring to express opinions and feelings in an indirect manner. Because "not hurting other people's feelings" and maintaining group harmony are their primary concerns, direct statements or emotional outbursts are believed to interfere with smooth interactions.

When declining a proposal, for example, Japanese people might say "I'll think about it", instead of saying "It's impossible". They worry that if they say "No" bluntly, their counterpart may feel hurt as well as shamed, and both parties will face an uncomfortable moment. The speaker will let the counterpart know that the proposal is being declined by using one of several different actions, depending on the situation – through body language or tone of voice, or by asking a third party to convey the message, or by simply not responding to further requests from the counterpart, hoping that eventually the counterpart will get the message.

Japanese people sometimes even show positive feelings indirectly because appearing to be happier than other people may jeopardize harmony.

Silence is a typical tool Japanese people use. They become silent when they do not understand the meaning of a message, because they do not feel comfortable asking for clarification. They worry that by doing so, they might appear unintelligent, or that they might make the speaker look unprepared. People are especially likely to remain silent if the speaker is of higher status.

A popular saying in Japan is that "silence is golden". Japanese people feel that if they put everything into words, the value of the message will be lessened – as a result, many things are left unsaid. Instead of effusing over how much they appreciate a favor someone did, they may give that person an expensive gift to show their gratitude. Rather than praising a subordinate for good performance, a manager may just buy the subordinate a meal.

Avoiding Confrontation

Confrontation and argument are often perceived negatively because most Japanese people believe they harm relationships. As a result, direct confrontation in many situations is avoided. If conflicts are minor, issues may be ignored until they cause greater problems and require attention. If it is essential that a conflict be resolved, people may try to settle it indirectly. For example, a person who disagrees with a counterpart might hint to that person by saying "I like your idea but I would also like to examine other alternatives". If the conflict is serious, he or she might ask a third person to mediate, or use silence and not say anything, delaying action so that the counterpart realizes something has gone wrong.

It is difficult for Japanese people to separate differences in opinion from personal relationships. When someone does not agree with them, they tend to perceive the feedback as personal criticism and start wondering what they did to upset the other person. Of course, this is very different from some Western cultures where debate is considered stimulating and constructive. In many Western societies, people can still be friends and have no hard feelings after an intense debate. In Japan, people may become overly emotional if they experience direct confrontation and find it difficult to heal the relationship after a heated discussion.

Using Apologies

In an attempt to maintain harmonious relationships, Japanese people frequently apologize for what may seem to be trivial matters. Such apologies, however, do not always indicate an admission of fault. People usually apologize for the inconvenience caused but not necessarily for mistakes made. For example, after a car accident, one driver may apologize to the other, but this does not necessarily mean that the driver was at fault. Rather, it may mean,

"It was very unfortunate that the accident happened. I hope we can discuss this calmly". Sales clerks will immediately apologize when a customer complains, regardless of the reason for the complaint, and even if they were not responsible for what happened. In other words, apologies are often used to sympathize and show sincerity towards those involved in the incident. In many cases, a word of apology soothes the negative emotions of all involved and makes problem solving easier.

Humility

"The nail that stands up will be pounded down" is an expression that shows very clearly how important humility is in Japanese society. Because of the group focus and the emphasis on group harmony, people are constantly aware of mutual dependence and generally wish to avoid standing out from the group. Thus, they tend to attribute any success in performance to other people's support rather than to their own abilities.

For example, Japanese people frequently say *Okagesamade*, which means "Owing to (all of) you". When greeting each other, if a Japanese is asked how he or she is doing, that person might reply "Owing to (all of) you, I am fine". Similarly, when praised, a Japanese may say, "It is owing to (all of) you. I did not do anything". It is rare to hear people say, "I think I did a good job. I am proud of myself", even if they actually think so. If one acknowledges one's own achievements without mentioning what is "owed to others", one could be perceived as being arrogant.

Understanding Nonverbal Cues

Nonverbal cues can provide much information about the meaning of messages, but as these cues and their meanings vary from culture to culture, they can be easily misinterpreted.

Some of the nonverbal cues used by Japanese people support their indirect communication style. For example, they rarely maintain direct eye contact. As a matter of fact, looking into another person's eyes can be perceived as being challenging or threatening; instead, Japanese people may look in the direction of the other person's forehead or throat. People try especially not to sustain eye contact with those senior to them (either in age or rank). During a presentation, the speaker may read from notes and may not look at the audience frequently. Also, members of the audience may just read handouts or take notes instead of looking at the speaker. Direct eye contact is also generally avoided between males and females unless they are very close.

A smile can have several different meanings in Japan. Of course, people smile when they think something is funny, but they might also smile to convey indirectly a negative message. For example, they might smile when they do not understand what is said to them. This is highly preferable to asking directly for clarification. Japanese people might even smile when they feel uncomfortable with a situation or when they are in trouble. They smile and let the situation pass because they do not want to be put on the spot, or bother others with their discomfort.

Here are some gestures that may be observed in Japan and which may be different from those used in other cultures:

- Japanese people often refer to themselves by pointing their index finger toward their noses. For example, to claim ownership to an item, an individual might point to his or her nose with the index finger indicating "It's mine".
- When asking someone to approach, Japanese people will usually extend their hands with the palm down and move the fingers back and forth toward the palm, while the same gesture performed with the palm up is used when beckoning to somebody very junior to them, or a dog.
- A hand waved in front of the face indicates "No". For example, if you ask a Japanese woman something in English and she does not understand you, she may wave her hand to signal that she does not understand English.

- During conversations, Japanese people nod frequently to indicate that they are listening. Note that a nod does not necessarily mean that the listener agrees with the speaker.
- Japanese women generally cover their mouths with one hand when they laugh.

UNDERSTANDING THE JAPANESE LANGUAGE

The language barrier is the challenge most frequently mentioned by foreigners living in Tokyo. It is highly recommended that you study the Japanese language while you are in Tokyo, or ideally, before you go. Your daily life will be made much easier if you are able to say even a few phrases in Japanese, and the more you learn the more you will improve the quality of your experience. Even if you are fluent in Japanese, people will appreciate your effort and are more likely to open up to you.

Overview

The exact origin of the Japanese language is not known. Some scholars claim it is similar to other languages in the Altaic language family (which includes Turkish, Mongolian, and Korean); other scholars observe similarities with Polynesian languages. Japanese people developed a writing system based on the Chinese written language, but the two languages are completely different in terms of grammar and pronunciation, and are not mutually intelligible.

The Japanese language used in the media and taught in schools (including language schools) is called *hyojungo* (standard language). In addition, large number of dialects are spoken throughout the country. In these dialects, some words are pronounced in unique ways and/or some vocabulary is different. The dialect spoken in Tokyo is very similar to the standard language. People from other parts of Japan think that people in Tokyo speak very fast and some people feel that the Tokyo dialect sounds cold.

Writing Systems

The Japanese writing system consists of three different sets of symbols: *kanji, hiragana,* and *katakana*. Japanese people use a mixture of these symbols when writing.

Kanji is the set of Chinese characters imported into Japan about 1,500 years ago. Chinese characters originated as pictographs and each character has a meaning. In the Japanese language, the same character can be pronounced differently depending on its usage (for example, whether the character is used independently or in combination with other characters). The Japanese government has identified about 2,000 *kanji* that are used in daily communication. Even Japanese people have difficulty memorizing what their meaning, writing, and pronounciation. The widespread use of computers and word processors now allows people to choose the character they want from a list of homonyms, so less time and energy is spent memorizing how to write the characters.

Hiragana is a simplified symbol system created from Chinese characters about 1,000 years ago. There are 51 *hiragana* symbols – they represent sounds, but do not have any meaning. *Hiragana* is often used after *kanji* to form verb endings and is also used for particles. ("Particles" are used to indicate the function of words in sentences.) While entire sentences can be written in *hiragana*, Japanese people find them cumbersome to read, sometimes ambiguous in meaning, and too simplistic.

Katakana is the third writing system. It contains 51 symbols just as *hiragana* does and represents the same sounds, but the symbols look different. *Katakana* is used to express words or concepts imported from other languages. For example, when computers were introduced into Japan, there was no Japanese word for "computer", so *katakana* symbols were used to simulate the English pronunciation of "computer".

Romaji, the fourth writing system, uses Roman letters to spell

Japanese words. In Tokyo, most train stations' names are displayed in *romaji* in addition to Japanese symbols. Many Japanese language textbooks are written in *romaji* so that foreigners can study the spoken language without having to learn the writing system.

In the past, Japanese script was usually written vertically and from right to left, but because of increased exposure to Western languages (especially English), more people today write Japanese horizontally and from left to right. Most Japanese books are still written vertically, however, and open from the right.

Pronunciation

All Japanese syllables end either in vowels or a nasal *n*. There are five vowels: *a* (as in "father"), *i* (as in "machine"), *u* (as in "dude"), *e* (as in "end"), and *o* (as in "over"). If two vowels appear together, they should be pronounced separately (such as the *a-i* in "naïve"). Because vowel sounds are prominent in the Japanese language, Japanese people tend to add vowels to the ends of syllables and words when they speak in other languages. For instance, they tend to pronounce the English word "house" as "how-su" and the word "stop" as "su-top-pu".

There are 14 consonants, most of which are pronounced approximately as they are in English. However, the Japanese language does not distinguish between "r" and "l" and there is no "th" or "v"; thus, it is difficult for Japanese people to pronounce these sounds when speaking in English or other languages containing these sounds.

Grammar

In the Japanese language, verbs normally come at the end of a sentence, and the indication of positive or negative also comes at the end. In other words, people must listen carefully until the end of the sentence for what is sometimes the most important part of the message. Verbs are not conjugated based on the gender or the number of subjects.

The subject of a sentence is often omitted in Japanese. People guess what the subject is, based on the context, such as the subject of the previous sentence, the nature of the topic, or the choice of words. In particular, they will often omit "I" or "me," so one must infer from the context that the subject is themselves – this frequently becomes a source of confusion to many foreigners.

Japanese people change the way they speak depending on whom they are speaking with. First, there are several levels of formality and informality that can be expressed by the choice of verbs and their conjugations. For example, *arigato gozaimasu* (thank you) is more formal than *arigato* (which also means "thank you"). Japanese people use more formal forms when speaking to people they are not well acquainted with, when they do business, or when they talk to older people. As individuals get to know each other better, they often change to more informal forms, although they will continue using formal forms when speaking with older people.

To reduce confusion for foreigners learning the Japanese language, Japanese language textbooks are usually written in the formal form. As a result, foreigners who studied Japanese abroad may find that the Japanese they speak is too formal for daily life in Japan, especially when dealing with people similar in age to themselves. Not that this should hold you back from studying Japanese prior to your arrival, as you will quickly learn the more informal forms through daily interactions with Japanese people.

In addition to the distinction between formal and informal forms of Japanese language, there is a distinction between honorific forms and humble forms. In conversation, people use the honorific form to refer to others and the humble form to refer to themselves when they want to show respect to their counterparts. The honorific form is used to "elevate" the other person and the humble form is used to "lower" the speaker. People generally use these forms when speaking with clients, with someone senior to them in either age or rank, or with people they do not know well. Both forms are expressed by different patterns. For example, the word "to come" can be expressed in three different ways: *kuru* (neutral formal form); *irassharu* (honorific form); and *mairu* (humble form).

Finally, there is a distinction between some word choices made by males and females. For example, when people refer to themselves (that is, when they say "I"), both males and females use either *watashi* or *watakushi*, but only males may say *boku* or *ore* in casual conversations. In addition, males and females often use different word endings, especially in informal settings. For example, to say "This is good, isn't it?", a man might say *"Kore ii daro?"* and a woman may say *"Kore ii desho?"*. In general, females tend to use more polite language than males do, although gender differences in language are less obvious among younger people.

COMMUNICATING WITH JAPANESE PEOPLE IN ENGLISH

While some Tokyoites you meet or work with may speak English fluently, most people you interact with on a daily basis will have limited experience in speaking English. Communicating effectively with them requires some effort and patience from both sides.

English Language Education in Japan

Most Japanese people study English in school for at least six years (three years each in junior high school and in senior high school). Those who go on to university usually study English for an additional four years. Many children and adults also attend private English schools or hire tutors.

Japanese youths tend to develop greater proficiency in reading and writing, than in comprehension and speaking, for a couple of reasons. Firstly, Japanese schools emphasizes the learning of correct grammar and sentence structure, and the memorization of vocabulary and phrases. In general, a significant portion of the entrance exam for high schools and universities is devoted to the testing of students' mastery of those aspects of the English language. As a result, schools tend to

teach *juken eigo* (entrance-exam English), focusing on drills and memorization, while largely neglecting comprehension and practical application.

A second reason is based on cultural values and communication styles. Because of the focus on group dynamics mentioned earlier, Japanese people care greatly about what others think of them. In consequence, they speak cautiously to avoid making any mistakes. This attitude often hinders them from developing fluency in English or other foreign languages, as in order to improve one must practice and make mistakes. Many Japanese who can speak English fluently do so because they spent some years abroad when young. Children have fewer cultural filters and will try out phrases in a new language with less hesitation. This is one reason why Japanese schools are trying to implement English education in primary schools when children's learning styles are more flexible.

Japanese English

Japanese people have adopted and sometimes modified the pronunciation of many English words, using them in daily conversations when speaking in Japanese. They also try to use these words when they speak in English, but these words can sometimes cause misunderstandings when pronounced differently or used with a slightly different meaning. Here are some examples:

- *terebi* – "television" (The original word has been shortened; the sound "b" replaces "v", which does not exist in Japanese.)
- *G-pan* – "jeans" ("Jeans pants" is abbreviated, with "G" standing for "jeans".)
- *OL* – "female support staff" ("OL" stands for "Office Lady", which is not widely used among native English speakers.)
- *kura* – "air conditioner" ("cooler")
- *manshon* = "apartment" or "condominium" ("mansion")

Effective Communication with Japanese People

Many Japanese people feel ashamed when they do not understand what foreigners say in English or when their English is not understood by foreigners. This tendency adds further pressure, making it more difficult for them to speak in English. (What a vicious cycle!) Consequently, one approach for communicating effectively in English with Japanese people is to create a safe environment for them, so that the stress is reduced as much as possible. Some general tips include:

1) Modify your English

~ Simplify your English and try to put only one idea into a sentence. Avoid using too many pronouns, adjectives and adverbs.

~ Speak slowly, pausing between sentences. Japanese people feel more comfortable when speaking in turns, and will wait until you finish your sentence. Pauses give them room to digest your message and to form a response in English.

~ Avoid negative questions. Japanese people tend to answer negative questions opposite from how a native English speaker would answer them. In order to avoid confusion, it is better to state questions in the positive. For example, to the question, "Didn't you know that there was a class this afternoon?", native English speakers would indicate the negative by responding "No", or "No, I didn't". Japanese people who are not fluent in English would probably indicate they did not know by saying "Yes" (meaning, "Yes, I didn't"), which is a direct translation of how they would answer in Japanese. To avoid misunderstanding, ask instead, "Did you know that there was a class this afternoon?"

~ Avoid tacking questions onto statements. It is difficult to understand both the statement and the question at the same time, and to determine how to respond. For example, "You didn't know that there was a class, did you?" is difficult for non-native speakers to understand because they cannot tell if it is a positive or negative question. Again, use a simple direct question: "Did you know that there was a class?"

~ Avoid idioms and colloquial expressions. Japanese students do not learn conversational English in school and usually do not understand colloquial expressions. For example, instead of saying "Shall I give you a hand?", say "May I help you?". Instead of saying "Are you all set?", say "Are you ready?" or "Have you finished?"

2) Check for Understanding
   ~ Do not assume that everything is understood if Japanese counterparts remain silent. This could simply mean they did not understand your message.
   ~ Check frequently for comprehension. (The question "Do you understand?" is not effective for confirming comprehension because Japanese people often feel it is rude to say "No".) Rephrase your statements and ask probing questions to confirm comprehension (such as asking for a specific date, figure, or action plan).

3) Use documents to support your message
 ~ Japanese people comprehend better reading English rather than listening or speaking it. Support what you say in writing. When you ask questions, write down key words. When making a presentation, prepare handouts, and if possible, distribute them to the audience in advance.

4) Speak in small groups of people
 ~ When several native speakers of English are involved in a conversation, it is extremely difficult for Japanese people to understand all that is said. Limiting the number of native speakers can slow the pace of the conversation and make it easier for Japanese people to participate.
 ~ When Japanese people are in a group, they are expected to observe group dynamics and pay attention to what others might think about their comments. You will probably get more honest reactions when you interact with Japanese people one-on-one.

5) Be personal
 ~ Having good relationships is important for Japanese people. They feel more relaxed when they speak with someone they know. Try to get to know them personally. Face-to-face communication is usually more effective than telephone conversations.

6) Be patient
 ~ Modifying your English and checking frequently for comprehension requires energy and can sometimes be frustrating. Understand that your Japanese counterpart is equally frustrated. Effective communication depends on mutual effort.

GETTING TO KNOW PEOPLE

To create good first impressions, it is important to know how to address people and how to greet people.

Japanese Names

Japanese people usually call each other by their family (last) names; given (first) names are used only among close friends, couples, or family members. They usually add *"-san"* after the family name; for example, a person whose family name is Suzuki will be addressed as Suzuki-*san*. The suffix *"-san"* is never added to one's own name, and is sometimes omitted when teachers speak with students, when older students speak with younger students, and when managers speak with subordinates. In other words, older people may call younger people by their family names without *"-san"* if they know each other.

The suffix *"-sama"* can be used instead of *"-san"* to indicate more formality, for instance, an important customer or a senior person named Tanaka may be addressed as Tanaka-*sama*. Following this custom, Japanese people may also attach *"-san"* to the family names of foreigners, or to their given names if the foreigners have invited Japanese counterparts to use the latter. In any case, it is best not to call Japanese counterparts by their given names unless they have invited you to do so more than once.

Japanese people write their family names first followed by their given names when writing in Japanese – they generally switch the order when writing in *romaji*. Sometimes, they do not write their given names at all. Similarly, they often mention only their family names when introducing themselves.

Greetings

Japanese people bow when greeting, not only the first time they meet but also each time they see one another. How deeply they bow depends on the relationship with the other party and the relative rank between the two. Deeper bows indicate more respect. People bow more deeply the first time they meet and on more formal occasions. A college graduate at a job interview, for example, bows almost 90 degrees in front of the interviewers.

People try to bow more deeply than their counterparts if the counterparts are more senior to them either in status or age. In other words, at the job interview, the graduate bows deeper than the interviewers to show respect (The interviewers would probably just nod to acknowledge the candidate.). When people greet others in informal settings (such as passing a neighbor on the street) they may bow only about 30 degrees. As they get to know each other, in relatively informal settings, they may bow less deeply or perhaps just nod when they see each other.

In Japan, people also bow when they depart, when they thank others, when they apologize, when they offer gifts, etc. In other words, Japanese people almost always bow when interacting with others. Because bowing is a way of showing respect, those who do not bow are often considered rude or arrogant. However, those who bow too frequently can be considered insincere. Obviously, bowing is an activity fraught with cultural nuances. As a foreigner you will not be expected to be aware of all these nuances, and Japanese people will most likely appreciate any efforts you make to show respect by bowing.

Shaking hands is not common except on ceremonial occasions such as press conferences and meetings of political leaders. Some people offer to shake hands with Westerners, knowing that this is their custom, but Japanese people tend to bow even when shaking hands.

Exchanging business cards is the most important part of the greeting ritual among Japanese people. People exchange business cards the first time they meet in business situations as well as on non-business occasions. Neighbors may exchange business cards to introduce each other or people may exchange cards at social gatherings. (*Refer to* "Greetings" *in Chapter 9*).

As for topics of conversation, people usually do not talk much about personal matters (such as health, families, or significant others) unless they know each other quite well. Safer topics of conversation among neighbors or people one has just met are food, weather, seasonal events, places to visit in Japan, customs and traditions in Japan or in your culture, and so forth. Unless you know a Japanese person well, you probably should not make negative comments about Japanese culture, because they might be taken as personal criticism. If you have experienced some problems due to cultural differences, you might describe what happened (try not to include your own interpretation) and ask the person for an analysis. Japanese people are generally very willing to help foreigners who seek their advice.

Visiting and Hosting
By visiting and hosting Japanese friends' and colleagues you will have a wonderful opportunity to get to know them better.

Visiting a Home
Japanese people do not often invite others to their homes because most homes are not large enough to accommodate many people at once. A Japanese person who invites a friend, especially a foreign friend, to his or her home is showing a deep commitment to the relationship.

Unless specified otherwise, an invitation to someone's home is only for you; it does not include a spouse or other family members. Japanese people generally keep personal friends and family members separate, and tend not to introduce them to each other (which is another reason why friends are not often invited to their homes). However, your family may be included if the person inviting you has already met them, or knows them well.

Arrive up to five minutes later than the specified time so that the host can relax a bit after completing preparations for your arrival. If the invitation is for dinner, you will probably be asked to arrive between 6pm and 7pm and will be expected to depart around 10pm. (How late you stay depends, of course, on your relationship with the host.)

Always take a gift when you are invited to the home of a Japanese person. You can ask what to take if you share a very close relationship with the host. Even if the host declines your offer, take something anyway as a symbol of reciprocity. Popular gifts are fruits, chocolates, cookies, and flowers. If you know that your host drinks alcohol, you can take a bottle of wine (beer may be considered too casual except for a barbecue party). You can also bring gifts such as small toys for any children in the house. The hosts might not open the gifts before you, but this is not an indication that they do not appreciate your gift. Opening a gift and showing a reaction is considered too risky. (What if they do not like it?) They will open it after you leave and thank you later.

You are supposed to remove your shoes when entering a Japanese home, so come prepared and wear a clean, hole-free pair of socks! Most Japanese people will offer you a pair of slip-

Photo by Akiko Watanabe

A three-generation family enjoys a New Year dinner at home.

pers to wear inside their home. You should remove them when you enter a traditional *tatami* mat room, as well as the bathroom; you usually will find another pair of slippers inside the latter, which should be used exclusively in that room. Some guests (not just foreigners) make the mistake of wearing these slippers out to other rooms and then feel very embarrassed!

Japanese people show their hospitality by putting a lot of time and effort into preparing a big meal for guests. If there is an item you cannot eat, simply leave it aside untouched. Sometimes your host will notice and will not offer you the same thing again.

Your host will very much appreciate receiving a thank-you letter or thank-you call the following day. When you see your host later, thank him or her again for the occasion even if you have already made a thank-you call or sent a letter. Japanese people like to experience continuity in relationships and reinforce them by referring back to past events. Additionally, they will feel happy to hear that you appreciated their efforts.

Hosting Japanese People in Your Home

If you have been invited to a Japanese friend's home, you may want to reciprocate the invitation. If you were the only guest at your friend's home, you might want to invite only your friend to your home. In general, Japanese people prefer to develop in-depth relationships with a small number of people rather than to meet many people at one time. In other words, they may feel more comfortable visiting you individually or as part of a small group rather than attending a large party with strangers. Their comfort level in speaking English will also affect their preferences.

Some people do not feel comfortable accompanying their spouses to a party if they do not already know the hosts. In Japan, husbands and wives tend to have different groups of friends and it is not as common as in the West to accompany each other to social occasions. Also, single people feel hesitant to bring dates unless they are engaged (a socially approved status). All of this,

153

of course, depends on several factors including the nature of the relationship, English proficiency and past overseas experience.

When offering food or drink, make the offer a few times. Japanese people usually decline the first offer out of politeness. In Japan, people often feel that it is not polite to ask for a drink or an item, so they tend to wait until their host has offered a few times. Therefore, good hosts should be attentive to the needs of their guests.

Select the menu based on what you already know about the food preferences of your guests. They may not tell you what they like or dislike even if you ask directly, but in general, Japanese people tend to prefer hot meals over cold and prefer foods that are not greasy; some do not like cheese. Meats other than beef, pork, or chicken are not popular in Japan (and are not readily available). These are just general guidelines; some people are more adventurous than others and love to try foods from other cultures.

GIFT-GIVING

Japan is a "gift culture". Gifts play an important role in building and nurturing relationships.

There are official gift-giving periods twice a year: one in mid-July (*ochugen*) and the other at the end of the year in December (*oseibo*). People send gifts to superiors, colleagues, and neighbors, and to others who have done them favors. To show appreciation and nurture relationships, companies also send gifts to their clients and other business associates. Department stores and retail shops regard these gift-giving periods as sales opportunities and offer special discounts to attract customers. Food, wine, and household goods such as towels and linens are popular gifts. The amount spent on each item varies depending on the relationship, but usually ranges from 3,000 to 10,000 yen.

Japanese people generally do not expect foreigners to follow these formal gift-giving customs. Even among Tokyoites, gift-giving is becoming less popular. Few younger people practice the custom of ritualized, obligatory gift exchange, preferring more casual relationships. Some companies have discontinued the practice of sending gifts to other companies in order to reduce expenses, and others have banned gift exchanges among employees in order to abolish ritual formalities. But if you like, you can use these opportunities to deepen relationships and to show appreciation for the help your Japanese friends have given you. Be aware that once you have started the custom, it will be reciprocated and will continue over the years.

Another occasion when Japanese people give gifts is upon return from a vacation or a business trip. They bring souvenirs (*omiyage*) to colleagues, neighbors, and friends. For a group of colleagues, people bring something inexpensive that can be shared (cookies, chocolates, or finger foods). For colleagues who have done work for them while they were absent, they may bring specially chosen souvenirs. They also bring gifts to their neighbors, particularly if they have asked the neighbors for a specific favor (such as watering the plants or looking after the mail), or if the neighbors have previously brought them *omiyage*. (Reciprocation is important in Japan!) Finally, they may also bring *omiyage* for close friends if they have received *omiyage* from them before or if they have found something that their friends would like. *Omiyage* do not have to be expensive, but should be reminiscent of the place the person has visited.

People often give farewell gifts when colleagues, neighbors, or friends move to another location, or when colleagues leave the company or retire. Expatriates who leave Tokyo after their assignments are finished are likely to receive a lot of gifts from Japanese colleagues and friends. It is also common for people who are leaving to give gifts to those whom they leave behind to thank them for their support and companionship. When giving farewell

155

gifts, people try to choose items that are reminiscent of the relationship or place.

Japanese people do not celebrate the anticipated birth of a baby by attending a "baby shower" (a party for giving gifts before babies are born). Instead, they give clothes, toys, or other baby-related items within a month after the birth.

Christmas and birthday gifts are only exchanged among adults if they are quite close. School-aged children may exchange birthday gifts and invite each other to birthday parties. The value of gifts varies by age and school, so if you have children you might want to check on this with other parents.

Japanese people have a tradition of giving *otoshidama* (pocket money) to children at the New Year. Adults are expected to give *otoshidama* to children present at New Year parties. The amount varies according to the age of the children and ranges from 2,000 to 10,000 yen. The money is placed in small envelopes specifically designed for *otoshidama*. (Such envelopes are sold in stationery stores.) *Otoshidama* is a major source of children's savings.

Wrapping is another important aspect of gift-giving in Japan. You might be surprised to find that everything is neatly and sometimes densely wrapped in several layers. Actually, some shops are criticized for using excessive wrapping. Nevertheless, the appearance of a package is as important as the contents. Japanese people tend to think that attention to detail (such as wrapping) reflects the degree to which a giver cares for or respects the gift recipient. Most department stores or large retail shops will gift wrap at no additional cost; the first thing a new department store clerk learns is how to wrap a gift! Even more attention is paid to the wrapping of gifts presented on formal occasions.

WEDDING AND FUNERALS
Attending a Wedding

Expatriates may be invited to wedding cocktail parties or receptions; this is especially true for expatriates who are managers of Japanese workers, as in Japan, the boss is often the most important guest at wedding parties.

Wedding receptions are usually held in the banquet rooms of hotels or at wedding convention halls. It has also become popular to hold wedding receptions at restaurants. You are likely to receive a written invitation from the bride and groom, and you are supposed to RSVP by sending a postcard back by a certain date. Unless it is specified otherwise in the invitation, your spouse is not invited. Sometimes you may also be invited to the wedding ceremony before the reception, but often invitations are issued only to relatives and very close friends.

Guests at wedding receptions generally give gifts of money. The amount depends on the guest's relationship with the bride and groom and ranges from 20,000 to 50,000 yen. If you have been invited to a wedding and do not know how much to give, consult your Japanese friends or colleagues. Guests put the money into special envelopes (*shugibukuro*) purchased at stationery stores, and take them to the reception. In return, guests receive souvenirs (such as plates, teacups, or glasses) from the bride and groom at the reception.

Wedding receptions are rather formal occasions. Men are expected to wear suits; preferably black ones. Women are expected to wear party dresses or suits of any color except white, which is reserved for the bride. A full-course meal (usually Western food) is served at the reception. Guests begin eating and drinking only after a formal toast is made by one of the honored guests. Predesignated speakers give speeches and someone may sing a song during the meal to celebrate the marriage. If you are the boss of either the bride or groom, you will be asked to give a speech. The bride and groom usually leave to change their clothes once or twice during the reception. These days more couples prefer to wear Western wedding clothes, but some still wear traditional

Japanese *kimono*. The reception usually ends with a speech by the newlywed couple and/or their parents.

Wedding cocktail parties, organized by friends of the bride and groom, often follow the formal wedding reception. While wedding receptions are for family members and close friends, cocktail parties are mainly for casual friends and colleagues. To attend wedding cocktail parties, guests are usually asked to pay an entrance fee, ranging from 5,000 to 10,000 yen. The dress style for a cocktail party is less formal than for a wedding reception; regular suits for men and dresses for women will suffice.

People who are not invited to either the reception or the cocktail party, but still want to congratulate the newlyweds, sometimes send the couple a gift with a value of 3,000 to 10,000 yen. Some items which are not appropriate as wedding gifts are scissors or knives (which can "cut" the relationship) and anything in fours (because the pronunciation of the number "four" is the same as "death" in Japanese). People also often send telegrams to the place where the reception or party is held in order to pass their personal congratulations along to the bride and groom.

Going to a Funeral

Most funerals in Japan, except those for the followers of Christianity or other religions, follow Buddhist rituals. For Buddhist funerals, people mourn in two different days. The first day is called *otsuya*; it literally means "to spend a night" with the deceased. A ceremony is usually held the same night or the following night after the deceased has passed away. The second ceremony is called *kokubetsushiki* and is usually held the day after the *otsuya*. The purpose of the second ceremony is to say goodbye to the deceased; the body is cremated shortly after this ceremony.

Those who are not particularly close to the deceased attend only the second ceremony. However, there is no rule regarding who should attend a funeral. Japanese people often help out at the funeral ceremonies of their colleagues' close family members.

People give *koden* (condolence money) to express their condolences. The amount depends on the guest's age and relationship with the family. When close family members of colleagues or friends pass away, people may give 5,000 to 20,000 yen. If you attend a funeral, it is always best to consult with Japanese friends or colleagues to determine the amount that is appropriate to give. The money should be put into a special envelope (*kodenbukuro*) and presented when you arrive at the funeral. Put your name, address, and the amount you enclosed on the outside of the envelope, as the family will need this information later when they send a gift to thank you for your generosity. The gift they return will usually be about one-third to half of the value of the money they received. This custom is called *kodengaeshi* (*koden* return).

People should wear black clothing when they attend funerals. Men usually wear black suits (or dark gray suits if they do not have black ones) with a black tie. Many kiosks at train stations sell black ties for men who suddenly have to attend funerals. Women also wear black suits or black dresses; their handbags and shoes should be black, too. Pearl jewelry is the only type worn.

During the funeral, Buddhist priests recite a sutra while mourners listen, and towards the end of the ceremony mourners are asked to offer incense. It is best to observe what others do and to do the same. The entire ritual is conducted in silence and guests do not speak to family members during the ceremony.

❊ ❊ ❊

The communication styles and customs of Japanese people are deeply affected by their cultural values. Foreigners may not be expected to behave exactly like Japanese people, but it is important to observe and respect the way things are done. Rather than memorizing do's and don'ts, ask Japanese friends to assist you by offering cultural insights and suggestions for what to do in each new situation you face. Enjoy your intercultural encounters!

159

—CHAPTER NINE—

WORKING IN TOKYO

Foreigners working in Tokyo will be working in a business environment that has, in some respects, seen dramatic changes over the past few decades. In the 1980s, the country experienced a "bubble" in its economy; in the 1990s, it suffered a significant downturn. Many companies were forced to restructure to cut costs, drastically altering their business strategies. Many were also forced to modify certain traditional business practices that were impeding their ability to keep up with their competitors in global business. While these factors have changed some aspects of how business is done in Japan, much remains the same.

To assist you in navigating the Japanese workplace, this chapter discusses issues that will affect foreigners working in Tokyo, including etiquette, business style, and challenges.

BUSINESS ETIQUETTE

While working in Tokyo you might encounter several features of protocol and business practices unique to Japan. In Tokyo, business etiquette is generally formal, especially in government circles and conservative industries such as banking and manufacturing.

What to Wear

In most work places in Tokyo, businesspeople normally wear business suits. Men working in government agencies and in the financial and manufacturing industries tend to wear conservative suits in navy blue, gray, or dark brown, with white, beige, or light blue shirts. Those working in fashion-related or mass communication industries may wear more trendy and colorful shirts and suits. In some high-tech companies or subsidiaries of foreign companies, casual wear is gradually being introduced. Many companies have also introduced "casual Friday", a day when employees are allowed to dress less formally; the definition of "casual" varies, but most companies do not allow male employees to wear shorts or sandals.

Similar customs apply to the business attire worn by women, although a greater variety of colors is acceptable. Career women usually wear suits or jackets with skirts (pantsuits are acceptable but less common.) They usually avoid large jewelry, excessive makeup, and strong or flashy colors such as bright yellow or hot pink. In many Japanese companies, female workers who are not on a career track wear uniforms provided by the employer. On casual days, women may wear T-shirts, pants, or dresses; shorts and tanktops are usually not allowed. In general, Japanese women dress rather formally.

Greetings

Japanese people customarily bow when they meet. (Some Japanese businesspeople may also offer to shake hands with Westerners, knowing that this is their custom.) As the depth of the bow

161

indicates the level of respect one desires to show, people try to bow more deeply than their counterparts if those counterparts are customers, senior in rank to them, or are otherwise important people. A formal bow is made by holding the hands at the sides of the thighs with the fingers straight, and bowing deeply with the eyes facing the floor.

When two people meet for the first time, they generally bow and then exchange business cards (*meishi*). This is an essential part of greeting others in Japanese business settings. It is recommended that you have your business cards printed in both Japanese and your native language, as this will help your Japanese counterparts pronounce your name and your company's name (if it is a foreign firm), and also indicates your strong willingness to do business in Japan.

Business cards are considered to be representations of their owners, and should be handled properly and with respect. When offering your card, hold it with both hands, the lettering on the card facing the recipient so that they can easily read your name, and introduce yourself by saying your name clearly.

When someone offers you a business card, receive it with both hands and glance at it for a moment to read the information. You can even say your counterpart's name aloud to make sure you are pronouncing it correctly. (It is not impolite to ask for the pronunciation if you are uncertain.) Put the cards you receive into a business card holder; do not put them into your pocket. (In particular, do not put them into the back pocket of your trousers, as it would be disrespectful to sit on the cards.) If you receive cards prior to a meeting, you can lay them on the table before you in the order in which their owners are sitting. Do note that it is generally considered rude to write on another person's name card.

Japanese businesspeople generally use their family (last) name in business settings, and when addressing others they usually add the prefix "*-san*". Follow this custom unless Japanese counterparts invite you to call them by their given (first) names; even then, address them by family name plus "*-san*" when in groups and formal settings. Knowing that many Westerners use given names in business, Japanese people often address Western counterparts by their given names plus "*-san*". Sometimes people add the title of a person instead of "*-san*"; for example, a person with the family name Sasaki who is the president (*shacho*) of a company would be addressed as Sasaki-*shacho*, or President Sasaki.

Seating Arrangements

Japanese people pay careful attention to seating arrangements. People are usually seated according to their rank in the hierarchy. In general, seats of honor, which are those furthest from the door, go to senior persons and guests. A businessperson visiting a client's office for a meeting, for example, might be led to a conference room and invited to sit farthest from the door. At a round table or when seating arrangements are unclear, guests wait for senior members of the hosting group to show them where to sit.

When business counterparts are invited out for meals, the host will formally invite the principal guest to sit in the seat of honor (middle of the table, farthest from the door). To show modesty and respect for the host, the guest may then decline at least once, claiming to be underserving of the honor. The host will persist however, and eventually the guest will acquiesce. Senior members of each group usually sit across from each other.

Entertainment

Entertaining for business purposes has long been popular in Japan. With success in business based largely on interpersonal relationships, companies have spent large amounts of money on dinners, drinking at clubs, and golfing in order to build and maintain such relationships.

Given the changes in the economy over the past several years,

163

many companies have implemented cost-cutting measures, significantly reducing their entertainment budgets. As a result, businesspeople do not entertain clients as extravagantly, and as often, as they once did, and treating them to lunch instead of dinner, or foregoing after-dinner drinks.

Business dinners are still a common venue for relationship building, however, and if you work in Japan, you will surely be expected to participate. (*For hosting business dinners, refer to* "Business Entertainment" *in Chapter 12.*)

Nightclubs are popular venues for after-dinner entertainment. In these nightclubs, hostesses sit next to customers to serve drinks and to chat with them. Although most nightclub customers are men, hostesses usually welcome the opportunity to serve women customers. Foreigners who realize that their business counterparts are planning to take them to a hostess club but who feel uncomfortable going, can turn down the offer by saying they are tired; an indirect communication style that is more tactful than saying you do not want to join in. (*See* "Japanese Communication Styles" *in Chapter 8.*)

Golfing is the most popular sport among Japanese businesspeople, and knowing how to golf has long been an essential component of conducting business. Because many golf courses are far from Tokyo, when people invite business associates for a day of golfing, they often arrange transportation in advance or personally drive their associates to the course.

Gift-Giving

Gift-giving was once a popular way of building interpersonal relationships with colleagues and customers, but in recent years budget constraints have made this practice less popular.

One interesting gift-giving custom unique to the Japanese workplace is that women workers give male colleagues chocolates on Valentine's Day (February 14), which traditionally in

Japan, is the day when a woman confesses her love through gifts of chocolates. This custom has been so vigorously promoted by chocolate companies and the media that women feel pressured to follow the custom, even if they do not actually "love" any of their male co-workers.

Usually all the women in a work group will pitch in and buy *giri-choko* (obligatory chocolate) for their male colleagues. This custom has become so popular that a significant portion of annual chocolate sales takes place around Valentine's Day! More recently, a new marketing opportunity, what's come to be known as "White Day" (March 14), has been vigorously promoted. "White Day" sees men giving "return" gifts (there's that reciprocity again!) to the women who gave them *giri-choko*, and of course, to their sweetheart(s) as well. (*See* "Gift-giving" *in Chapter 8*.)

THE JAPANESE WORK FORCE

In order to better understand Japanese business counterparts, it is useful for foreigners to gain some insights into current issues influencing the Japanese work force such as hiring and promotions, lifetime employment, and the employment of women.

Hiring Practices, Job Security, and Promotion

In general, Japanese companies prefer to hire inexperienced staff (typically fresh university graduates) with good potential and then train them, rather than to hire people with work experience. The assumption is that people who have established their careers elsewhere would not blend well into a new corporate culture.

The hiring of university graduates takes place once a year and all new staff start work on the same date, April 1. Recruitment of candidates takes place more than a year before the actual date of hire. Students find information about job openings through university bulletin boards, job fairs, and alumni networks. Qualifications looked for are: a degree from a good university (students from the top public universities are the first choice of most employers); good grades; and suitable personal characteristics (for example, team orientated, diligent and sincere).

These days many companies cannot afford the time and expense of developing a young work force, so some experienced and skilled staff are employed, in addition to university graduates. Some companies have also realized the benefits of recruiting executives who can compete effectively in the global business arena, and who can drastically change the way the companies operate; thus they are turning increasingly to foreign executive search firms for assistance in locating such talent.

Foreign companies in Japan have traditionally hired more mid-career workers than have Japanese companies, because training inexperienced workers was not cost effective and because Japanese companies offered more stability. Younger Japanese are now attracted to foreign companies because salaries and advancement opportunities are generally better there.

Many Japanese companies used to guarantee lifetime employment, so workers were reluctant to change jobs. Those who did so were regarded as lacking in patience or as troublemakers. Now few companies offer job security, so some people choose to change companies to advance their careers, while others have been forced to do so as a result of restructuring and downsizing. As a result, employers are becoming less prejudiced toward those who change jobs. Nevertheless, the percentage of people who change jobs in mid-career is still lower than in the United States and some European nations, and Japanese people still try to stay as long as possible in the company they joined immediately after university.

In the past, a strong sense of loyalty to their employers and colleagues meant workers were hesitant to take vacations or leave on time at the end of the official workday. Given the decline in job security and greater emphasis on life outside of work, younger employees are less hesitant about enjoying time for themselves.

To cut costs, many companies are hiring part-time employees for administrative, data entry, or simple manufacturing jobs. Most part-timers are women; many of whom are married and are trying to earn additional income for their families or themselves. The number of men applying for part-time jobs is increasing, however. While some men choose this route because they cannot find full-time work, many young men do so because they prefer the flexible lifestyle that part-time jobs offer.

In an attempt to boost productivity, the practice of promotion based on performance has been introduced in a number of Japanese companies, but some observers think that it will not be effective in Japan – the strong emphasis on teamwork makes evaluating individual performance difficult. Young talent may be promoted to managerial levels if they are exceptionally competent, but in most cases, age and seniority still take precedence.

The Employment of Women

Many Japanese organizations are still male-dominated. The percentage of women at managerial level in Japan is less than 10 per cent. After the economic downturn, finding a job has become especially difficult for women – companies have reduced the number of new staff, and when they do hire, they prefer males.

Large Japanese companies usually offer college-graduate female applicants two different tracks: career track (*sogo-shoku*) and administrative track (*ippan-shoku*). Those who choose the former can potentially be promoted to management level in exchange for working long hours and accepting transfers to other locations. Those who choose the administrative track will be engaged in support jobs and are rarely offered transfers. There is the unspoken expectation that women in administrative jobs will get married and leave the company after four or five years of work.

Some talented women find that certain foreign firms offer more opportunities for meaningful work and advancement than

167

do Japanese companies, because these companies, modeling the cultures of their home countries, encourage equal treatment of women and men.

Many women who do not actively pursue careers or who prefer to have flexible schedules work as independent contractors. They register with human resource agencies that have contracts with mid- and large-sized companies, and are then sent to work at these companies when there is demand. The agencies take a certain percentage out of the contract fees as commission.

The business environment is especially difficult for women with children, regardless of their work status. In general, employees are expected to spend long hours at the office and socialize with co-workers afterwards. It is difficult for working mothers to do so, as their working husbands face the same pressures, and because the number of child-care facilities, though growing, is still inadequate. As a result, women lose precious opportunities to gather inside information and build rapport with co-workers, both of which are keys to success in Japanese organizations.

JAPANESE BUSINESS STYLES

One outcome of Japan's economic success in the 1980s was intense international interest in Japanese business style and practices. Now that the Japanese economic bubble has burst, it is Japan's turn to analyze its business practices to determine its shortcomings. This has resulted in a gradual modification of the country's business culture, although many traditional practices, especially those that reflect wider cultural values and beliefs, remain in place.

Following are corporate characteristics found mostly in large, older Japanese firms. Young companies and subsidiaries of foreign firms are more similar to those found in the West, but with a Japanese flavor.

Hierarchy

Within most Japanese organizations, hierarchy is highly respected. Employees are expected to defer to the authority of people who are senior to themselves (either in title or age), and to follow the chain of command. When a decision is needed, for example, a proposal has to be brought up through the chain of command, even if the work of some people in the chain is not directly related to the proposal. When holding a meeting, senior members of the company are sometimes invited just as a sign respect for their rank, even if they do not have expertise in the areas of discussion. In addition, subordinates will never confront their manager in front of customers, and even in internal meetings, subordinates are unlikely to correct the mistakes of superiors in front of others.

A typical Japanese company has several tiers of hierarchy, with only subtle differences between each level. Because most people have stayed with the same company for a long time, they know to which positions they will be promoted and at what age. Generally most employees in an organization with similar qualifications advance to the same level at the same pace, with a few rising more rapidly and higher than others. Young employees, however, are generally not promoted beyond the level of older employees, because seniority is highly valued.

The layers in the hierarchy are so thin that there are no major differences between them in terms of responsibility or salary. It is interesting to note that although hierarchy is respected in Japan, the actual salary difference between a junior rank employee and a top manager tends to be far smaller than in other countries.

Manager-Subordinate Relationships

A good manager in a Japanese organization is someone who takes care of subordinates and who acts as a professional and personal mentor to them. A manager is also, of course, expected to have technical expertise, but that is not always a priority – they are

169

more often than not expected to be generalists than specialists. The manager's job is to use effectively their subordinates' talent and knowledge and to increase the group's morale so that performance increases.

Employees in Japan are rotated among several departments for the first couple of years to learn how the entire company operates. An engineer may spend a few years in Human Resources, and a salesperson may learn accounting before finally being assigned to Sales and Marketing – even then employees may still be transferred to another department if there is an opening. Employees in the management track are rotated among key positions more frequently than are those in the engineering track. As a result, employees who have worked in the same group for a long time may have gained more technical expertise than their manager.

Good manager-subordinate relationships often resemble family relationships in that the manager's role is similar to that of a parent or older sibling. In addition to assigning tasks, a manager ensures that the emotional and psychological needs of subordinates are met. When a subordinate appears to have a problem, it is the manager's responsibility to recognize and take care of it, even if it is personal in nature (such as a family matter or a conflict with a loved one). Thus, a manager must develop interpersonal relationships with subordinates, taking them out for drinks or dinner; that is, spend time with them outside the office. Business may or may not be discussed on such occasions. The goal is to create trusting relationships so that when problems arise, subordinates feel comfortable approaching their manager.

Good subordinates support their managers by making them "look good" and by keeping them informed about every aspect of work. In private, the communication between a manager and a subordinate with a close relationship can be very direct and open. However, when they are in public, such as in front of a client, a good subordinate is expected to show the manager respect.

rvice) in the form of free maintenance check-ups or repairs are ommon. Salespeople use very formal language with customers d apologize profusely if they have made even a minor mistake.

Decision-Making

ne prominent characteristic of the Japanese internal corporate usiness style is the decision-making process. Japanese organizaons are very consensus oriented. Decision-makers must seek put and acceptance from all those who will be affected by the cision to ensure implementation. It is rare for a single person to ave decision-making authority, except in a one-person company.

Many Japanese companies employ a document system called *ngi-seido* to make a decision. When people at the operational level me up with a new idea, they prepare a *ringi-sho* (written proposal quiring a decision). To compose the document, they hold a series informal meetings or conversations to gain input and endorsement from colleagues of the same level. The proposal is then sent people one level higher to request their input and endorsement. hose who agree, stamp their seals on the proposal so that others n see who has already agreed to it. If any modifications are sugsted, the proposal is sent back to the lower level. Once the odified proposal is endorsed by all members on the first two vels, it is sent to the next highest level for review. The same ocess takes place and continues until the seals of all people, cluding top management, have been added.

As mentioned previously, in order to garner the approval of ers, the composers of a proposal often conduct a series of inmal meetings with key people. This process of influencing opins is called *nemawashi*, which literally means "to dig around the ts" (of a tree before transplanting); that is, for a transplanted e to grow, thorough preparation is necessary. In the decisioning process, this means that for proposals to be endorsed, key ple must be adequately informed and persuaded. Originators

Customer Relations

"Customers are gods" is a phrase that describes aptly the expe
tion of how customers should be treated in Japan. Customer s
faction is not just a priority; rather, it is the premise on w
most businesses are based. Product and service consumers
express their opinions directly and exhibit a superior attitude v
interacting with merchants and suppliers, who are expecte
meet the buyers' needs, even when those seem unreasonable
example, changing product specifications on short notice, or
ering the price after a contract is signed). Salespeople must de
good relationships with clients by regularly taking them ou
entertainment such as golf or dinner. When transfe
salespeople usually introduce their replacements to their custo
personally in order to foster the continuance of smooth rela

Because of this personal emphasis in business, personal
rals are critical when pursuing new customers. Even when
ucts are of high quality and good value, many Japanese b
hesitate to work with unfamiliar suppliers. Introductions
other organizations, such as banks, or from influential people
existing bonds to the potential customer, can help establish
relationships. Some foreign companies have difficulty enteri
Japanese market because they do not have strong netwo
place. Many successful foreign firms in Japan partner wi
companies to gain access to customers via existing netwo

Many foreigners are impressed by the quality of J
goods and services, and the goal of Japanese salespeo
meet their customers' needs. Rather than using "hard s
work hard to learn the customer's preferences so that
offer exactly (or sometimes more than) what the custom
Although retail customers seldom bargain in shops, s
sometimes offer discounts and other *sabisu* ("service",
items and services included free of charge) to frequent
or those who buy in bulk. For example, *afuta sabisu*

of proposals use socializing, "confidential" private conversations, and small, informal meetings as forums for encouraging colleagues to exchange information, express ideas and air disagreements. By the time a proposal gets to the top level of an organization, everybody has been informed about it and has agreed to go along with it, so last-minute conflict or changes are unlikely to occur.

A large formal meeting is usually held at the end of the decision-making process to announce the proposal, ensure comprehension, and confirm endorsement. Again, by this time, everyone who is affected by the proposal has been fully informed and consensus has been reached, so no surprises or disagreement will be expressed during the meeting.

The benefits of going through this elaborate process are that potential mistakes are avoided and implementation of the decision will be smooth. On the other hand, this formal process is time-consuming and with so many people involved, it is unlikely any one person will take responsibility for identifying and remedying any problems that may arise down the line.

Working Hours

The official working hours for most offices in Tokyo are from 9am to 5pm, but many people stay at work until 10 or 11pm. There are several explanations for why people work such long hours.

Firstly, as "customers are gods", employees are expected to deliver products or services of exemplary quality to ensure customer satisfaction; these expectations create extra work for the detail-oriented Japanese worker.

Secondly, the typical Japanese decision-making process involves a lot of people, and much information, time and data are required to build consensus. People stay late to handle all the groundwork and paperwork before and after decisions are made.

Thirdly, in Japanese organizations, performance evaluations are based on teamwork and attitudes toward work as well as on

173

results produced, so working late is one way for employees to show their commitment. Thus even those who accomplish their tasks in fewer hours may be evaluated negatively, if they leave while others are still toiling. In addition, people are expected to help others, so if they leave the office after meeting their individual responsibilities when others are still working, they can be perceived as not being team players. In addition, because of adherence to hierarchy, younger people feel they should not leave the office until their manager and other senior people have left.

Given these long working hours, *karoshi* (death from over-work) has become a serious problem in Japanese society. If it is determined that an employee died from the stress and fatigue of working too hard, a company can be held responsible for the employee's death, and be made to provide his or her family monetary compensation; compensation, however, is rarely paid as it is usually difficult to determine *karoshi* with legal certainty.

Photo by Yuko Morimoto-Yoshida.

Riding the subway after a long day's work.

Japanese people often arrive home late because they spend a lot of time socializing with colleagues after work, in order to develop essential personal relationships with colleagues and managers. Socializing provides employees with the opportunity to complain openly to their managers about work and to share inside information about certain issues. As neither of these things is likely to occur at the office, socializing plays an important role in building good working relationships and in allowing employees to air potentially explosive or sensitive issues.

FOREIGNERS WORKING IN TOKYO

Foreigners in Tokyo work in many capacities, such as businesspeople, diplomats, engineers, teachers, professors, and service personnel. Most arrive in Japan with a job; a few search for a job after arrival.

Job Searches for Foreigners

Foreigners who arrive in Tokyo looking to work here generally face many challenges in finding a job. First, to be eligible to work in Tokyo, foreigners must obtain a valid employment visa, and to obtain this visa, they must receive sponsorship from a prospective employer. Many employers are reluctant to hire foreigners, however, because of the mountain of paperwork involved. Secondly, to be effective in most jobs, foreigners must have a certain command of the Japanese language, thus employers prefer a Japanese candidate, unless the foreigner has experience or skills (such as computer skills) that significantly outweigh the need for fluency in the language.

In spite of these challenges, some foreigners do find work, the most common of which is teaching their native languages. In particular, numerous English-language schools in Tokyo are constantly looking for native speakers. Some schools require candidates to possess certain credentials for teaching English, while others are more flexible. Foreigners also sometimes find jobs related to writing and editing materials in English. Modeling, particularly for advertisements, is popular with Westerners.

To begin a job search, check employment listings on the Internet, or in English-language magazines and newspapers. The Tokyo Employment Service Center for Foreigners (Tel: 03-3586-8609; **http://www.tfemploy.go.jp**) is a public organization offering foreigners in Tokyo placement services. You will also find advertisements for job placement agencies in the media (on Mondays, *The Japan Times* classifieds features a large "Help Wanted" section; and a list of agencies can be found in the book *Tokyo Finder* (listed in the "Further Reading" section).

Challenges for Foreigners

Expatriates working in Tokyo report challenges due to cultural differences in language, communication styles, working hours, decision-making styles, and gender issues.

The Language Gap

The most frequently mentioned challenge for expatriates working in Japan is language.

Expatriates who work for the Tokyo subsidiaries of foreign firms may assume that English is commonly used for written and verbal communication, and that they will have few problems communicating with Japanese colleagues. However, this is an erroneous assumption. In most subsidiaries, a mixture of Japanese and English is used, and while a few employees can speak English fluently, especially those who have have lived or have obtained degrees abroad, most will not feel comfortable speaking English, and some have very weak command of the language.

Furthermore, English-speaking expatriates who interact with employees of Japanese companies will find that the number of Japanese staff fluent in English to be very limited. If you have a chance to visit Tokyo before beginning your assignment, talk to some of your potential colleagues so that you will start work with realistic expectations regarding this issue.

Studying Japanese prior to your move and continuing to do so in Tokyo will help bridge the language barrier. Your knowledge of the Japanese lan-

guage, as well as the effort made to communicate, will be much appreciated by Japanese colleagues and can create a good impression. Speaking a second language often requires a lot of effort and is stressful for some people; but by doing so, you can empathise with your Japanese colleagues who are struggling to improve their command of English.

Differences in Communication Style

Misunderstandings are not solely caused by differences in language, but also by differences in communication style. Expatriates who have worked with Japanese people often feel that they do not receive enough information from Japanese colleagues about a variety of work-related topics such as personnel issues, decision-making, and ongoing projects.

As Japan is a group-oriented culture, its people place priority on maintaining harmony within groups and therefore often employ an indirect communication style. (*Refer to* "Japanese Communication Styles" *in Chapter 8*)

For example, Japanese people think twice before voicing their opinions (especially negative ones), and sometimes convey messages through a third person. Other approaches employed to maintain group harmony are using hints and suggestions, and avoiding direct confrontation.

As Japanese people usually convey negative feedback or

suggestions subtly, foreign workers sometimes do not take their Japanese counterparts' comments seriously, and sometimes do not even notice that a message has been communicated. On the other hand, Japanese workers are not used to being confronted directly and may feel offended or threatened by such encounters.

Expatriate managers sometimes fail to recognize the capabilities of Japanese employees because, in general, Japanese workers tend to downplay their abilities and performance in front of others, in order not to stand out from the group. They expect managers to recognize their abilities and effort, and to promote them accordingly. In addition, Japanese workers who do not feel comfortable speaking in English may not mention their achievements at all. It is thus likely for an expatriate manager to overlook an employee's contributions or neglect to use the employee's talents.

Even positive feedback is communicated indirectly in order to maintain harmony among group members. Praising an individual worker openly may make that person stand out from the group, and make both the individual and group members feel uncomfortable. Thus, in Japan, managers generally reward and praise the entire group instead of just the individual, or give positive feedback to an individual employee only in a private setting or through a third person. One of the greatest frustrations of foreigners who work with Japanese people is the lack of feedback on their achievements; thus, it is hard to know whether Japanese people think they are performing well. On the other hand, Japanese people often feel that they are being coddled when they receive constant praise from a foreign manager.

What can you do to reduce misinterpretation and maximize your working experience with Japanese colleagues? First, try to cultivate multiple sources of information and feedback. Differences among Japanese employees, in terms of communication styles and proficiency in English, may mislead you if you rely only on feedback from a small group of people. Learn what is really going on by listening to people from different areas and positions in the company. At the same time, be sensitive to the company hierarchy – junior staff members sometimes may not feel comfortable talking to you unless their bosses have been informed. There is a delicate balance between respecting the hierarchy and getting to know enough people to be effective in your work.

By building personal relationships with Japanese workers, you will be able to receive more candid and direct feedback from them. After-work socializing is a prime opportunity to develop relationships with your colleagues and to get to know them better; they may behave very differently when they are away from the office. People who are usually business-like in the office might be open and casual at dinner or at a bar, offering valuable feedback that you would have never had the chance to hear in the office. It may only be through such informal interactions that you discover important information, such as who's the most influential person in a particular work group, as an individual's level of influence may not be reflected in the organizational chart!

Of course, because of the language barrier and differences in communication style, both you and your Japanese colleagues may initially feel uncomfortable socializing after work. But what matters to Japanese workers is that you are willing to spend some time with them; it is not important what is actually discussed on such occasions. Issues raised during after-work gatherings are considered off-the-record and people generally do not bring them up at the office the next day.

However, if you are successful in building rapport with Japanese colleagues through such gatherings, they are likely to provide you with more work-related information in the future. Try to speak with colleagues regularly outside the office, even if the occasion is only lunch or a coffee break. Some may be more open when you meet with them individually than in the presence of others.

Another way to develop and nurture relationships with Japanese colleagues is to brief them thoroughly about the background of a particular project. When people from different backgrounds work together, shared goals or common interests tie them together. As Japanese people value group goals and achievements, their motivation will increase when they understand the aims of the group and how their roles fit with that of the group. Regular group meetings should be held to keep track of progress, remind the group of the goals and redefine direction. This will help to establish common ground among group members; an essential ingredient of teamwork and productivity, as Japanese people can be very open and direct with people with whom they share similar interests. In addition, share with Japanese colleagues what is going on at headquarters or in other international offices of your company. This will increase their sense of being part of the company and your credibility will rise because you are able to provide such information.

Long Working Hours

Many expatriates find that they spend a lot more time at work in Tokyo than in their home countries, primarily because their Japanese colleagues and clients work long hours. Because a large part of this work ethic can be attributed to cultural values and societal norms, expatriates find that it is not easy to change either the working style of their Japanese colleagues or of themselves. Many expatriates are not willing to stay at the office longer than necessary and may even be among the first to leave the office at the end of the day. One risk associated with this approach is that as Japanese people often get more creative after hours and may discuss new ideas or make important decisions late at night, the person who leaves early may remain uninformed.

Again, building good personal relationships with Japanese colleagues can be an effective strategy for bridging these differences. If you have developed good communication channels, you will be informed properly about decisions made in your absence, so you would not feel the pressure to be present at all times.

Through the informal communication channels that you cultivate, you should also be able to learn the main factors behind your Japanese colleagues working late. If the reason is due to a heavy workload and you are a manager, you may be able to reduce it, for example, by changing work procedures, or by reducing the number of reports workers must generate for the headquarters.

Due to the time difference between Japan and your home country, you may frequently have to work from home. Usually people in the home country are not particularly sensitive to the time constraints of expatriates; thus, expatriates feel that they work around the clock. It is important to let Japanese colleagues know that you work from home so that your leaving early or arriving late will not become an issue. It is also important to be clear to people in your home country about your working hours, so that they will not call you regularly in the middle of the night.

You may get tired of frequent after-work gatherings, so be sure to pace yourself and do not feel pressured to attend every gathering you are invited to. Try to go out more often in the early stages of your Tokyo assignment, as declining initial offers might make people hesitant to invite you again. Ideally, after a couple of months, you will be able to find a way to balance your time between work and personal life.

Lengthy Decision-Making Process
When conducting business with Japanese people, many foreigners feel very frustrated with the long decision-making process. You might not experience this as much in your Tokyo office if you work for the subsidiary of a foreign company, but you might find that it affects your work with Japanese customers. Consequently, you might have to factor in more lead time when you do business with Japanese companies. If people at your company's headquarters will be affected as well, let them know that the

181

decision-making process is somewhat different in Japan and encourage them to modify their expectations.

Patience is the key in dealing with this lengthy process. To find out what is going on with a customer, use several different channels. Your formal contact person within the customer organization might be able to tell you at what stage of the decision-making process the company is or how long it might take to reach a decision. If your contact seems hesitant to explain the situation, it might be that he or she simply does not know.

It might also be a good idea to take the contact person out for a get-together (for example, lunch, dinner, or drinks) to get sensitive information off-the-record. If your contact is not willing to divulge the information, you might ask your Japanese colleagues to find out the information through their personal contacts. Your contact person might not be able to tell you because of hierarchy or obligations to others, but people in other areas in the customer organization may feel free to disclose the details. Also, if you know other expatriates who have dealt with this organization before, you could ask for their insights.

Gender Inequality

Female expatriates frequently mention that they observe gender inequality in the Japanese workplace. They often see that Japanese women, equally as competent as their fellow male workers, are promoted less frequently than men, even in the Tokyo subsidiaries of foreign firms. Foreign women, however, generally do not feel that they are affected by gender inequality; that they are treated almost equally (but less so than in their home countries) because they are foreigners. However, due to their gender, many initially encounter difficulty in establishing their credibility.

For foreign women to establish credibility, either in Japanese organizations or in the subsidiaries of foreign firms, it is essential that they receive support from an immediate supervisor. Women should work to create good personal relationships with their managers through individual meetings, informal get-togethers, and after-work socializing. Once they have gained credibility in the eyes of their managers, these managers will generally speak highly of them to others, making it easier for them to establish relationships with other key people at work.

Foreign women in managerial positions sometimes want to promote female Japanese colleagues in an attempt to resolve gender inequality in the organization. This approach can backfire if there is a lack of consensus in the organization regarding the issue. Before promoting a particular woman, it is essential to check on her reputation with different people and to be aware of possible reactions to the promotion. If a Japanese woman is promoted without the full agreement of others, she could experience harsh treatment. Try to gain compliance from other workers before making the promotion so that it seems legitimate to most people.

❊ ❊ ❊

Obviously, the key for foreigners to work effectively in Tokyo is to build good personal relationships with their Japanese colleagues and customers. Learning and following certain business customs unique to Japan is one way to leave a good impression on others. Spending some time with colleagues, subordinates, and customers outside of the office will contribute toward developing open and trusting relationships. Once you are successful at building such close relationships, those relationships are likely to last for a long time – even after you have departed for your home country.

183

—CHAPTER TEN—

RAISING CHILDREN IN TOKYO

Many expatriates moving to Tokyo with children will be pleased to discover that the metropolis is, to a great extent, child-friendly. High-quality education is available at Japanese and international schools, and there is a wide variety of entertainment and extra-curricular activities.

THE JAPANESE EDUCATIONAL SYSTEM

In Japan, the basic educational system consists of six years of primary school, three years of junior high school, and three years of senior high school. Many parents also send their children to kindergarten and university. School attendance through junior high school is compulsory for all children.

Photo by Akiko Watanabe.

High School girls in typical attire—mini-skirts and 'loose' socks.

Both public and private schooling are available for children at all levels. Tuition is free for public primary and junior high schoolchildren, and parents need only pay for textbooks, uniforms, and additional expenses, such as lunch fees. Tuition fees are charged for public kindergarten, senior high school and university, but the fees are generally less than half of that for private schools.

The school year starts in April and ends in March. In most primary, junior high, and senior high schools, it is divided into three terms: term one from April to late July; term two from September to late December; and term three from January to late March. Between each term there are summer, winter, and spring vacations, in addition to national holidays. No public schools hold classes on Saturdays and Sundays, but some private schools do.

Examinations are not necessary for entry into public kindergartens, primary schools, or junior high schools. However,

185

examinations are required for entrance into public senior high schools and universities, as well as private schools at all levels.

Entrance examinations for the best schools are rigorous. As graduates of the top universities are prime candidates for jobs with the most prominent companies and government organizations, many parents want their children to enter these universities. Students from premier high schools have the best chances of entering top universities, so students feel the pressure to enter good high schools. The same principle applies to entrance into junior high schools, so competition starts at a very early age, just to ensure that children will have good careers!

Parents often send their children to tutoring classes to assist them in preparing for entrance examinations. Many children attend these classes almost every day after school. Consequently, life for junior and senior high school students is strenuous. Japanese people call this period *juken jigoku*, which means "entrance examination hell". Nowadays, many parents try to send their children to good private schools that provide continuous education

Photo by Yuko Morimoto-Yoshida .

Young school children wear bright yellow caps when out on field trips.

from primary school through to university, so that their children do not have to take examinations to move up to senior levels, and can enjoy their school life. As a result, competition for entry into these primary schools has become extremely intense, and even small children must attend tuition to prepare for the exams.

EDUCATION FOR FOREIGN CHILDREN
Tokyo offers several options for the education of foreign children, and most expatriate parents are quite satisfied with the quality of education available.

Japanese Schools
Foreign children are eligible to attend Japanese public schools in the districts in which they reside. If you are considering this option, you can get detailed information by contacting the Board of Education at the ward or municipal office nearest your residence.

Language is an important issue to consider when choosing a school. Most Japanese public schools do not offer "Japanese as a Foreign Language" classes, so if your child does not understand Japanese, keeping up with lessons and other activities can be extremely difficult, especially at the higher levels. In addition, as Japanese society is relatively homogeneous, teachers are not specifically trained to accommodate cultural diversity in their classes. Consequently, foreign children may not receive adequate assistance to help them adjust and thrive in the new culture.

As Japanese schools are now in the process of changing their curricula to support the goal of developing students to be successful in the global arena, they are gradually becoming more accepting and accommodating of foreign students.

While attendance at a Japanese public school can be a nearly insurmountable challenge for children from other countries, some foreign parents are pleased with the experiences their children have while attending Japanese schools. This is especially true for

187

parents of young children, as they tend to develop fluency in the Japanese language quite easily. Parents are often impressed by how attentive and committed the teachers are to the students.

There are some customs and systems unique to Japanese schools that may surprise foreign students and parents. They include: 1) students take off their street shoes and wear indoor shoes at school all day; 2) students are required to clean their classrooms (at most schools); 3) students stand up and bow when teachers enter the classroom; and 4) students stay in the same classroom most of the day while teachers move from class to class to teach.

International Schools

Tokyo has many international schools that serve the needs of the foreign community. In selecting a school, consider various factors such as academic standards, philosophy of education, level of discipline and facilities. It is strongly recommended that prior to enrolling you child, you should visit the school and speak with the staff – many schools welcome parents to tour the school. Some schools host official open houses or regular school tours.

Please note that in Tokyo, demand for places in international schools is greater than the supply, and at many schools, openings fill up far in advance of the beginning of the school year. Thus, the availability of an opening may actually be the most important factor in determining which school your child will attend.

Most international schools begin the school year in September and end in June. However, many schools will accept students at any time the school is in session if there is an opening.

The application process varies from school to school. Most schools ask applicants to submit application forms as well as official transcripts from previously attended schools; some schools require recommendation letters. After school officials review these documents they may request that applicants attend an interview and/or take certain tests. Check with each school for specific application requirements and procedures.

Tuition for international schools is generally quite high, ranging from 1.7 million to 2 million yen annually. Additional expenses can easily add up to 1 million yen, and typically include registration fees, building maintenance fees and school bus service fees.

Schools with English-Language Curricula

The American School in Japan

1-1-1, Nomizu, Chofu-shi, Tokyo 182-0031

Tel: 0422-34-5300; **http://www.asij.ac.jp**

Founded in 1902, this is the largest and oldest international school in Tokyo. It offers co-educational classes from Kindergarten through Grade 12 and is attended by 1,500 students from 40 countries. The curriculum follows the American system but is modified to fit the Japanese environment. Nursery School and some Kindergarten classes are held at the school's second campus in Meguro.

Aoba-Japan International School

2-10-7 Miyamae, Suginami-ku, Tokyo 168-0081

Tel: 03-3335-6620; **http://www.a-jis.com**

Founded in 1980, this is a co-educational school offering classes from Kindergarten through Grade 9. The school accepts students who are fluent in English as well as those with limited English proficiency. Japanese language study is an integral part of the curriculum. Currently enrollment is at 600. Its Nursery School is located in Meguro.

The British School in Tokyo

1-21-18, Shibuya, Shibuya-ku, Tokyo 150-0002

Tel: 03-5467-4321; **http://www.bst.ac.jp**

Founded in 1989, this school provides a British-style primary education. Co-educational classes are offered from Kindergarten through Year Eight (age 13). Majority of the nearly 400 students are British.

The Christian Academy in Japan
1-2-14 Shinkawa-cho, Higashi Kurume-shi, Tokyo 203-001
Tel: 0424-71-0022; **http://caj.or.jp**
Founded in 1950, this school offers a co-educational
environment based on the American system, from Kindergarten
through Grade 12. Of the more than 400 students enrolled,
54% are the children of missionaries; just over half are
Americans, with nearly 30 per cent Japanese, about 10 per
cent Korean, and the rest from other countries.

International School of the Sacred Heart
4-3-1 Hiroo, Shibuya-ku, Tokyo 150-0012
Tel 03-3400-3951; **http://www.iac.co.jp/~issh3**
Founded in 1908 by the Society of the Sacred Heart, this school
offers a co-educational Kindergarten and all-girls' classes
through Grade 12. It has approximately 650 students, and the
curriculum is based on both the American and British systems.

Nishimachi International School
2-14-7 Moto Azabu, Minato-ku, Tokyo 106-0046
Tel: 03-3451-5520; **http://www.nishimachi.ac.jp**
Founded in 1949, this co-educational school offers classes from
Kindergarten through Grade 9. Among the 400 students
enrolled, approximately 40 per cent are American, 33 per cent
are Japanese, 14 per cent are Australian or British, and 13 per
cent are from other countries. The curriculum is based on the
American model. All students study Japanese as their first or
second language.

Saint Mary's International School
1-6-19 Seta, Setagaya-ku, Tokyo 158-8668
Tel: 03-3709-3411; **http://www.smis.ac.jp**
Founded in 1954 by the Roman Catholic Brothers of Christian
Instruction, this is a boys-only school and offers classes from
Kindergarten through Grade 12. It has more than 900 students
representing 75 different countries. The school uses a

curriculum that follows the American model and provides an International Baccalaureate course of study.

Seisen International School
1-12-15 Yoga, Setagaya-ku, Tokyo 158-0097
Tel: 03-3704-2661; http://www.seisen.com
Founded in 1962, this school is run by the Handmaids of the Sacred Heart of Jesus. It offers a co-educational Kindergarten and all-girls' classes from Grade One through Grade 12. With a student body of nearly 700 representing over 60 countries, the school serves the international community as well as Japanese children who have lived abroad. Like Saint Mary's it offers an International Baccalaureate course of studies.

Tokyo International School
4-17-26, Mita, Minato-ku, Tokyo 108-0073
Tel: 03-5484-1160; http://www.tokyois.com
Founded in 1994, this co-educational pre- and primary school is attended by more than 200 students from over 35 nations and boasts the best student/teacher ratio (15:1) of any primary school in Tokyo. The primary school moved to its current location in 2001, while the preschool is still located at the old Meguro campus.

Schools with Curricula in Other Foreign Languages

Several international schools in Tokyo offer curricula in languages other than English. They include the following:

Lycée Franco-Japonais de Tokyo
1-2-43 Fujimi, Chiyoda-ku, Tokyo 102-0071
Tel: 03-3261-0137

Tokyo Chinese School
14 Gobancho, Chiyoda-ku, Tokyo 102-0076
Tel: 03-3261-5894; http://www.tcs.or.jp

Tokyo Indonesian School
4-6-6 Meguro, Meguro-ku, Tokyo 153-0063
Tel: 03-3711-8842

Tokyo Korean School
2-1 Wakamatsucho, Shinjuku-ku, Tokyo 162-0056
Tel: 03-3357-2233

PRESCHOOLS
Tokyo offers a variety of educational opportunities, both international and Japanese, for children who are not of school age.

International Preschools
Plenty of international preschools are available in Tokyo. Most international schools have affiliated preschools, while independent preschools are also available, such as:

Child's Play
18-8 Motoyoyogi, Shibuya-ku, Tokyo 151-0062
Tel: 03-3460-8841

Classic Montessori International School
2-10-8 Hiroo, Shibuya-ku, Tokyo 150-0012
Tel: 03-5468-6456

Gregg International School
1-14-16 Jiyugaoka, Meguro-ku, Tokyo 152-0035
Tel: 03-3725-8000

Kids World
Has more than 10 sites in central Tokyo and surrounding areas.
Tel: 03-3252-1162

Komazawa Park International Preschool
4-26-17 Fukasawa, Setagaya-ku, Tokyo 158-0081
Tel: 03-5707-0979

Maria's Babies' Society
Tomy's House #101, 3-36-20 Jingumae, Shibuya-ku, Tokyo 150-0001
Tel: 03-3404-3468

Japanese Preschools

Japanese kindergartens (*yochien*) can provide wonderful cultural experiences for both children and parents. Japanese kindergartens are of two types: private and public; but private facilities are more numerous. Many private kindergartens accept children as young as three, while most public kindergartens accept children four years of age. Fees for tuition are higher for private kindergartens.

Language is initially an issue for foreign children who do not speak Japanese, and the first couple of months can be difficult. Most children pick up the language rapidly, however, and soon adjust to the new environment. Language can also be an issue for parents struggling to communicate with the teachers. Be patient and expect some miscommunication periodically.

It is a common custom in Japanese kindergartens for teachers and parents to exchange notebooks, called *renrakucho*, on a daily basis. Parents are supposed to write down in the notebook things that teachers should know (health problems, for example). The teachers will write, in Japanese, about how the children behaved in class. Foreign parents who cannot read Japanese well can inquire if any teachers are able to write the notes in English (or the foreign language spoken by the parents), or request that the notes at least be written in simple Japanese.

Another common custom involves boxed lunches (*obento*). Children may be asked to take boxed lunches on special occasions (such as field trips), a few days per week, or every day. Japanese mothers spend much time preparing, wrapping and arranging the contents of the boxed lunches for their children. They fill the boxes with several foods, such as sausages, small tomatoes, boiled vegetables, small hamburgers, etc., arranging the contents so carefully that the lunch sometimes looks like a piece of artwork.

The appearance of the containers is as important as the contents. Most children have cute containers that feature famous comic-book characters. There seems to be hidden competition among children concerning whose boxed lunches look best – it becomes the mothers' responsibility to prepare nice boxed lunches so that their kids feel proud. Not wanting their children to feel embarrassed about having "substandard *obento*", foreign mothers do usually try to make their lunch creations look attractive.

Japanese Child-Care Facilities

Child-care facilities, called *hoikuen*, both private and public, are available; they usually care for children of working Japanese parents, but foreign working parents are also eligible to apply. Some of these facilities even accept children who are less than one year old. Prior to accepting children, the *hoikuen* verifies the parents' employment status and income, and sets the fee accordingly. Private child-care facilities are more flexible in their requirements for enrollment, as well as designated time for picking up the children, but they also cost more. Also, some private facilities are not adequately staffed because they are not inspected as stringently and as frequently as are public facilities.

Lunches are provided at *hoikuen*, so children are not required to take boxed lunches. The number of *hoikuen* is increasing, but not fast enough to support the needs of working parents in Tokyo.

EXTRA-CURRICULAR ACTIVITIES

Children in Japan are kept busy after school. This is especially true when they are young and have not yet begun intensive studying. Many of them engage in two or three extra-curricular activities. Popular activities among Japanese children include ballet, piano, and swimming lessons for girls, and soccer, baseball, and martial arts for boys. Japanese parents are enthusiastic about developing well-rounded children, and are willing to pay the fees for these extra-curricular activities.

The number of extra-curricular classes taught in English is increasing. Generally, more than half of the children participating in such classes are Japanese, because English-language instruction for young children is something which Japanese parents are very eager to pay for. Children tend to learn foreign languages relatively faster when the languages are combined with activities. Thus, many classes (including dancing, drama, and gymnastics) are now taught in English; instructors of some of these classes are native English speakers. Fees for these classes are generally higher compared to similar activities taught in Japanese. Most international schools also offer a variety of extra-curricular activities; once your child has entered school, finding appropriate activities should be easy.

A note about martial arts: studying martial arts can be a unique cultural experience for foreign children living in Tokyo, because several popular martial arts (such as *judo*, *kendo*, and *karate*) were developed in Japan, and many classes are offered. Although martial arts are more popular among boys, girls are also welcomed to participate. (*Refer to* "Martial Arts" *in Chapter 14*.)

ENTERTAINMENT FOR CHILDREN

Tokyo and the greater Tokyo area offer many types of recreation for children. Both adults and children will enjoy many of popular recreation spots available.

Amusement Parks

Tokyo has several amusement parks. Those with specific themes draw more crowds than general amusement parks with rides, and tend to get quite crowded on weekends. Costs of visiting can be high, because most places charge a fee for each ride or performance in addition to the entrance fee, but parents usually feel that they get their money's worth because children enjoy themselves and are kept busy for an entire day.

195

Korakuen Amusement Park

1-3-61 Koraku, Bunkyo-ku, Tokyo 112-0004

Tel: 03-3811-2111

Korakuen is part of Tokyo Dome City, which contains a baseball field, a bowling alley, and a skating stadium. Korakuen also has thrilling roller coaster rides and a carousel, and offers shows and events geared toward children.

National Children's Castle *(Kodomo no Shiro)*

5-53-1 Jingumae, Shibuya-ku, Tokyo 150-0001

Tel: 03-3797-5666

This 10-story building offers facilities designed to help children develop their artistic, athletic, and imaginative talents. Facilities include play halls, music studios, a video library, a swimming pool, and a computer room.

Sanrio Puroland

1-31 Ochiai, Tama-shi, Tokyo 206-0033

Tel: 0423-72-6500

Shows are performed here starring Sanrio's famous cartoon characters (such as Hello Kitty). The theme of the park is "love and dreams" and attractions highlight that theme.

Tokyo Disneyland

1-1 Maihama, Urayasu-shi, Chiba 279-0031

Tel: 045-683-3333

Modeled after the original Disneyland in California, many features such as landscaping, attractions, and services were imported from the U.S. This is definitely the most popular amusement park in the Tokyo area. Be prepared to spend a long day here because the wait for popular rides such as Space Mountain can easily be more than an hour. DisneySea, a new amusement park located nearby, features water attractions.

Tokyo Sesame Place

600 Kamiyotsugi, Akiruno-shi, Tokyo 197-0832

Tel: 042-558-6511

This theme park featurs the famous TV show "Sesame Street",

and caters to children from ages one through 12 as well as their families. Children can play with simple but creative educational tools such as plastic bowls and nets. The park also offers shows which feature Sesame Street characters.

Tokyo Summer Land
600 Kamiyotsugi, Akiruno-shi, Tokyo 197-0832
Tel: 042-558-6511
Located just next to Tokyo Sesame Place, this is a place of ever-lasting summer. Man-made waves dash against the shores of a huge indoor pool and tropical rains create a summer atmosphere all year round. An outdoor pool is also open during the summer. In addition to swimming, children can enjoy several rides, a picnic area, a golf range, tennis courts and a bowling alley.

Toshimaen Amusement Park
3-25-1 Mukoyama, Nerima-ku, Tokyo 176-8531
Tel: 03-3990-3131
The park offers a variety of rides for children of all ages. Other popular attractions are water slides and seven different swimming pools.

Yomiuri-land Amusement Park
4 Sugesengoku, Tama-ku, Kawasaki-shi, Kanagawa 214-0006
Tel: 044-966-1111
In addition to taking thrilling rides such as the roller coaster and the free fall, children can watch sea otters and enjoy performances by seals. The park also features a swimming pool in summer and an ice-skating rink in winter.

Aquariums
Tokyo has several aquariums which feature exhibits that will fascinate children.

Enoshima Aquarium
2-17-25 Katase Kaigan, Fujisawa-shi, Kanagawa 251-0035
Tel: 0466-22-8111

The first modern aquarium in Japan, it consist of three sites: 1) an aquarium; 2) a marine land featuring dolphin and whale shows; and 3) a marine zoo where seals, penguins, sea lions and sea otters live.

Kasai Rinkai Aquarium

6-2-3 Rinkai-cho, Edogawa-ku, Tokyo 134-8587

Tel: 03-3869-5152

Located in Kasai Rinkai Park, the aquarium has a large doughnut-shaped tank where huge tunas swim in groups. A guided tour (in Japanese) is offered, taking visitors behind the fish tanks which contain a total of 62,000 fish belonging to 540 species.

Shinagawa Aquarium

3-2-1 Katsushima, Shinagawa-ku, Tokyo 140-0012

Tel: 03-3762-3433

The theme of this aquarium is "communicating with the river and the sea". It offers the only dolphin show in Tokyo and displays more than 10,000 different fish. A big tunnel-shaped glass tank offers visitors a 180-degree view of the fish.

Sunshine International Aquarium *(Sunshine Kokusai Suizokukan)*

Sunshine City 10Fl., 3-1-3 Higashi Ikebukuro, Toshima-ku, Tokyo 170-8630

Tel: 03-3989-3467

This large aquarium showcases fish from all over the world. One of the most popular events is an underwater feeding show during which a diver enters the tank to feed the fish and also answers questions from the audience.

Yokohama-Hakkeijima Sea Paradise Aqua Museum

Hakkeijima, Yokohama-shi, Kanagawa 236-0006

Tel: 045-788-8888

This is a sea paradise built on a little island called Hakkeijima. The aquarium is one of the largest in Japan and displays

100,000 fish representing 500 species. There is also a playground for small children, and a place to feed the penguins.

Zoos
Zoos located in Tokyo and the greater Tokyo area will provide children and parents with hours of family entertainment.

Inokashira Zoo
1-17-6 Gotenyama, Musashino-shi, Tokyo 180-0005
Tel: 0422-46-1100
Both the main zoo and the annex are located in Inokashira Park. More than 200 species of wildlife live here, including elephants, monkeys, and raccoons. Inokashira Park also has a pond where visitors can ride boats, and is a good place for family picnics. The cherry blossoms are beautiful in spring.

Tama Zoo
7-1-1 Hodokubo, Hino-shi, Tokyo 191-0042
Tel: 042-591-1611
This huge zoo tries to recreate the animals' natural environment. It features a savanna with herbivorous animals and a bus tour that allows visitors an up-close view of the resident lions.

Ueno Zoo
9-83 Ueno Koen, Taito-ku, Tokyo 110-8711
Tel: 03-3828-5171
The oldest zoo in Japan, its most famous exhibit is the giant panda donated by the Chinese government, and on weekends and holidays, visitors must wait in a long line to view the panda.

Zoorasia
1175-1 Kamishirane-cho, Asahi-ku, Yokohama-shi, Kanagawa 241-0001
Tel: 045-959-1000
Built in 1999, this zoo's goal is to replicate six different climate zones so that animals can live in their natural environments. It also exhibits rare animals in order to protect the species.

Museums

Tokyo has many museums showcasing fields such as science, history, and culture. (*See* "Art Museums" *in Chapter 14 for a list of art museums.*)

Fukagawa Edo Museum *(Fukagawa Edo Shiryokan)*
1-3-28 Shirakawa, Koto-ku, Tokyo 135-0021
Tel: 03-3630-8625

Here visitors can experience downtown Tokyo in the mid-19th century (Tokugawa Period). Inside the four-story building, shops, restaurants, residences, and traffic from the Fukagawa district (in the eastern part of Tokyo) are reproduced. Visitors can touch certain exhibits to gain a "feel" for life at that time and also listen to sounds simulating daily life then.

Ghibli Museum
1-1-83 Shimo-renjaku, Mitaka-shi, Tokyo 181-0013
Tel: 0422-40-2277

Hayao Miyazaki, a famous animation producer known overseas for his works, "Princess Mononoke" and "The Neighbor Totoro", is the director of this museum. It is designed to be a fantasy world for children and features famous characters from movies as well as the museum's original animated films. Advance tickets specifying time and date are required for entrance; tickets are sold at Lawson convenience stores throughout Tokyo.

National Science Museum *(Kokuritsu Kagaku Hakubutsukan)*
7-20 Ueno Koen, Taito-ku, Tokyo 110-8718
Tel: 03-3822-0111 Monday through Friday; Tel: 03-3822-0114 Saturday, Sunday, and national holidays

This museum covers all the wonders of nature and science, including evolution, meteorites, the solar system, and the analysis of sound waves. Children can participate in many hands-on exhibits.

National Museum of Emerging Science and Innovation
(Nihon Kagaku Miraikan)
2-41 Aomi, Koto-ku, Tokyo 135-0064
Tel: 03-3570-9151
Opened in 2001, this museum features numerous exhibits and activities to help visitors understand the latest science and technology developments. The director of the museum is the Japanese astronaut Mamoru Mori.

Sunshine City Planetarium
Sunshine City 10F, 3-1-3 Higashi Ikebukuro, Toshima-ku, Tokyo 170-8630
Tel: 03-3989-3466
Here children as well as adults can enjoy the spectacular panorama of stars through the use of advanced telescopes.

✿ ✿ ✿

Finding the best educational and recreational opportunities for children while living overseas can be a challenging task for parents. Nonetheless, you will be delighted with the wide variety of educational, recreational, and cultural experiences Tokyo has to offer; and the more you explore, the more you'll discover.

—Chapter Eleven—

TAKING CARE OF YOUR HEALTH

Medical standards in Tokyo are very high, and up-to-date medical treatments are available at most hospitals and clinics; though some aspects of medical care may differ from that in found in other countries. One thing that might surprise newcomers about Japanese hospitals and clinics is that while much of the cost of health services is generally covered by one of two national health insurance plans, some payment is required upon services rendered, and most service care providers accept only cash. Thus, expatriates living in Japan learn to keep on hand a certain amount of cash on hand in case of medical emergency. This chapter will give you some insight into the Japanese medical system and the cultural differences you might encounter when seeking treatment.

THE HEALTH INSURANCE SYSTEM

All residents of Japan, including foreigners, are required to join a public health insurance program. To participate, people pay monthly fees (according to their income), and in return, receive coverage for a large portion of their medical expenses. Private insurance is also available, but serves primarily as supplementary coverage for complex treatments or luxury hospital rooms. The biggest advantage of public health insurance is that it can be used at any hospital or clinic, so patients are free to choose their doctors and to change hospitals. Public health insurance covers medical treatment and prescribed medicines, but not preventive care.

Although foreign residents are expected to enroll in the public health insurance system, some do not. Instead they buy foreign-based private insurance policies, especially if they will be living in Tokyo for only a short period of time, the reasons being: 1) people who are not fluent in Japanese and who are in Tokyo for short stays often prefer private clinics that cater to foreigners – some of these clinics do not accept Japanese public health insurance because they operate independently from the national health care system; 2) Japanese public health insurance is valid only in Japan – most expatriates need insurance that will cover treatment not only in Japan, but also in their home countries and other nations.

Expatriates with overseas-based private insurance are usually required to pay the full costs of any medical treatment or prescriptions provided. They then apply to their insurance companies for full or partial reimbursement. Foreigners who plan to visit a doctor, clinic, or hospital in Japan may wish to inquire in advance about policies regarding insurance acceptance and billing, as some health care providers may be hesitant to treat patients who are not enrolled in one of the public health insurance programs.

Japan has two types of public health insurance: Employees' Health Insurance (*Shakai Kenko Hoken*) and National Health Insurance (*Kokumin Kenko Hoken*).

Employees' Health Insurance

This type of insurance is generally provided to full-time employees and any of their dependents residing in Japan. Previously, it covered most basic and emergency health care at the rate of 80 per cent for employees and 70 per cent for dependents, but since 2003, this has been revised to a flat 70 per cent. It also covers a portion of the cost for prescriptions, but not for preventive care, childbirth, cosmetic surgery, or luxury hospital rooms.

Expatriates on assignment in Japan often qualify for this type of insurance. If you are eligible, your employer will ask you to complete an application form that will be submitted to the Employees' Health Insurance Office.

Only one insurance card (*hoken-sho*) is issued per family, and family members must show this card each time they see a doctor. Patients who visit a doctor in an emergency without their insurance cards must pay all fees in full. They can then submit receipts to the Employees' Health Insurance Office to request partial reimbursement. It is highly recommended that all family members carry a photocopy of the family insurance card, as in an emergency, some medical institutions accept a photocopied version.

Insurance premiums are calculated based on the individual employee's standard income and are automatically deducted from the monthly salary. Many employers pay a portion of the premium on the employee's behalf. The premium remains the same no matter how many dependents an employee has.

National Health Insurance

This insurance is generally provided to residents of Japan who are not covered by other insurance plans. It covers most basic and emergency health care at the rate of 70 per cent for policyholders and their dependents. The insurance also covers a percentage of the cost for prescriptions, but not for preventive care, childbirth, cosmetic surgery, or luxury hospital rooms.

Foreigners who are not full-time employees can enroll in the National Health Insurance program if they meet one of the following criteria: they are residing in Japan for one year or longer; or they have resided less than one year, but can prove intent to stay one year or longer (for example, to students who are admitted to schools for one year or longer). If you qualify, submit an application to the National Health Insurance Section of your local ward or municipal office within 14 days of completing your Foreign Resident Registration. When applying, take your Foreign Registration Card, your seal (although your signature will be accepted if you do not have one), and a document that proves your stay will be one year or more (for example, a copy of your visa). (Refer to "Obtaining Necessary Documents" in Chapter 4.)

As with the Employees' Health Insurance plan, participants will receive one insurance card per household and will be required to present it whenever they receive treatment. Insurance premiums are calculated according to income and the number of dependents covered. Payment can be made in installments at banks, post offices, or local ward or municipal offices.

HEALTH CARE FACILITIES AND PROCEDURES
Hospitals and Clinics

Medical facilities with 20 or more beds are categorized as hospitals, and those with fewer than 20 beds are categorized as clinics. Hospitals vary greatly in size, areas of expertise and medical equipment available. Some large hospitals are affiliated with universities and serve as research and teaching facilities. There are also many small private hospitals. Some hospitals offer services in all major medical fields and others specialize in one particular field, such as oncology or cardiovascular medicine.

There are two types of clinics: those run by one doctor with expertise in a single field (pediatrics or dermatology, for example), and those run by a few doctors with different expertise. Patients have a choice of either seeing a doctor at a hospital or going to a clinic; both have advantages and disadvantages.

Advantages of visiting hospitals: 1) large ones, especially, have advanced medical equipment, enabling them to conduct complex examinations; and 2) hospitals that provide services in various areas mean different specialists can be consulted under one roof. Disadvantages: 1) at many hospitals, unless a patient's symptoms are life threatening, the wait to see a doctor can be more than an hour – most hospital doctors do not accept appointments, especially for initial visits; 2) because hospital doctors see so many patients each day, they can seem rather impersonal and may not give patients their full attention; and 3) in many hospitals, more than one doctor is assigned to see outpatients, so there is no guarantee that patients will be seen by the same doctor each time they visit the hospital.

The advantages and disadvantages of clinics are just the opposite of those for hospitals. As there are more clinics than hospitals, patients can easily find one near their home or office. The waiting time at clinics is usually shorter than at hospitals, and some clinics now accept appointments. The disadvantage is that clinics cannot usually afford to buy the most advanced medical equipment, and doctors may not be up-to-date in some fields.

Generally, people go to clinics when they think that their symptoms are not serious, and only when the symptoms persist do they visit a hospital. On occasions, clinic doctors will refer patients to hospitals when they think that further testing and more in-depth examinations are necessary.

International Clinics

Certain clinics in Tokyo serve almost exclusively the foreign community. They are popular among expatriates because the doctors as well as some staff members, including nurses and receptionists, speak English. Physicians in these clinics are usually either foreigners or Japanese doctors who have been educated abroad.

As previously mentioned, many of these clinics operate independently from the Japanese health care system and do not accept public health insurance. Thus, they are not bound by certain regulations stipulated by the Japanese government. For example, they are free to use medications that have not been officially approved for use in Japan, and to charge whatever fees the market will bear. Consequently, such clinics and the medication they prescribe tend to be more expensive than the regulated versions.

International clinics , like those listed below, are located primarily in Minato-ku and Shibuya-ku where many expatriates live. Foreigners living in other areas usually seek out a neighborhood doctor on whom they can rely on in urgent situations.

International Clinic
1-5-9 Azabudai, Minato-ku, Tokyo 106-0041
Tel: 03-3583-7831
National Medical Clinic
5-16-11-202 Minami-Azabu, Minato-ku, Tokyo 106-0047
Tel: 03-3473-2057
The King Clinic
6-31-21 Jingumae, Shibuya-ku, Tokyo 150-0001
Tel: 03-3409-0764
Tokyo British Clinic
Daikanyama Y Bldg. 2 Fl. 2-13-7, Ebisu-Nishi, Shibuya-ku, Tokyo 150-0021
Tel: 03-5458-6099
Tokyo Medical and Surgical Clinic
32 Mori Bldg. 2 Fl. 3-4-30 Shiba-Koen, Minato-ku, Tokyo 105-0011
Tel: 03-3436-3028

Doctors in Japanese Hospitals/Clinics

When symptoms warrant, many people go directly to a specialist. Others consult a general practitioner (primary care physician) first and then to specialists when referred. When consulting a specialist, especially one who is well known or affiliated with a prominent hospital, an introduction or referral is very important; without an introduction, patients often must wait several months for an appointment. Doctors sometimes charge patients a fee for writing a referral letter to another physician. If your doctor does not personally know a particular specialist whom you would like to see, ask colleagues and friends if they know someone who knows the specialist and who can make an introduction.

Asking for a second opinion from another doctor is not frequently practiced in Japan. Some doctors are reluctant to share data with other practitioners, so patients who seek another opinion may have to undergo duplicate medical testing. Nonetheless, this practice is becoming more widespread and is often worth the trouble, as it may result in valuable information on diagnosis and options for treatment.

Communicating with most Japanese doctors can be a challenge for those who do not speak Japanese. Although many doctors know certain medical terminology in English or German, they may not understand casual descriptions of symptoms. Doctors who have spent a couple of years in an English-speaking country, however, will probably have a good command of the language. The best places to find such doctors are at large hospitals and international clinics.

Japanese doctors tend to be authoritative, although their styles vary depending on personality and age. It is widely believed that doctors are experts who know what is best for patients; thus patients tend to follow the instructions of their doctors without asking many questions. The concept of "informed consent" (that patients should be informed about options for and risks of treatment, and agree to a plan of treatment prior to implementation) is relatively new in Japan. Although the importance of such a concept is widely recognized, doctors are not required by law to discuss treatment options and risks with patients, and many physicians are still not used to doing so.

In dealing with Japanese doctors, be patient and persistent, and do not be discouraged from asking questions. Be prepared for initial resistance from them, however, or in some cases a continuing refusal to discuss your case to your satisfaction. You may decide that it is necessary to find a more receptive doctor. Although more doctors now think it is important to share information with patients, some still think that patients who ask too many questions are challenging their expertise and decisions.

Payment for Medical Services

Charges for tests, medical treatments, consultations, and prescriptions must be paid when services are provided. People who enroll in one of two public health insurance plans and who present their insurance card will be charged only their co-payment (30 per cent of the total cost). If they do not carry their insurance card (such as in cases of emergency), they will have to pay the full amount and then apply for reimbursement. People enrolled in foreign-based private insurance plans have to pay in full, and then submit an application to their insurance company for reimbursement.

Most clinics and hospitals do not accept credit cards, and as checks are not widely used in Japan, all patients should carry cash when visiting any kind of health care provider. (See "Emergencies" later in this chapter)

Medication

Most medicines prescribed by doctors in Japan can be purchased at the clinics or hospitals with which the doctors are affiliated although an increasing numbers of doctorjust write prescriptions and ask their patients to purchase the medication at pharmacies. As public health insurance covers a large portion of the costs of prescribed medications, they are often cheaper than over-the-counter medications. Doctors usually prescribe a three- to four-day supply and ask patients to return if symptoms have not improved over that period of time.

Recommended dosages of both prescribed and over-the-counter medications (especially painkillers) are generally lower in Japan than in the West because the average body size of Japanese people is relatively smaller. Let your doctor know if the dosage of the prescribed medication seems ineffective. Prior to moving to Japan, it may be useful to obtain a note or a copy of your prescription from your previous doctor to show as reference to your doctor in Japan. Foreign prescriptions cannot be filled in Japan, so any prescriptions written by doctors in other countries must be rewritten by doctors in Japan.

The following pharmacies cater to the foreign community and may carry some imported products. Do note that some foreign over-the-counter medications that contain narcotic, psychotropic, and/or hallucinogenic ingredients are prohibited for sale in Japan (Tylenol Cold,, Nyquil,, and Sudafed, for example).

American Pharmacy
Hibiya Park Bldg. 1-8-1 Yurakucho, Chiyoda-ku, Tokyo 100-0006
Tel: 03-3271-4034

Medical Dispensary
32 Mori Bldg. 3-4-30 Shiba-Koen, Minato-ku, Tokyo 105-0011
Tel: 03-3434-5817

National Azabu Pharmacy
4-5-2 Minami Azabu, Minato-ku, Tokyo 106-0047
Tel: 03-3442-3181

Roppongi Pharmacy
6-8-8 Roppongi, Minato-ku, Tokyo 106-0032
Tel: 03-3403-8879

Hospitalization

Sometimes doctors prescribe a stay in the hospital for further examination, specialized treatment, or surgery. Patients of doctors who work at large hospitals are eligible to be hospitalized whenever a bed is available. Depending on the patient's condition, the waiting period can be more than one month.

The average length of stay in a hospital is generally longer in Japan than in many Western countries. This can be attributed to several factors: 1) there is an assumption that it is the responsibility of hospitals to see that patients have fully recovered before release; 2) as homes in Japan (especially in Tokyo) tend to be small, most families do not have private rooms in which convalescing family members can rest; and 3) because public health insurance covers a large portion of the costs of hospitalization, it is not overly expensive for patients to stay in hospitals for extended periods. During hospital stays, patients usually must share their room with a few other patients. Private hospital rooms are available, but these are not covered by public insurance; patients thus have to pay a rather substantial fee per day for such rooms.

Health Examinations

Companies in Japan are required by law to provide free annual health check-ups for their workers. The standard procedure includes chest X-rays, a blood pressure test, and blood tests to check cholesterol levels and liver function. Schools also offer students basic annual health check-ups (such as blood tests, eye and dental examinations, and examination by a doctor).

Each ward or municipal district in Tokyo offers free or low-cost basic health check-ups for residents who are self-employed or unemployed, including foreigners. These check-ups are conducted at public health centers, and at designated clinics or hospitals. Check with your ward or municipal office for information about dates and locations. Thorough physical examinations are also available at designated clinics and hospitals at relatively low charges for people with some form of public health insurance.

CHILDREN'S HEALTH CARE

Parents whose children will be accompanying them to Tokyo should look for a good pediatrician (*shonika*) soon after their arrival. One way of finding a pediatrician is to ask friends, neighbors and the parents of your children's classmates; another is to check the international clinics mentioned earlier; and yet another is to ask staff members at the international schools for a list of English-speaking pediatricians. The books *Japan Health Handbook* and *Japan for Kids* also list pediatricians who speak English.

When contacting these doctors, check whether they will see patients after-hours, as many Japanese doctors will not. Parents who choose a pediatrician who does not offer after-hour care should identify a hospital or clinic that will accept children in case of emergency. (See "Emergencies" later in this chapter)

Vaccinations

While no longer compulsory in Japan, certain vaccinations are strongly recommended and are provided free of charge at designated clinics, hospitals and public health centers. Shortly after registering your residence with your local ward or municipal office, you will receive a notification letter indicating the dates and places that vaccinations will be administered (contact your local ward or municipal office for more details). Recommended vaccinations include the following:

- Polio
- DPT (combined triple vaccine for diphtheria, pertussis, and tetanus)
- Measles
- Rubella
- Japanese Encephalitis

- BCG (tuberculosis)

Other vaccines such as those for influenza, chicken pox, mumps and hepatitis B are available at clinics, hospitals and public health centers for a fee.

WOMEN'S HEALTH CARE

Women go to either a gynecologist (*fujinka*) or an obstetrician-gynecologist (*sanfujinka*) when they want to consult a doctor on female health matters.

General Care

Few Japanese women go for routine checkups by a gynecologist, because this type of preventive care is not covered by public health insurance. Also, some Japanese women are psychologically resistant to an internal examination gynecologists typically conduct. For many Japanese women, the first time they visit a gynecologist is when they become pregnant. The importance of early detection of breast and uterine cancer is increasingly publicized, and some doctors now encourage women to receive routine gynecological checkups. In Tokyo, ward and municipal districts offer female residents (generally only to those over 30) free examinations for both uterine and breast cancer at designated clinics, hospitals and public health centers.

Gynecologists will generally accept public health insurance for checkups if patients claim that something is wrong with them, even if the problem appears to be minor. The routine exam is similar to that conducted in most other countries; however, a mammography is conducted only if a doctor finds some abnormality.

Family Planning

Condoms are the most popular form of contraception and are sold at drugstores and supermarkets. In 1999, the Japanese government officially approved the birth control pill as a contraceptive,

213

but public health insurance does not cover the cost of the pills. The pills can be obtained only with a doctor's prescription, and a doctor's visit is required each time a refill is needed. As Japanese doctors usually only prescribe up to a three-month supply of the pills, and because the variety is still small compared to some other countries, many foreign women who use them bring an ample supply to Tokyo and get refills when they travel back home. Other forms of contraception available in Japan (although not popular) are spermicidal jellies, intrauterine devices and diaphragms.

Many couples in Japan struggle with infertility problems, and the number of clinics and hospitals that specialize in infertility has been increasing. Several advanced treatments have become available, including medication, surgery, artificial insemination and in-vitro fertilization. Infertility treatments can be quite expensive, as they can continue for long periods of time and are not covered by public health insurance.

Abortion is legal in Japan, and can be performed if a woman has the nominal consent of her partner. Doctors seldom ask many questions and the paperwork is minimal. Fees are not covered by public health insurance if the abortion is done by choice rather than due to health considerations, but the cost is relatively low.

HAVING A BABY IN TOKYO

Some foreign couples decide to have a baby while living in Tokyo. Factors to consider are the quality of health care and the fact that accompanying spouses may not be able to find work.It can also be useful to know how pregnancy and childbirth are handled in Tokyo.

During Pregnancy

Pregnant women in Tokyo regularly see obstetrician-gynecologists for checkups. Note that in Japan, doctors calculate the human gestation period as 10 months (in 28-day increments since the last period), whereas Westerners generally calculate it as nine months (in 31-day increments since the last period). Thus, in Japan a typical pregnancy is said to last 10 months.

After a pregnancy is confirmed, a woman is expected to register her pregnancy at the ward or municipal office where she lives. She will then receive a booklet called *Boshi Kenko Techo* (*Mother and Child Health Handbook*). This booklet should be taken to every doctor's visit before and after delivery, in order for doctors to record the mother's and baby's health information and immunization histories. The booklet also contains the schedule and coupons for vaccinations as well as coupons for regular checkups.

Some wards and municipal offices carry free copies of bilingual handbooks. The booklets can also be ordered at a small charge from the Mothers' and Children's Health Organization (Tel: 03-3499-3111). Bilingual editions are available in eight different languages: English, Thai, Spanish, Chinese, Korean, Tagalog, Portuguese and Indonesian.

Japanese doctors are concerned about difficult deliveries and various diseases (such as diabetes) associated with weight gain during pregnancy. Consequently, they are strict about weight gain and recommend that women limit the gain to between eight and 10 kilograms (about 16 to 20 pounds). Because the body sizes of many foreign women and Japanese women are different, doctors may adjust their standards for foreigners. Genetic testing is not routinely performed unless the family has a history of some congenital disorder. However, such testing can be performed if requested by the patient.

Giving Birth

Usually women give birth at the same medical facility where they have received prenatal care. There are many options, ranging from small clinics to large hospitals. In general, clinics are more personal and open to accommodating individual needs, whereas hospitals tend to abide by rules and are less likely to make exceptions or cater to individual requests. One benefit of large hospitals, however, is that they are capable of handling complicated births and have access to a wide variety of drugs.

Additional issues to consider when choosing a place for delivery are, the availability of pain relief medication, rules regarding the presence of the father at delivery, and the length of the recommended postnatal stay.

In Japan, it is quite common for women to give birth without taking painkillers, as people are concerned about possible side effects on both mother and baby. Also, there is a fundamental belief that giving birth is a natural human process that should not be interfered with. Nevertheless, as it becomes more evident that the appropriate administration of pain medication is unlikely to have negative consequences, more doctors are willing to agree when patients request such medication. Hospitals are more likely than clinics to have several pain relief options available.

Many hospitals in Japan do not allow fathers to be present during the delivery. This may be due to a general assumption that delivery is a woman's job. Actually, many Japanese women do not want their husbands to see them at the delivery scene, and as more than one woman is likely to be undergoing labor in the same room, the lack of privacy could be a factor. However, the trend is slowly changing and it is becoming more common for fathers to participate in prenatal care and childbirth.

In Japan, new mothers and babies are kept in the hospital longer than in some other countries. Generally, mothers stay in the hospital at least five days to one week. If they have given birth by Caesarean section, they may be required to stay even longer. Some Japanese women who give birth overseas are surprised at how quickly they are sent home when they would prefer to stay and rest a little longer. In contrast, some foreign women in Japan

216

feel that they are confined to the hospital for an unnecessarily long period of time. (Some hospitals are open to negotiation concerning the length of stay in hospital after childbirth.)

After delivery, babies are usually kept in a central nursery monitored by nurses and are brought to mothers, or the mothers go to them, only for breast-feeding. The main reasons for this separation are to protect babies from exposure to a plethora of germs and to allow mothers to recuperate. Some Western mothers dislike being separated from their babies, so they look for a hospital with which they can room with or negotiate the length of time they spend with their infants.

Midwives play an important role in the delivery of babies in Japan. Depending on the hospital or clinic, it is often the midwives, rather than the doctors, whom women consult for prenatal advice, and midwives assist in deliveries at clinics and hospitals. Some will also assist with home delivery, especially if no complications are anticipated.

Costs associated with normal pregnancy and childbirth are not covered by public health insurance. However, people enrolled in public health insurance can apply for a Lump-Sum Childbirth Subsidy of 300,000 to 350,000 yen when a child is born. The amount is roughly equivalent to the cost of hospitalization and delivery. Expenses for medical treatment related to any complications of pregnancy and childbirth (such as Caesarean section delivery) are, however, covered by public health insurance.

Resources and Support Groups

Giving birth in a foreign country can be stressful for prospective parents, but this stress can be significantly reduced by talking to others who have gone through the process. In Tokyo, there are a number of resources and support groups for expatriates who are expecting or caring for newborns, such as those listed below.

Support Groups

La Leche League Japan
http://www.lalecheleague.org

La Leche League is an international non-profit organization that provides education, information, and support for mothers and pregnant women who wish to breast-feed their babies. They arrange monthly meetings and offer telephone counseling.

Tokyo Pregnancy Group
http://www.geocities.com/tokyopregnancygroup

This group holds regular meetings featuring keynote speakers and provides a forum for attendees to exchange information and share experiences with others.

Tokyo with Kids
http://www.tokyowithkids.com

This website hosts discussion forums on several topics including giving birth in Tokyo and children education.

DENTAL CARE

Japanese dentists (*shika* or *haisha*) perform all regular dental care procedures, including fillings, root canals, and cleanings, but they do not perform orthodontics.

As not all dentists have the same knowledge or use the same techniques, Japanese people often ask friends and colleagues for recommendations. For routine treatments, Japanese people visit dental clinics; for complex procedures, they sometimes go to dental hospitals affiliated with dental universities. Dentists, unlike other doctors, usually take appointments.

Basic dental procedures are covered by public health insurance, so insured patients should take their insurance cards with them to dental appointments. Optional treatments and better-quality crowns are not covered by insurance, and thus can be quite expensive.

The notion of preventive dental care (for example, regular

teeth cleaning) is not yet widespread in Japan. Theoretically, public health insurance is accepted only for necessary procedures and not for preventive care; therefore, most dentists do not accept insurance for simple checkups and cleaning. However, when patients claim that "something is wrong", dentists will often accept the insurance. Some Japanese doctors who have received training in overseas are more aware of the importance of preventative care and are more open to accepting public insurance for regular checkups.

Orthodontic treatment has recently become popular in Japan, mainly as a result of influence from the United States. Previously, people considered certain misalignment (such as crooked teeth) to be charming; as a result, few children and almost no adults wore braces. Now, the benefits of tooth alignment on health and beauty are being emphasized. More parents are having their children's teeth straightened for health reasons, while many young women do so for aesthetic purposes. Orthodontic treatment is not yet covered by public health insurance and can be expensive.

Photo by Akiko Watanabe .

Peaceful Shinjuku Gyoen Garden.

MENTAL HEALTH CARE

Although it is not common for Japanese people to seek mental health services such as psychiatry or counseling, in Tokyo these services are readily available, and some are geared towards the foreign community.

Counseling

When experiencing symptoms of stress, or more serious emotional or relationship problems, many Japanese people are reluctant to visit a mental health professional. There are two main explanations: firstly, people are not comfortable expressing feelings and emotions to a third party whom they do not know well; and secondly, among Japanese people there is still a negative bias attached to mental illness, so people are concerned about how they will be perceived if others learn that they are being treated for mental problems. As a result, in Japan, the field of counseling is still immature. However, the need for professional treatment and the number of counselors are increasing, especially in Tokyo where people experience a great amount of stress due to busy lifestyles and the hectic pace of work.

Several organizations, including the following, offer counseling in English and other languages by counselors overseas training. The Japan Health Book provides further options.

Ikebukuro Counseling Center
Tel: 03-3980-8718; **http://www.gol.com/hozumiclinic** (They have an English language page accessible from the homepage) Professional counselors provide services in English and other languages. If necessary, they can refer patients to medical doctors and psychiatrists at the Hozumi Clinic.

TELL Community Counseling Service
Tel: 03-3498-0231; **http://www.telljp.com**
Professional counseling for adults, teenagers and children in English, Japanese and other languages.

Cultural Adjustment

Adjusting to life in Tokyo is not always easy. At some point during the first several months after arrival, many people experience a degree of emotional stress and even depression. Some people lose self-confidence because it is often difficult to accomplish even small tasks such as buying laundry detergent or mailing a package. People who work may discover that their business styles, very effective in their home country, are not only less effective in Japan, but could even be counterproductive. People sometimes feel isolated, lonely and homesick. Some even feel physical symptoms such as fatigue, stomachache, or a lack of appetite. Such distress and symptoms are natural reactions to adjusting to a new environment.

If you suffer any emotional or physical distress, do not be too hard on yourself, or be judgmental about things and people around you. You are going through a transitional phase and things will get better. However, if your physical symptoms persist for an unreasonable period of time, do check with a physician.

To cope with such stress, it may help to talk to others who are also going through it or have already gone through it. Seek support from members of international clubs or organizations; perhaps you can exchange experiences with others. Participate in cultural activities or study the Japanese language. Take short trips out of Tokyo to gain a fresh perspective. Eventually, as you accustom to life in Tokyo, you will begin to accept cultural differences and will be able to define a way of living that is fairly comfortable for you, even though it may be quite different from what you were accustomed to in your home country.

ALTERNATIVE HEALTH CARE

Although mainstream Japanese medical procedures are similar to those practiced in the West, a wide variety of alternative medical treatments have been used in Japan for centuries. Many people today rely on these alternative treatments to help them relax and reduce the effects of work stress, or to treat chronic pain and diseases that Western medicine could not cure. A growing number of doctors now regard alternative treatments as complementary to their allopathic treatments.

There are numerous practitioners of alternative medicine in Tokyo, although finding one who can alleviate specific symptoms may require some time and experimentation. Also, as not many such practitioners accept public health insurance, the cost of seeing them regularly can be high.

Acupuncture (*Hari*)

Acupuncture was introduced from China early in Japanese history, and was used as a basis for developing a unique set of techniques and tools for treatment. Acupuncturists stimulate specific points (*tsubo*) along body meridians by inserting fine needles through the surface of the skin. Sometimes these needles are removed after brief stimulation, and sometimes they are left there for several hours. Discomfort is usually minimal. Different *tsubo* are related to various areas or functions of the body, and inherent healing powers are activated by the stimulation. Among other benefits, acupuncture treatments can contribute to the relaxation of muscles, an increase in circulation, the stabilization of blood pressure, and an improvement in immune system functions.

Acupuncturists must pass a national licensing examination. Traditionally, many professionals in this field were blind people with an acute sense of touch that enabled them to easily locate *tsubo*. Although blind acupuncturists contributed greatly to the development of the field, today they make up a small percentage of acupuncturists in practice.

Public health insurance covers acupuncture treatments prescribed by medical doctors, but some acupuncturists do not accept insurance.

Massage

There are three different types of massage available today in Tokyo: *anma*, European-style massage and *shiatsu*. In each of these types of treatments, practitioners directly stimulate certain parts of the body with their hands to relax muscles and improve blood circulation. Massages are known to help stabilize blood pressure, increase immunity and relieve pain.

Anma was introduced centuries ago from China and has the longest history among the three styles. Practitioners mainly knead muscles, moving from the center of the body outwards.

In Japan, practitioners of European-style massage (typically referred to simply as "massage") lightly stimulate the skin surface, moving from the outer extremities of the body towards the center (the heart). This is believed to improve the circulation of blood and lymphatic fluid.

Shiatsu combines techniques from a variety of treatments including *anma* and chiropractic, and even includes elements from *judo*. Practitioners mainly apply pressure to *tsubo* with the fingers with the goal of relaxing muscles and adjusting the function of the nervous system.

Practitioners of all three types of massages must pass a common national licensing exam. As with acupuncture, many early practitioners of massage were blind. Public health insurance covers massage treatments for certain types of illnesses if prescribed by doctors; however, some practitioners do not accept insurance.

Chiropractic

Compared with other alternative healing methods, chiropractic was made available in Tokyo only fairly recently. Practitioners adjust the alignment of a patient's spine to release healing powers. Chiropractic care is believed to be effective in lessening the symptoms of spinal misalignment such as headache, stiff shoulders, and back pain.

Although chiropractic has been approved as a medical practice in some countries, it has not yet been approved by the Japanese government. Therefore, there is no formal certification procedure for practitioners. Some of them are graduates of chiropractic schools in the United States or other countries, and others studied at one of many private chiropractic schools in Japan. When looking for a chiropractor, it is a good idea to research carefully – some practitioners have limited training and experience. Because chiropractic care is not officially approved by the government, public health insurance does not cover this type of treatment.

Herbal Medicines

Many of the formulas used in modern-day Japanese herbal medicines (known as *kanpo yaku*) have their roots in medical concepts first encountered centuries ago by Japanese people through contacts with China. These herbal remedies are believed to enhance the harmony of the entire body and to increase natural recuperative powers. Various clinical studies have shown the efficacy of *kanpo yaku* in boosting the immune system, alleviating menopausal symptoms, and improving nervous disorders and ailments of the elderly. Some cases have been reported in which *kanpo yaku* are believed to have cured cancerous growths.

More than 100 herbal medicine formulas have been approved by the Japanese government, and public health insurance covers the cost of these formulas if they are prescribed by medical doctors.

EMERGENCIES

Knowing what to do and where to go in case of emergency is important, especially for people who have small children.

Calling an Ambulance

The number to dial for an ambulance is **119**. Many public phones allow callers to connect directly to 119 without inserting a coin, simply by pushing a button. On telephones that do not have this type of button, just dial 119; the call will go through directly without the insertion of a coin. Pink and red phones (which are very rare now) require a 10-yen coin to dial 119.

Dialing 119 connects you to the central calling center of the Tokyo Fire Department. You must tell the operator that you need an ambulance (*kyukyu-sha*), because this number is also used to call fire trucks. Give the following information to the operator:

- The address where an ambulance is needed.
  Jusho wa _____ desu. (Address is _____.)
- The name, age, and the gender of the patient.
  Namae wa _____ desu. (Name is _____.)
  _____ sai desu. (Age is _____.)
  Josei desu. (It is a woman.)
  Dansei desu. (It is a man.)

If you do not speak Japanese, ask to speak to an English-speaking operator. They are on duty 24-hours a day. Do not hang up if you are not transferred immediately to an English-speaking operator, or if you think the operator did not understand what you said. Emergency operators will try to trace the origin of any telephone call, determine the location, and send an ambulance.

While waiting for the ambulance, it is important to prepare the patient's passport, Foreign Registration Card, and insurance card (if the patient is enrolled in public health insurance plan). Also, gather some cash – at least 30,000 yen – to cover any initial medical costs at the hospital (the ambulance ride is free). Patients who do not have their insurance cards available or who are not enrolled in a public health insurance plan will probably have to pay the full amount of any expenses in advance and receive reimbursement afterwards.

If you have insufficient cash, try borrowing from family and friends, or withdraw money from ATMs (which are abundant in Tokyo). If that is not possible, hospitals or clinics are likely to accept whatever money the patient has as a deposit, and/or keep a form of the patient's identification until full payment is made.

The Tokyo Fire Department has paramedics available who sometimes perform emergency medical procedures under the guidance of doctors working at a Command and Control Center. The ambulance usually transports the patient to the nearest hospital capable of handling the patient's condition. A patient can request to be sent to the hospital with which his or her personal doctor is affiliated. The ambulance personnel may comply if the doctor agrees to see the patient and if the hospital accepts ambulances.

Emergency Medical Services

Not all medical practitioners are available to their patients outside of regular office hours. Check with your doctor and dentist and ask them what you should do in case of an emergency.

Generally speaking, when illnesses or injuries are life threatening, it is best to go to the emergency room of a facility designated by the government as an "emergency hospital". Problems that are not life threatening can usually be handled at certain clinics located throughout Tokyo, known as "Holiday/Evening Clinic Centers", that provide after-hours emergency medical care.

In some neighborhoods, hospitals take turns accepting patients at night and on holidays (ask the ward or municipal office for a schedule). Check with hospitals and clinics in your neighborhood to locate one where you can go in case of an emergency.

ADDITIONAL RESOURCES
Books
Japan Health Handbook
By M. E. Maruyama, L. P. Shimizu, and N. S. Tsurumaki. Published by Kodansha International.

The authors are experts in nursing and childbirth education. The book provides detailed medical advice as well as information about clinics and hospitals for foreigners.

Japan for Kids: The Ultimate Guide for Parents and Their Children

By Diane Wiltshire and Jeanne Huey. Published by Kodansha International.

The book covers a wide range of topics about raising children in Japan, and includes detailed information about clinics, hospitals, and support groups.

Directories

NTT TOWNPAGE

This is an English-language telephone directory, and can be obtained free of charge at any NTT office or by calling 03-3459-7511.

TELL Calendar

Published by Tokyo English Life Line, this calendar contains a list of clinics and hospitals. It can be ordered by calling 03-3498-0261.

Telephone Services

Tokyo English Life Line (TELL)

Tel: 03-5774-0992

It provides free information and counseling in English on a variety of topics of interest to foreigners living in Tokyo.

Tokyo Metropolitan Government Office

Tel: 03-5285-8181

Provides information on hospitals with doctors or staff who speak foreign languages.

❖❖❖

It is reassuring to know that high-quality medical care is readily available in Tokyo. You are also encouraged to identify suitable medical facilities (especially for emergencies) soon after your arrival, and to memorize a few useful Japanese phrases. To you health!

—CHAPTER TWELVE—

EATING WELL IN TOKYO

If you enjoy trying different kinds of food, you will not be bored in Tokyo. There are numerous Japanese and international restaurants, while shops and supermarkets stock products from all over Japan, and an increasing selection of imported goods.

JAPANESE FOODS AND BEVERAGES
Popular Japanese Foods

The traditional Japanese diet is very healthy. It includes a lot of vegetables and features fish and soybean products (both of which are low in cholesterol) as the main sources of protein. In addition, the popular Japanese cooking methods of boiling, steaming, and grilling require little use of oil. A typical dinner served at a Japanese home includes cooked rice, *miso* soup (broth seasoned with *miso*, a fermented and salted soybean paste), an entrée (fish or meat), and steamed or cooked vegetables.

The Japanese diet has been influenced by Western tastes, and in the past couple of decades people have increased their consumption of meat, dairy products, and oily foods. Traditional Japanese cuisine is regaining popularity, however, especially among health conscious people and women who want to stay slim.

Certain Japanese foods seem unusual and, in some cases, even unappetizing to many newcomers to Japan. Over time, however, many foreigners grow to enjoy Japanese cuisine.

Sushi

Sushi comes in many forms. *Nigiri-zushi*, typically known simply as *sushi* in the West, is a pressed oval of rice covered with a piece of raw fish fillet. Popular toppings include tuna, yellow tail, and flounder, but other types of fresh seafood can be used as well. *Sushi* rice is flavored with vinegar, pressed into a bite-sized oval, dabbed Japanese horseradish (*wasabi*), and topped with a slice of carefully cut fish (slices of raw fish are called *sashimi*, and can be served as an appetizer or as a main course).

To eat a piece of *sushi*, dip it lightly in soy sauce and eat it in one bite (not always an easy task!). *Sushi* is usually accompanied by slices of pickled ginger (*gari*), which in olden times was thought to kill any bacteria in the fish. Now *gari* is usually eaten in between different types of *sushi* to cleanse the palate and refresh taste buds.

The best place to eat *sushi* is at the counter of a *sushi* restaurant. True *sushi* restaurants serve only *sushi* and a few varieties of appetizers. Diners often make their selections after viewing the fresh fish in the counter display case, or they may ask for recommendations from the *sushi* chef working behind the counter – diners can watch the chef prepare their *sushi*.

There is one drawback to eating at a *sushi* counter. Often there is no written menu or price sheet; the chef decides the price of each kind of *sushi* based on the market price of the fish. Thus,

229

diners do not know the cost of the *sushi* until they pay the bill, and as they never receive a detailed receipt, they cannot tell the price of each kind of *sushi*. The bill can be a shock. In order to eat more reasonably priced *sushi*, people sometimes sit at a table (instead of the counter) and order a set meal with a fixed price.

Another option for eating *sushi* is to go to a *kaiten-zushi* (which means "rolling *sushi*") restaurant. Here diners sit at a counter as small plates of *sushi* move past on a conveyor belt – diners simply take the dishes they want off the belt. Prices are indicated by the color of the plate on which the *sushi* is placed. The quality of the *sushi* at these "conveyor belt" counters may not be as high as that at the gourmet *sushi* counters, but they usually cost less.

Although the preparation of *sushi* looks easy, long years of practice are required to learn the techniques, such as cooking rice to the appropriate consistency, shaping it with the right pressure, slicing the raw fish fillets, etc. Thus, few Japanese people try to make this kind of *sushi* at home. Instead, they prepare other kinds of *sushi*, such as *maki-zushi* (*sushi* rolls) and *gomoku-zushi* (*sushi* rice covered with bits of seafood and vegetables).

Photo by Yuko Morimoto-Yoshida.

An itamae-san, *or sushi chef.*

Tempura

Tempura is seafood and vegetables dipped in batter and deep fried. The dish is thought to have been introduced by the Portuguese, who came to Japan in the 16th century. Some scholars believe the word *tempura* is derived from the Portuguese word for flavoring, "tempero". Large prawns, eggplant, sweet potatoes, and asparagus are popular choices. The batter is made from flour, water, and egg. *Tempura* is usually eaten dipped in salt, or in a broth flavored with soy sauce and a small amount of grated Japanese radish. It is sometimes served on top of noodles or over rice.

Some restaurants specialize in *tempura*, but it is also available in restaurants that serve other traditional Japanese foods. Many people make *tempura* at home, although learning to prepare the batter and frying the seafood and vegetables at the right temperature generally takes some practice.

Sukiyaki

Sukiyaki is prepared by cooking thinly sliced beef and vegetables such as *shiitake* mushrooms, bamboo shoots, and Japanese leeks, along with other ingredients such as *tofu*, in a large iron pan. The ingredients are seasoned with soy sauce, rice wine (*sake*), and sugar. *Sukiyaki* is usually prepared at the table – diners take the cooked food directly from the pan, dipping them in beaten raw egg before eating them.

The quality of the beef determines the quality of the *sukiyaki*. Fatty beef is considered better for *sukiyaki* because the fat adds a rich flavor to the broth. Expensive *sukiyaki* restaurants serve beef that is almost white (rather than red) due to the high fat content. *Sukiyaki* is easy to prepare at home. Supermarkets sell thinly sliced beef cut specifically for *sukiyaki*; prices however, can be very high!

Shabu-shabu

Shabu-shabu is Japanese-style fondue. Thinly sliced beef is dipped and cooked briefly in a boiling broth flavored with seaweed. *Tofu*

231

and vegetables such as Chinese cabbage, Japanese leek, and *shiitake* mushrooms are added to the broth. After the ingredients are cooked, they are dipped in a sauce made from either soy sauce and Japanese lime, or from sesame paste. Like *sukiyaki*, *shabu-shabu* is generally shared by parties of four to five people.

Sukiyaki and *shabu-shabu* are often served in the same restaurants because the key ingredient for both dishes is good-quality beef. *Shabu-shabu* is quite easy to prepare at home. Thinly sliced beef cut specifically for *shabu-shabu* (it is thinner than that for *sukiyaki*) is sold in meat shops and supermarkets.

Yakitori

Yakitori is skewered grilled chicken. Small chicken cubes are skewered onto a thin bamboo spike (sometimes alternated with small pieces of Japanese leek), seasoned with salt or glazed with a special sauce, and then grilled on a gas or charcoal grill. Old *yakitori* restaurants use their own secret sauce recipes that have been passed down through several generations. The smell of sauce that has dripped onto the grill can really stimulate one's appetite!

Yakitori is considered a snack or an appetizer rather than a main dish and is often accompanied by a glass of beer. Colleagues and friends often meet at *yakitori* restaurants for after-work social gatherings. *Yakitori* is easy to prepare at home – the basic ingredients for the glaze are soy sauce and sweet rice wine (*mirin*).

Ramen

Ramen is thin egg noodles in soup. Originally a Chinese dish, Japanese people modified the recipe, resulting in hundreds of versions of *ramen* made from different ingredients and soup bases. Ingredients added to *ramen* include corn, boiled egg, and sliced pork. The soup is made from pork, beef, or chicken broth, or a combination of these; some chefs even use fish broth.

Japanese people are crazy about *ramen*. They eat it for lunch, as a snack, or after drinking alcohol, and may wait in line for an hour just to eat at a popular *ramen* shop. Japanese television frequently airs shows introducing new *ramen* shops and the best *ramen* in the city.

Karé Raisu

Karé raisu (curried rice) is meat and vegetables in curry sauce served over rice. This dish was imported from India, and then modified to suit Japanese tastes. Because *karé raisu* has developed a distinct flavor very different from the original, Indian people eating curry in Japan have been known to comment, "Well, it was a very good meal, but what was it?" Compared to Indian curries, Japanese curries are less spicy and the sauces are thicker because flour is usually added. There are hundreds of different recipes for *karé raisu* in Japan.

Karé raisu is a very popular dish to prepare at home and is a good choice for beginner cooks. Many people use an instant curry mix (which comes in the shape of a solid bar) to make *kare raisu*. The process is simple: stir-fry your favorite ingredients, add water, simmer for 10 to 15 minutes; then add the curry bar and let it melt into the mixture. Supermarkets carry instant curry bars in various flavors and levels of spiciness.

Japanized Foods

Japanese people like to modify foods imported from other countries to suit their own tastes. In addition to *ramen* and *karé raisu*, Japanized foods include other curry-related items, pasta, and breads. Japanese people like curry so much that they have created many different curried dishes, including *karé udon* (curry sauce over broad wheat noodles) and *karé pan* (deep-fried bread rolls stuffed with curry sauce). For another culinary adventure, Italian pasta is mixed with Japanese ingredients to make *natto* spaghetti (fermented soybeans seasoned with soy sauce and served over pasta) and *tarako* spaghetti (pasta with fish eggs and olive oil). Finally, Japanese people are very creative with breads, and have popularized *an-pan* (buns filled with sweet bean paste) and *yakisoba-pan* (buns containing fried noodles!).

JAPANESE FOOD CHALLENGES FOR FOREIGNERS

For many foreigners, especially Westerners, sampling certain Japanese foods for the first time requires courage. The most famous challenge is *natto* (fermented soy beans). *Natto* smells a bit like strong cheese and is gooey; the taste, however, is not so bad – it simply tastes like beans. Once you have acquired a taste for *natto*, you cannot live without it! The best thing about it is that it is full of protein and calcium and therefore, very nutritious.

Anko, or sweet bean paste, is used frequently in Japanese confectionery. The paste is made from cooked red beans and sugar. Some foreigners object to the idea of adding sugar to beans, because in many countries beans are supposed to taste salty. Others say that the look of particularly dark *anko*, which can be almost black, does not seem appealing.

Finally, although *sashimi* and *sushi* are probably the foods for which Japan is most famous internationally, foreigners are often reluctant to try them. Many are squeamish at the thought of eating fish raw and some are concerned with the freshness of the meat. It may be reassuring to know that Japanese restaurants usually cook any fish not fresh enough to eat raw. Give *sashimi* and *sushi* a try – you may become a connoisseur!

BEVERAGES
Non-alcoholic Beverages

Green tea has been a popular beverage in Japan for centuries. It goes well with Japanese foods and is purported to be beneficial to one's health. Green tea is available in several varieties; the flavor, color, and aroma vary according to the tea leaves, the way they are grown, and when they are picked. The most popular green tea is *sencha*; the leaves are picked in May, dried, and sold immediately. *Hojicha* is the roasted version of *sencha* and has a nice aroma; it is less expensive than *sencha* and is suitable for daily consumption. *Gyokuro* is one of the most expensive green teas; extra care is taken to avoid exposing the leaves to direct sunshine, creating a tea with a perfect balance of bitterness and sweetness.

Restaurants specializing in Japanese food serve hot or cold green tea, as well as cold barley tea (*mugicha*) in the summer; other restaurants serve water. Soft drinks and orange juice are available, although Japanese people seldom consume them with meals. Coffee and English teas are also popular drinks. People drink coffee throughout the day – for breakfast, lunch, after dinner, and during breaks. Vending machines selling canned soft drinks, coffee and tea can be found throughout Tokyo.

Alcoholic Beverages

Alcohol consumption in Japan is fairly high. The most popular alcoholic beverage is beer. Many people like to start dinner or drinks with it, and they may continue drinking it during the meal. Beer consumption increases substantially during summer when people go to "beer gardens" (pubs serving beer and appetizers) located on outdoor patios or on the rooftops of buildings.

Another popular alcoholic beverage is *sake*, or Japanese rice wine. There are thousands of *sake* breweries in Japan; the taste and flavor of the *sake* produced vary according to the type of rice and brewing process. Some types of *sake* taste better served warm, while others taste better cold. *Sake* is a wonderful complement to Japanese foods such as *sushi* and *sukiyaki*.

Hard liquors such as whiskey and brandy are less popular now as Japanese people become more health conscious, but wine has gained in popularity. Most Western restaurants and some Japanese restaurants now serve wine, and a few have developed special menus of Japanese foods that go well with wines. Wine is often drunk at home, too. French and Italian wines, as well as Australian, Californian, and Chilean are popular, with an increasingly wide range of quality and prices available at many liquor shops and grocery stores.

Japanese people like to make toasts when they drink, especially at parties and formal occasions. People usually begin drinking only after the glasses of all guests have been filled and someone has made a toast. Occasionally a senior person or host will make a short speech, followed by everyone saying *kanpai* (meaning "dry your glass"). It is customary for people to fill the glasses of the people sitting next to them. To show that they are paying attention to the needs of others, they try to pour refills before the glasses are empty. People do not fill their own glasses.

TABLE ETIQUETTE

In earlier times, Japanese people followed a detailed set of table manners carefully, but many now prefer to enjoy eating in a more casual setting. Foreigners are not expected to follow all the rules of traditional Japanese table etiquette, which is fortunate because Japanese people do not like to embarrass foreigners by letting them make a *faux pas*; but foreigners who do follow some of the traditions demonstrate respect for Japanese culture, and thus make a good impression.

For many foreigners, the most difficult part of eating the Japanese way is learning to use chopsticks (*hashi*). Japanese people use chopsticks for most meals at home, in restaurants that serve Japanese food, and many other Asian food restaurants. At home, family members each have their own

TRIGG.

Photo by Yuko Morimoto-Yoshida

chopsticks. One form of chopsticks, known as *waribashi,* is made from a long piece of wood that is partially split; users complete the split when they want to eat. *Waribashi* are often provided at restaurants or given to dinner guests in homes. You might see people rubbing the two sticks together to remove tiny splinters, but this is not considered good manners.

When using chopsticks, hold one (by the thick end) at the base of your thumb, steadying it with your ring finger. Hold the other one (also by the thick end) in between your index finger and middle finger, supporting it with the tip of your thumb. Use the first chopstick as a stable base, and move the second chopstick toward the first as necessary to lift or cut foods (*see above photo for proper way of holding chopsticks*). Use the thin ends to carry food to your mouth.

Chopsticks (the thin ends) are customarily placed on a chopstick rest in front of you before and after meals. When no rest is provided, people sometimes fold the piece of paper in which the *waribashi* was wrapped to make an instant chopstick rest.

When using chopsticks, certain movements should be avoided. First, do not stick your chopsticks straight up in your rice bowl, as this reminds people of how Buddhists make offerings to the deceased. Also, do not give another person food by passing it from your chopsticks to their chopsticks, as this resembles the Buddhist funeral custom where two people use chopsticks to hold a piece of bone from the cremated body (instead, place the food item on their plates). Finally, do not use your chopsticks to move plates or bowls, do not wave your chopsticks in the air while you speak, and do not hold chopsticks in a fist.

There are some rules of dining etiquette that Japanese people still follow. In formal Japanese restaurants, dishes are served one after another, with rice, *miso* soup, and pickled vegetables served at the end of the meal. In regular restaurants, rice and soup are served together with the entrée and vegetables. When foods are served simultaneously, it is good manners to eat them in an alternating fashion rather than to finish one dish first and then move on to the next one. When eating rice or *miso* soup, it is better to lift the bowl up to one's mouth than to lean toward the table; it is also customary to place the rice bowl on the table in front of the diner and put the *miso* soup bowl to the right of the rice bowl. Pouring soy sauce over rice is considered exceptionally bad manners. It can also make the rice very difficult to eat with chopsticks!

When eating noodles, Japanese people make a slurping noise. This is surprising to some foreigners, but they soon learn that in Japan such noise is not only appropriate, it is even recommended. Noodles are supposed to be eaten quickly before they get soggy, especially when they are served in soup. Making noise while eating noodles indicates that one is enjoying the experience. Incidentally, some people also make noise when sipping soup or even coffee, but as in Western etiquette, this is not considered good manners.

Japanese people usually begin eating only after everyone at the table has been served. To be polite, people who are waiting to be served invite those already served to begin eating. The people who have been served may then start eating, or they may continue to wait, especially if they are younger or of lower status than other diners. When people are about to begin eating, they say *Itadakimasu*, which is loosely translated as, "I humbly receive the meal." After the meal they say *Gochiso sama deshita*, which means "Thank you very much for the meal".

Japanese restaurants usually do not provide napkins, so many women carry nice handkerchiefs to place across their laps while they dine. Many restaurants provide diners with hot towels (*oshibori*) to clean their hands; some men use them to wipe their faces, but this is not considered to be the best of manners.

Seating arrangements at meals, especially formal meals, are an important consideration. (*Refer to* "Seating Arrangements" *in Chapter 9*).

SHOPPING FOR FOOD

Groceries can be purchased at Japanese supermarkets, small shops and department stores; convenience stores also carry basic food items. Expatriates often rely on international supermarkets when looking for imported products. Regardless of where you shop, a 5 per cent consumption tax is usually added to the stated price.

Supermarkets

People in Tokyo buy most of their groceries at supermarkets, and prefer to shop for a few necessities each day rather than buying in large quantities every few days. Over time, as people grew to prefer the convenience of finding a wide variety of foods in one place, supermarkets have overtaken small shops selling meat, fish, and vegetables. Major supermarket chains include Ito Yokado, Jusco, and Seiyu; in addition, there are many small local supermarkets.

Small Shops

There are still many reasons to shop at small stores, however. While small shops may not offer as large a selection as do the supermarkets, the products they sell may be fresher, and the prices lower. Also, once the clerks get to know you they may give you special discounts or let you know what is the best buy of the day. For foreigners, communicating with store clerks may require extra effort, but establishing relationships with them is a great way to learn about Japanese culture, and you will feel that you are part of the community.

Department Stores

A third popular venue for grocery shopping is the basement of department stores; most department stores dedicate the lower levels to selling foods of all kinds, including fish, meat, fresh fruits, and vegetables. Confectionery counters feature sweets and chocolates. The selection is large and upon request, purchases can be artistically wrapped. Delicatessen sections offer cold cuts and prepared foods. Aisles can get crowded in the late afternoon when people shop for ready-made entrées and side dishes for dinner. By the way, if you purchase ready-made foods, it is best not to eat them on the street, as doing so is not common in Japan.

Convenience Stores

Convenience stores (called *konbini*) are very handy for last-minute shopping. They are usually open 24-hours a day, and sell basic food items such as salt, sugar, and milk, as well as necessities such as batteries, stockings, toiletry products, and first aid items. They also sell ready-made and instant meals popular with people lacking time to cook.

Convenience stores also offer a variety of other services. Here you can send faxes, make photocopies, pay utility bills and withdraw or deposit money using ATMs. Some convenience stores even sell train, airplane, and concert tickets.

International Supermarkets

Foreigners who have lived in Tokyo for a long time are pleased to find that the availability of imported foods is ever increasing, paralleling the growth in the foreign population and the diversification of the tastes of Japanese people. Many medium- and large-sized supermarkets have "International Food Corners", and several supermarkets specialize in selling imported products. Popular supermarkets include:

Costco
1-4 Toyosuna, Mihama-ku, Chiba-shi, Chiba 261-0024
Tel: 043-213-4111
Kinokuniya International (Headquarters)
3-11-7 Kita Aoyama, Minato-ku, Tokyo 107-0061
Tel: 03-3409-1231
There is another store in Todoroki.
Meidi-ya (Hiroo Store)
5-6-6 Hiroo, Shibuya-ku, Tokyo 150-0012
Tel: 03-3444-622
There are eight other stores in Tokyo.
National Azabu Supermarket
4-5-2 Minami Azabu, Minato-ku, Tokyo 106-0047
Tel: 03-3442-3181
Nissin World Delicatessen
2-34-2 Higashi Azabu, Minato-ku, Tokyo 106-0044
Tel: 03-3583-4586

American products can be ordered through the **Foreign Buyer's Club** by telephone (078-857-9001) or via the Internet (**http://www.fbcusa.com**). This organization is based in Kobe in western Japan, but offers delivery to Tokyo for a fee. It carries more than 40,000 items including food, home products, and books.

FOOD SELECTIONS
Vegetables and Fruit
Most common vegetables (such as lettuce, cabbage, onions, eggplant, mushrooms, tomatoes, cucumbers, potatoes, and green peppers) can be found throughout the year in ordinary supermarkets and grocers. Some of these vegetables may look and taste a little different than those in your home country. Japanese eggplant, cucumbers, and green peppers, for example, are thinner and shorter than those generally found in Europe and the United States, and are more flavorful.

241

Photo by Desmond Ng

Japanese people pay exorbitant prices for exotic fruits. The famous Southeast Asian durian fruit is priced at 6,000 yen, about US$50 a piece!

Some vegetables are unique to Asia, such as *gobo* (burdock root), *daikon* (long radish), and *takenoko* (bamboo shoots). Japanese cookbooks written in English are available at major bookstores and feature a variety of recipes using these vegetables.

Fresh herbs have recently become popular in home cooking. Increasing numbers of supermarkets sell herbs, such as basil and mint, but the larger or international supermarkets offer the best variety.

Fruits are abundant in Tokyo and are best when purchased in season. Strawberries are tender and sweet in winter and spring. Cherries are luscious in early summer. Japanese cherries are a real treat but are incredibly expensive; a box may cost 3,000 yen! Less expensive American cherries are also available. Watermelons and melons as well as peaches are sweet and juicy in mid-summer. Persimmons, Asian pears (*nashi*), and grapes are at their peak in fall. Apples and tangerines ripen just in time for winter. Japanese people tend to prefer sweet over sour when selecting fruits; as a result, farmers put much effort into creating sweeter fruits.

Vegetables and fruits are generally priced and sold in packages or piles and rarely by weight. Some supermarkets and independent shops sell smaller portions to meet the needs of small families and single buyers.

Meat

Pork, beef, and chicken are available at most meat shops and supermarkets. Japanese people buy pork and chicken more often than beef because they are cheaper. Japanese beef is very expensive, one reason being that farmers take extreme care in raising their cattle. It is said that some farmers feed beer or wine to cows to make the beef tender. Less expensive, leaner beef from places such as the United States and Australia has become available since the liberalization of beef imports in 1990 – consumption of beef has since increased. However, as many popular Japanese recipes call for the more fatty and tender beef that is produced domestically, Japanese cooks still spend a lot of yen on their beef.

Other meats such as veal, lamb, and turkey are not popular and are generally available only at international supermarkets. Japanese people prefer to purchase meat in slices rather than in large chunks. If you want to buy meat for a roast, for example, you will probably have to buy it at an international supermarket or ask a butcher in a meat shop to cut it specifically for you. While supermarkets generally sell meat in packages, individual shops sell it in units of 100 grams (about one-quarter pound).

Fish

Fish shops and the fish sections of supermarkets are usually lively places. To attract customers, fish is nicely displayed and store clerks try to create an energetic and vibrant ambience through their interaction with customers, who are welcomed by shouts of "*Irasshai!*" which means "Welcome". (*Sushi* chefs and waiters in restaurants will often say this as well.) When hearing this forceful greeting for the first time, some foreigners feel like they are being scolded and wonder what they have done wrong!

A wide variety of fish is available throughout the year. Fall and winter are the best times to purchase certain kinds of fish, including Pacific saury, sardines, and mackerel. Large fish are usually filleted and sold in packages or piles containing two or three fillets. Smaller fish are also sold in packages or piles. Fish for *sashimi* are often cut into small pieces and sold in packages, or, sometimes, in large chunks so that people can slice them at home.

In order to choose the freshest fish, people check the color of the fillets (the brighter the better), the color of the scales (the shinier the better), and the color of the eyes (clear eyes are better than cloudy or red eyes).

Bread

Surprisingly, Japanese people are bread lovers, although their staple food has traditionally been rice. Many prefer bread for breakfast, and some restaurants offer customers the choice of rice or bread as a side dish. Fresh bread and pastries are sold at bakeries and in the basement grocery sections of department stores. People often stand in long lines to get bread hot from the oven.

In accordance with Japanese preferences, many bakeries in Tokyo produce soft, sweet white breads, but there are an increasing number of bakeries specializing in French, German, and Italian style breads. Chains such as Kobe-ya and Andersen offer breads that are every bit as good as anything you can find in Europe! Japanese people can be very creative with breads and have invented interesting pastries containing Japanese ingredients.

EATING OUT

People eat out often in Tokyo and there is no shortage of restaurants serving Asian foods, such as Japanese, Chinese, and Korean, and Western foods, especially Italian and French, as well as American. Some are world-class restaurants in terms of quality, atmosphere, and prices. However, there are also many inexpensive places with good food. Foreigners are surprised to find that the portions of food served in restaurants in Tokyo tend to be generally smaller than those to which they are accustomed.

Photo by Chihoko Tanefusa

Plastic food displays at Japanese restaurants look deceivingly like the 'real thing'.

For foreigners who are unfamiliar with Japanese food, deciding what to order at a Japanese restaurant can be an intimidating experience. Fortunately, many Japanese restaurants feature menus with pictures to which you can point. Also, many display plastic models of meals in glass cases near the entrance. It is fascinating to see how closely these plastic models resemble the actual dishes served. Even if you cannot read the names of the dishes, you can order by motioning to the server to accompany you to the window where you can simply point to the model.

After your food has been served, a server will place the bill on your table; you should pay at the cashier counter as you leave the restaurant. In fancy restaurants, the bill will not be provided until you request it; you should pay at the table. As many smaller restaurants still do not accept credit cards, you need to carry sufficient cash. A 5 per cent consumption tax is added to the total price of your meal. While tipping is not required at any restaurants in Japan, restaurants in hotels, as well as relatively expensive restaurants, automatically add a service fee of 10 per cent to the bill.

Smoking is permitted in most restaurants, although some have designated non-smoking areas.

245

Breakfast

Japanese people generally eat breakfast at home. Consequently, most restaurants are open only for lunch and dinner.

Hotel restaurants do serve breakfast, but a glass of freshly squeezed orange juice alone can cost a whopping 1,000 yen and a full breakfast can set you back 3,000 yen or more. After adding taxes and service fees, a breakfast in a nice hotel in Tokyo could well be the most expensive breakfast in the world!

A more reasonably priced option is breakfast at a coffee shop. Some coffee shops located near train or subway stations or in commercial areas of Tokyo offer a breakfast menu called "Morning Set" for around 500 yen. It comes with a thick slice of toast, coffee, and a small side dish such as a hard-boiled egg or salad. "Morning Set" is usually served from 7am to 9am.

Lunch

The standard lunch hour in Japanese companies is 12 noon to 1pm. Everybody goes out for lunch at the same time; thus, restaurants near office buildings can be extremely crowded during that one-hour period. People who can avoid the rush hour will have a more relaxing lunch.

In order to serve many customers in a limited time, restaurants in business districts generally serve various set meals (*teishoku*). In Japanese restaurants, a set meal usually includes an entrée (grilled fish or sautéed meat, for example), a vegetable dish, rice, and *miso* soup. In Western restaurants, a set meal might include soup or salad, an entrée, and rice or bread. The price of a set meal ranges from 700 to 1,500 yen. If the restaurant is crowded, customers may be asked to share a table with others.

Noodle shops are popular places for lunch. *Ramen* shops often serve side dishes such as fried vegetables, dumplings, or fried rice, in addition to noodles. Other noodle shops offer both buckwheat noodles (*soba*) and/or wheat noodles (*udon*). These are usually served hot in a broth seasoned with soy sauce and various other ingredients, or cold with a soy sauce-based dip accompanied by a small amount of Japanese horseradish (*wasabi*) and finely-chopped scallion. Noodles shops charge between 600 to 1,000 yen.

People who have time to enjoy a nice, leisurely meal often choose an up-scale restaurant, many of which offer lunches at reasonable prices. Full course meals might include an appetizer, one or two entrées, and desserts for 2,500 to 5,000 yen. Many famous Japanese restaurants also serve similarly priced boxed lunches. If you order a boxed lunch, you can enjoy small portions of various Japanese dishes (such as *sashimi*, *tenpura* and cooked vegetables), all artistically arranged in a lacquered box.

Dinner

In Japan, the largest meal of the day is dinner. When selecting a restaurant, Japanese people look for one with an atmosphere that complements the occasion.

Casual Dining

Italian restaurants are popular for dining with friends or colleagues. Tokyo is home to hundreds of Italian restaurants ranging from high-end establishments to pizza houses. Many offer high-quality full course meals for 5,000 to 10,000 yen. Some boast Italian chefs who prepare authentic dishes and Italian servers to wait on you, so you can almost imagine that you are in Italy.

When cost is not an issue, *sushi* restaurants are a favorite among Japanese people. When dining in large groups, they often choose Chinese or Korean barbeque restaurants where they can share the food. People who like culinary adventures can try food from different parts of the world such as Thailand, India, or Mexico, or they might try "Fusion" (a type of cooking that mixes the styles and ingredients of different cuisines).

Family restaurants (*famiri resutoran*) are places where families with children can enjoy food in a casual atmosphere at rea-

247

sonable prices. Many of them are open 24-hours a day, and are located in the suburbs where they can provide ample seating and parking spaces. Popular family restaurants include SkyLark, Denny's, and Jonathans. They can also be found within Tokyo itself, and often feature a wide selection of both Japanese and Western-style cuisine.

Restaurants for Special Occasions

Several Italian and French restaurants in Tokyo offer elegant settings and excellent food and wine. Famous French restaurants with branches in Tokyo include Taillevent Robuchon, Tour d'Argent, and Maxim de Paris. Dinner at these places may cost 20,000 to 30,000 yen per person or more, if wine is ordered.

After-Work Socializing

When people go out with colleagues they often choose *izakaya*, which are casual places serving drinks such as beer and *sake* (rice wine) along with lots of appetizers. The typical menu includes *edamame* (boiled soy beans), *tofu*, fried fish (*yakizakana*), and fried chicken. Most dishes are easy to share, so people order several for the group. Many *izakaya* offer *nomi hodai*, or "all you can drink" at a fixed price. These *izakaya* are very popular with young people.

When paying the bill, co-workers often divide the total by the number of people and everyone pays the same amount (usually around 3,000 yen). Some foreigners are surprised by this custom, called *warikan*, as it may be more common in other countries for people to pay only for what they have consumed. When a manager or older person accompanies the group, it is common for that person to pay a larger share, or even the entire bill.

After-work gathering spots also include *yakitoriya* and *odenya*. *Yakitoriya* are restaurants that serve *yakitori* (skewered grilled chicken) and drinks (mainly beer and *sake*). *Odenya* serve *oden* – a dish of stewed fish cakes and vegetables in soup that is especially good for staving off the cold winter, and drinks (beer and *sake*).

Business Entertainment

Japanese food restaurants called *ryotei* are formal places for entertaining important customers. They serve traditional Japanese multi-course menus that were originally served at tea ceremonies, and the portions are tiny. The courses usually include appetizers, grilled or steamed fish and vegetables, rice, and *miso* or clear broth. Considered a refined version of Japanese cuisine, great attention is paid to the appearance of the food as well as to the taste.

Many of these *ryotei* restaurants look like old Japanese houses and diners customarily remove their shoes when they enter. The food is served in private rooms, so *ryotei* are good choices for closed-door meetings. In fact, senior government officials use *ryotei* for their meetings so often that some joke that important Japanese political decisions are made at *ryotei* and not at the Diet building! Many *ryotei* only accept new customers with referrals. The price of entertaining here is beyond imagination; famous *ryotei* may charge more than 100,000 yen per person.

If *ryotei* are beyond your budget, Japanese restaurants that serve *sukiyaki* or *shabu-shabu* are also good places for entertaining. For those whose clients are wine connoisseurs should consider expensive French and Italian restaurants.

Fast Food Shops

Western fast food is popular in Japan, especially among the younger generation. Most major American fast food establishments have branches in Japan, among them McDonald's, Burger King, Wendy's, Kentucky Fried Chicken and Subway. In addition, there are several hamburger shops run by Japanese companies, such as MOS Burger – in addition to conventional burgers, they serve Japanese versions such as *teriyaki* chicken burgers and rice buns.

Pizza, too, is popular and shops that deliver are many. What is "pizza" to Japanese, however, may not look like "pizza" to foreigners. Japanese versions include toppings such as seafood and *teriyaki* chicken, and sauces such as mayonnaise and curry paste. Although some foreigners grow to enjoy these variations, at times they crave "regular pizza" with cheese and pepperoni! Do not worry, the regular version is also available at most places.

There are also several kinds of Japanese fast food outlets. One type serves *gyu-don*, a bowl of rice topped with cooked sliced beef. Noodle stands, known as *tachigui soba* (literally meaning "stand while eating noodles"), are also popular. These stands are located primarily at train stations. Most stay open all day and people stand there for lunch, snacks, or after-work drinks.

Coffee and Tea Shops

Coffee shops are everywhere in Tokyo and some are quite luxurious. Some Japanese are coffee connoisseurs and very particular about the kinds of coffee they drink. Because of the high cost of importing quality beans coupled with the high cost of rent, the price of a cup of coffee can reach 1,000 yen! Many coffee and tea shops serve a variety of cakes and pies; these shops are especially popular with young women. Casual coffee stands have become an alternative to the more expensive coffee shops. Branches of the American-based chain Starbucks are prevalent.

❊ ❊ ❊

Hopefully you will enjoy the wide variety of food options available in Tokyo. While eating unfamiliar food or ordering dishes in a restaurant can be a challenge initially, with time and practice you will find it easier. Learning how to cook Japanese dishes will also definitely enhance your cultural experience during your stay in Tokyo. Enjoy the feast!

CHAPTER THIRTEEN

SHOPPING IN TOKYO

Tokyo is a great place to shop with a wide variety of domestically manufactured as well as imported goods available. This chapter offers you some insight into the shopping scene and tips on things to buy.

THE SHOPPING SCENE

Things tend to be more expensive in Tokyo than in other cities in the world, but the durability of products and the services included in the retail price often justify the additional cost. By comparing prices and shopping during sale periods, savvy shoppers can actually find very good deals. Bargaining is not a custom in Tokyo, except at some small shops and flea markets. In most shops, a 5 per cent consumption tax is added to the stated price of goods. Credit cards are accepted at department stores and large retail shops, but not at some small shops. Shopping hours are generally from 10am to 7pm. Many shops are open on Sundays; some shops close for one day each week.

Returning merchandise is not a common practice in Japan. In case there is a need, ask the sales clerk about the return policy when you make the purchase and retain the receipts, as they will be required when making the return. Sales clerks are more likely to accept a return for reasons such as malfunction or a size problem.

PLACES TO SHOP

Shoppers in Tokyo can visit districts devoted to specific products, or large shopping districts and department stores that carry almost everything. To save money on everyday items, people shop at large supermarkets, flea markets, or second-hand shops.

Shopping Districts
The Ginza

Ginza is the most expensive place to shop in Tokyo. The area around the "Ginza 4-chome Crossing" (the intersection of Harumi Dori and Chuo Dori streets) hosts world-famous designer boutiques interspersed with traditional and exclusive Japanese shops. Merchandise from famous boutiques, such as Gucci, Chanel, and Prada, to name a few, can cost one-and-a-half times the price of the same items in other countries. Such mark-ups reflect the Japanese preference for high quality, luxurious items, as well as Tokyo's high real estate prices. Young Japanese women are the best customers at these boutiques, as wearing and carrying designer goods is considered very fashionable. It can be fun to window-shop in this area, even if you do not purchase anything.

The traditional Japanese shops located here carry conservative, high-fashion items popular with older, well-to-do people. Many of these shops have been in the Ginza are for a long time and have established reputations as premier retailers of specialized goods, including tailor-made suits, shoes, and *kimono*. The families of the shop owners and those of many of their clients have been doing business together for at least a few generations.

In an attempt to attract a wide variety of people to the area, the main street of Ginza, Chuo Dori, is closed to traffic during the day on weekends, and a few fast-food joints have opened among the finer restaurants and traditional shops. Although young people and families with children welcome the more casual atmosphere, many older people continue to resist moves to make the Ginza less exclusive. After all, the people who are attracted to this area enjoy the classy atmosphere that can only be experienced here.

Other Areas

People in search of trendy fashion frequent the fashionable boutiques in the **Aoyama** areas. There are many designer boutiques which sell more contemporary and less expensive clothes than those in Ginza. Also, **Daikanyama** and **Jiyugaoka** on the Tokyu Line and **Shimokitazawa** on the Keio and Odakyu Line are little neighborhoods with clusters of small interesting boutiques.

Both **Shinjuku** and **Shibuya** are large shopping districts with department stores, "fashion buildings" with small boutiques, discount electronics shops, and major bookstores. With different kinds of stores conveniently located in one place, these areas are always crowded with young people and families. Those tired from shopping can rest in one of the many restaurants in the area. Harajuku is another place popular with young people; its tree-lined boulevard and adjacent side streets are lined with numerous shops selling inexpensive clothes, jewelry, and cosmetics. A few famous European brand boutiques have opened branches here to attract older and more well-heeled customers,.

Photo by Akiko Watanabe.

Tree-lined boulevard in Harajuku.

DEPARTMENT STORES

Department stores are convenient places to shop because they carry a wide range of products (including clothes, household items, crafts, toys, and food) and you can compare items from different brands in the same place. Also, most department stores have special corners for extra small and extra large sizes, although the selections tend to be limited.

Regular prices of items in department stores tend to be high. However, department stores hold frequent discount sales (especially for clothing) due to intense competition. During sale periods, selected merchandise is often reduced by 30 to 40 per cent. Major credit cards are accepted at all department stores.

Customer service in department stores is quite impressive. Customers arriving at a department store at opening time are greeted by a number of uniformed store clerks lined up at the entrance. The clerks bow and say *Irasshaimase*, which means "Welcome". As customers leave the store at closing time, the clerks bow to them at the exit and say *Arigato gozaimashita*, which means

"Thank you". Some stores have "elevator girls" who operate the elevators; they would inform customers what products are sold on each level, as well as usher customers on and off the elevators. Many wear hats and white gloves.

Sales clerks are quite attentive. They will help you select merchandise by finding the appropriate size, color, and design. They will take your payment to the cashier and bring you back the sales receipt. And they will wrap up each purchase neatly for no additional fee.

Department stores also offer additional services that enhance the shopping experience. Most have restaurants and coffee shops, and some have small galleries exhibiting world famous paintings or cultural artifacts. Some offer child care and roof garden amusement facilities for children. Most have parking in the basement or in an adjacent building. Major department stores in Tokyo include the following:

Isetan
Tel: 03-3225-2514
Popular for its women's clothing. Foreigners can become members of the I-Club (at no charge) and receive shopping guidance and information about events (such as sales on tall- and large-sized clothing). There are four Isetan stores in Tokyo: Shinjuku, Kichijoji, Tachikawa, and Fuchu.

Marui
This chain of department stores targets young customers in their teens and twenties.

Mitsukoshi
Considered the most prestigious department store in Tokyo, Mitsukoshi carries traditional, conservative items. Its four main stores are in Ginza, Shinjuku, Nihonbashi and Ikebukuro.

Odakyu
The Odakyu flagship store is conveniently located at Shinjuku Station. Two other stores are located in Machida and Fujisawa.

255

Seibu
Targeted at younger clients, Seibu holds a big sale each time the company's baseball team (the Seibu Lions) wins the league championship. The three main stores in Tokyo are in Shibuya, Yurakucho, and Ikebukuro.

Takashimaya
This is another old establishment that targets both adults and younger customers. The four Tokyo branches are in Shinjuku, Nihonbashi, Futako Tamagawa, and Tachikawa.

Tobu
Located in Ikebukuro, Tobu is the largest department store in Tokyo.

Tokyu
The headquarters in Shibuya provides a luxurious shopping experience.

Large Supermarkets
There are several large supermarkets in Tokyo that are a cross between regular supermarkets and department stores. Most sell grocery items and a variety of products including casual fashion and household items. The quality of the products is often lower than that in department stores, but then, so are the prices. Many supermarkets belong to chains and are located in suburban Tokyo or just outside Tokyo in Chiba, Saitama, and Kanagawa. Popular stores are Ito Yokado, Jusco, Seiyu, and Daiei.

Flea Markets and "Recycle" Shops
Flea markets and used-items ("recycle") shops have recently become popular in Tokyo. Japanese people used to be hesitant to wear clothing or buy furniture that had previously been owned by strangers, but now they seem to realize the practicality of recycling these goods. Items sold at flea markets or in "recycle" shops tend to be in very good condition.

Several wards or municipal districts occasionally hold flea markets. You can obtain the schedule by checking with the ward or municipal office in your area. A few commercial organizations in Tokyo regularly hold large-scale flea markets in public spots such as Meiji Park in Sendagaya and Yoyogi Park in Harajuku. Contact the Tokyo Recycle Campaign Citizen's Association (*Tokyo Recycle Undo Shimin no Kai*; Tel: 03-3384-6666) and Citizens' Association of Recycling Campaign (*Recycle Undo Shimin no Kai*; Tel: 03-3226-6800) for information.

You can also obtain information about flea markets and recycle shops in the book *Japan with Kids: A Guide for Parents*. Visit the website "Tokyo with Kids"(**http://www.tokyowithkids.com**), or look for notices in English-language publications.

Internet Shopping

Shopping by computer is increasingly popular in Japan. People who cannot find their clothes and shoe size in Japan can order from shops in their home countries via the Internet. Bear in mind, however, that shipping and handling charges can be quite high (sometimes higher than the retail price of the products).

THINGS TO BUY
Clothes

Clothes sold in Tokyo are generally of good quality and can be pricey. You can find the most current styles because Japanese people like to follow world fashion trends. As young Japanese women spend a lot of money on clothing, many shops in Tokyo target them and selections are abundant. A large variety of men's clothing casual wear, trendy Italian fashions, and conservative suits can also be found.

As mentioned earlier, foreigners may find clothes sold in boutiques and department stores expensive if they do not shop during sale periods. However, less expensive items are available at individual shops in small neighborhoods, large supermarkets, and used-clothing shops, and the number of inexpensive domestic brands is also increasing.

American casual apparel brands such as the Gap, Old Navy, and Eddie Bauer are popular in Tokyo, and are located throughout the metropolis, including Shibuya, Harajuku and Shinjuku.

Sizes

Many Westerners find the clothing and shoes sold in Tokyo too small to fit Western bodies. If you require sizes larger than those readily available, you may want to pack a supply from home and then supplement that by shopping when traveling outside Japan. You can also try foreign-brand shops in Tokyo and the "large size" corners in Japanese department stores.

Comparison of Japanese, American and European Sizes

Women's Clothing

Japanese	7	9	11	13
American	4	6	8	10
English	6	8	10	12
Continental	36	38	40	42

Men's Clothing

Japanese	S	M	L	LL
American	34	36	38	40
English	34	36	38	40
Continental	44	46	48	50

Women's Shoes

Japanese	22.5	23	23.5	24
American	5.5	6	6.5	7
English	4	4.5	5	5.5
Continental	35	36	37	38

Men's Shoes

Japanese	25.5	26	26.5	27
American	8	8.5	9	9.5
English	6	7	8	9
Continental	40	41	42	42.5

Household Items

Most household goods (such as linens, tableware, and bathroom items) are available at department stores, but you can probably save money by shopping at large supermarkets or neighborhood shops. For a wide variety of reasonably priced kitchen utensils, go to Kappabashi (near the Asakusa area), where wholesale stores for kitchen items are located. You can even buy the plastic models of foods displayed at restaurants' entrances – while expensive, the *sushi* samples make good souvenirs.

Tokyu Hands specializes in household goods and items for home improvement and repairs. Here you can hire contractors to renovate your home for you. They also carry products for a variety of hobbies such as gardening, knitting, and crafts. The five main branches in Tokyo are in Shibuya, Shinjuku, Ikebukuro, Futako Tamagawa, and Machida.

Furniture

Nowadays most Tokyo residents use Western-style furniture, or a combination of Western and Japanese styles. The designs and colors of the Western-style furniture sold in Tokyo may not suit Western tastes, however. Many Japanese people prefer furniture with simple designs and in bland colors, so that it will blend in with other items in their homes. Furniture sold in Japan are smaller and shorter than those manufactured overseas, to fit the smaller-sized Japanese and their cramped homes. Out of necessity, Westerners in Japan often buy imported furniture.

Some department stores have furniture corners. While their inventories may be limited, by visiting a few you can get an idea of design, size, and price. There are also a few large furniture stores in Tokyo, of which IDC Otsuka (**http://www.idc-otsuka.co.jp**) has the largest interior showroom in Japan. In addition to furniture manufactured locally, it also carries an extensive inventory of American and European furniture. Considering the transportation and insurance costs of importing your own furniture, the imported furniture at IDC Otsuka is priced fairly reasonably. Several individual shops also sell specific brands of imported furniture.

Foreigners who are in Tokyo for only a short time can rent furniture through furniture leasing stores; most of these stores give customers the option of purchasing rented furniture at a reasonable price should they want to take it back to their home countries later. Relocation companies or real estate agents can often recommend leasing stores. Classified advertisements on furniture shops and leasing stores appear regularly in English-language newspapers and magazines, and in the NTT TOWNPAGE telephone directory.

Electronics

The quality and versatility of Japanese electronic appliances for the home is unbeatable. The high-tech appliances used in the course of daily life are amazing and include cordless irons and vacuum cleaners, and refrigerators that alert owners when the doors are open for too long. Like other products in Japan, electronic appliances cost more than in many other countries. Still, considering all the functions and the durability of the products, they may not turn out to be as expensive as they seem.

Akihabara is the place to go for reasonably priced electronic appliances and computers. In this district, there are more than 600 shops selling a variety of electronic products. The prices are

Photo by Yuko Morimoto-Yoshida

Busy shopping street in Akihabara Electric Town.

20 to 30 per cent less than the suggested retail and you may be able to get further discounts by bargaining – unlike in other shops in Tokyo, you can and should bargain in the shops in Akihabara Because this district is frequented by tourists, sales clerks are accustomed to dealing with foreigners and may speak some English.

There are also several discount electronics shops in major shopping districts (Shibuya, Shinjuku, and Ikebukuro, for example). Shops such as Yodobashi Camera, Sakuraya Camera, and BIG Camera, all carry a variety of electronic products (not just cameras!) at prices lower than those in department stores.

FOREIGN READING MATERIALS

Foreign books, magazines and newspapers are generally expensive due to the cost in importing them. Most major bookstores have a section featuring foreign reading materials. One of the largest, Kinokuniya, has materials in English and other languages. Listed below are some bookstores that carry foreign language books:.

Book 1st
33-5 Udagawa-cho, Shibuya-ku, Tokyo 150-0042
Tel: 03-3770-1023
Fiona Bookstore
5-41-5 Okusawa, Setagaya-ku, Tokyo 158-0083
Tel: 03-3721-8186
Foreign Books BIBLOS
1-26-5 Takadanobaba, Shinjuku-ku, Tokyo 169-0075
Tel: 03-3200-4531
Kinokuniya
Takashimaya Times Square, 5-24-2, Sendagaya, Shibuya-ku, Tokyo 151-0051
Tel: 03-5361-3301; **http://www.kinokuniya.co.jp**
There is another large branch in Eastern Shinjuku, and many smaller stores around Tokyo.
Maruzen
2-3-10 Nihombashi, Chuo-ku, Tokyo 103-0027
Tel: 03-3272-7211
Another store is located in Ochanomizu.
Tower Records
1-22-14 Jinnan, Shibuya-ku, Tokyo 150-0041
Tel: 03-3496-3661
There are several other branches around Tokyo.
Yaesu Book Center
2-5-1 Yaesu, Chuo-ku, Tokyo 104-0028
Tel: 03-3281-1811

American books can also be ordered through the **Foreign Buyer's Club** (Tel: 078-857-9001; **http://www.fbcusa.com**).

Compact Disks

A boon for music lovers, large compact disc (CD) shops in Tokyo carry substantial collections of American, European, and Japanese music in a variety of genres. A CD manufactured in Japan will cost about 1,500 yen for a single and 3,000 yen for an album. The prices of imported CDs are generally lower because they do not include the lyrics or comments about the music that are included in Japanese CDs.

You will find large CD shops in major commercial areas such as Shibuya, Shinjuku, and Ikebukuro. Tower Records has a huge store housed in a seven-story building in Shibuya as well as smaller branches elsewhere. Other large CD shops include HMV, Shinseido, and Tsutaya; all have branches throughout Tokyo.

Toys

Most department stores have relatively large toy corners in which children enthusiastically congregate to play with the toy displays.

Pokémon, a story that had its origins in Japanese comics, is famous worldwide. If you have a child who is a big Pokémon fan, the Pokémon Center in Nihombashi (Tel: 03-5200-0707) is a must-go. The size of the shop is only about the size of a tennis court, but it carries a tremendous amount of Pokémon merchandise.

Computer games and video games are very popular among Japanese children. In addition to department stores and individual toy shops, many stores in Akihabara and electronics shops around major stations sell electronic toys.

Kiddy Land (Tel: 03-3409-3431) in Harajuku has been a very popular toy store for a long time. It carries Japanese-made and imported toys for children of all ages. Giant American toy store, Toys 'R' Us (**http://www.toysrus.co.jp**), now has more than 100 outlets in Japan, including several in Tokyo. In addition to toys, they sell children's clothing and nursery items.

Japanese Crafts and Antiques

Japanese crafts make good souvenirs for friends and are nice to keep as mementos of your time in Japan. One interesting craft is *washi*, or Japanese hand-made paper. Hundreds of different items can be made from *washi* and include lantern covers, umbrellas, notebooks, and letter paper. Many little shops on the street (Nakamise Dori) leading to the Sensoji Temple in Asakusa sell such paper products and other crafts. Isetatsu in Yanaka (close to Asakusa; Tel: 03-3823-1453) also carries a lot of paper products specially made with patterned prints. Kyukyo-do (Tel: 03-3571-4429) near the "Ginza 4-chome Crossing" is an old store (founded in 1663) specializing in Japanese paper products such as postcards, stationery, calendars, and folding fans.

Traditional Japanese toys make good gifts for children. Although Japanese kids nowadays play more often with computer games, they still play with some traditional toys. A popular one is *kendama*, a ball and wooden cup at the end of a handle. The cup and ball are tied together with string and children swing the ball and try to catch it in the cup. Another traditional toy is the wooden top (*koma*); children spin it by hand or with a heavy string. They compete with each other to see how fast they can spin their *koma*. Kites are still popular among some children; in addition to modern kites made of plastic, there are traditional kites made from Japanese paper featuring *Kabuki* (traditional Japanese theater) actors or other Japanese motifs. Some adults use them to decorate their homes as they are too valuable to fly!

Like the colorful kites, Japanese paddle-shaped fans (*hagoita*) make wonderful household decorations; they are intricately crafted using quilted cloth and feature *Kabuki* characters. (Children used to play with plain wooden paddles during the New Year holidays.) A *hagoita* market is held in December at Sensoji Temple in Asakusa. The prices can be quite high, but the fans are beautiful. You can find all of these traditional toys in shops on Nakamise Dori.

The Oriental Bazaar in Harajuku (Tel: 03-3400-3933) also carries a variety of Japanese crafts. This is the largest craft shop in Tokyo. It carries typical souvenir items such as paper products and cotton robes, as well as more expensive items such as swords, block prints, chinaware, and antique furniture.

Some department stores also have a Japanese crafts corner, selling items such as accessories, paper products, *kimono*, and table linen. Tablecloths and place mats made from Japanese fabrics are great for daily use and for souvenirs.

If you are into antiques, you will find many antique shops along Kotto Dori (meaning "Antique Street") in Aoyama. Items sold here can be very expensive. Visiting antique flea markets is a way of finding unique antiques at reasonable prices. They are usually held at shrines on Sundays. (Check with each of the shrines for their schedules.) You can bargain at these flea markets. The following are quite famous:

Togo Shrine *(Togo Jinja)*
1-5-3 Jingumae, Shibuya-ku, Tokyo 150-0001
Tel: 03-3403-3591
Nogi Shrine *(Nogi Jinja)*
8-11-27 Akasaka, Minato-ku, Tokyo 107-0052
Tel: 03-3478-3001
Hanazono Shrine *(Hanazono Jinja)*
5-17-3 Shinjuku, Shinjuku-ku, Tokyo 160-0022
Tel: 03-3200-3093

❖❖❖

Since the economic bubble burst in early 1990s, the number of discount shops and inexpensive items available for purchase has increased, making Tokyo more attractive for shoppers. At the same time, the number of expensive brand-name shops has also increased; people love to mix and match their discount-store T-shirts with luxurious items. Experiencing such contradictions adds pleasure to your shopping experience in the bazaar that is Tokyo.

— CHAPTER FOURTEEN —

ENJOYING YOUR LIFE IN TOKYO

A great advantage about living in Tokyo is that there are plenty of options for leisure: exploring historic sites, watching baseball games, trying out the latest electronic gadgets, enjoying a Kabuki performance, are just a few.

PLACES TO VISIT

In addition to places mentioned here, there are numerous interesting neighborhoods waiting to be discovered.

Old Tokyo

Asakusa and its surrounding areas such as Nezu and Yanaka are the best places to experience the ambience of old Tokyo. Asakusa was developed in the 17th century (Tokugawa Period) as the commercial area of the capital (then called Edo). The old buildings and traditional atmosphere reflect the area's historic past. The main landmark is Sensoji Temple, the oldest temple in Tokyo. Kaminari-mon, the main gate to the temple, features a huge red lantern and is a favorite spot for taking photos. **Nakamise Dori,** the street connecting the gate to the temple, is lined with hundreds of small shops offering a variety of souvenirs. Deep inside the temple's Main Hall is an original statue of Kannon, the Buddhist Goddess of Mercy (known in Chinese cultures as Kuan Yin). Although tourists are no longer allowed in that part of the temple, they toss coins as offering into a box outside the Main Hall and pray to the goddess for their happiness. Several festivals are held in Asakusa throughout the year – the most famous is Sanja Matsuri, held each May. Try to catch this festival, during which portable shrines are carried within the Asakusa district by groups of people in traditional costumes.

The many temples and shrines scattered throughout Tokyo also provide glimpses of the past. Generally, temples are Buddhist structures and shrines are Shinto (*Refer to* "Religion and

Photo by Shu Ikkatai.

The lively Sanja Festival in Asakusa.

267

Beliefs" *in Chapter 2*). Occasionally, you will find them where you least expect to, such as between, or even on top of, tall buildings. Their traditional architecture will take you back in time. In addition to Sensoji, interesting temples include Kiyomizu-do Kannon in Ueno, Kan-eiji in Uguisudani, and Zojoji in Hamamatsu-cho.

The **Meiji Shrine** in Harajuku, built in honor of the Meiji Emperor, is the most famous in Tokyo and the most visited on New Year's Day. The gate to the shrine is the largest wooden gate (*torii*) in Japan and the main building is an example of refined Shinto architecture. Although Harajuku tends to be noisy and chaotic due to its large concentration of youths, once you enter the shrine you will feel insulated from the outside world – dense woods around the shrine block out the sound of traffic, and the only "noise" to be heard are that of birds singing and footsteps on the stone-paved path. Other famous shrines include **Nezu Jinja** in Nezu, **Yushima Seido** in Yushima, and **Sanno-Hie Jinja** in Akasaka.

Tokyo's most prominent historical landmark is the **Imperial Palace (*kokyo*)**, located near Tokyo Station. It was at one time much larger and called Edo Castle, and served as the headquarters of the Tokugawa Shogunate (1603-1868); today it is the residence of the imperial family. The palace itself is new. Remnants of the old castle, including a few towers, gates, and part of the foundation, are still visible in Higashi Gyoen, a garden on the east side of the palace; the surrounding stone walls and moat, built to protect the castle from potential attacks, are also original. The palace is open to visitors only on New Year's Day and on the Emperor's birthday. On both days, the imperial family stands on the balcony to greet people. Standing in the center of the business district, the old stone walls provide a contrast to the modern office buildings, a reflection of Tokyo culture where the old co-exist with the new.

A comfortable way to visit many of Tokyo's landmarks is to take a **Hato Bus** tour. Hato Bus offers a few different guided tours in English, covering major sights in Tokyo, including historical sites. Call Hato Bus (Tel: 03-3435-6081;**http://www.hatobus.co.jp**) for more information.

Vista Points

The observatory deck in the **Tokyo Metropolitan Government Office** in Shinjuku offers spectacular 360-degree views of Tokyo and the surrounding area; on a clear day you can even see Mount Fuji. (The Metropolitan Government Office buildings were designed by the world renowned architect Kenzo Tange.) This part of Shinjuku, with its magnificent skyscrapers, is the center of modern Tokyo. The observatory deck on the top floor of the 60-story **Sunshine City 60** in Ikebukuro, with its shops, restaurants and a magnificent vista of the city, is also worth a visit. Before these superstructures existed, the **Tokyo Tower** in Shibakoen was the most popular observation spot. Built in 1958 and modeled after the Eiffel Tower in Paris, it is still included in city tour itineraries and is usually crowded with tourists.

Photo by Chihoko Tanefusa.

The Skyscrapers of the Tokyo Metropolitan Government Office in Shinjuku seen from a children's park.

269

Tsukiji Fish Market

This wholesale fish market is the largest of its kind in Japan, where fish from all over the world gets auctioned off. Although visitors cannot join the auction, they can observe the auctioneers running through the market stalls that overflow with the day's catch. Bidding begins around 3 a.m. and most activities end by 5 a.m.

Many restaurants in the market's vicinity serve breakfast to those attending the auction (including tourists). This is probably the only place in Tokyo where you can have *sushi* for breakfast, and the experience is well worth rising early. You can also buy fresh seafood at the fish shops located here; while the retail price is not much different from that charged elsewhere, the quality is better. This is a fun place to take visiting friends and family.

Waterfront Area

Odaiba is a new area developed on reclaimed land in Tokyo Bay. In addition to the office buildings, which themselves are worth seeing for their contemporary designs, Odaiba offers various at-

Photo by Hikaru Kobayashi.

Rainbow Bridge over Tokyo Bay.

tractions for both adults and children: strolling on the boardwalk that runs along the bay, and an amusement park for kids. Several good restaurants are located in the shopping complexes and nice hotels overlook the bay. One indoor mall, Venus Fort, gives shoppers the impression that they are outside, because its ceiling is painted to resemble the sky, complete with clouds. Visitors driving to Odaiba at night will cross a vividly illuminated **Rainbow Bridge**.

Shopping Districts
(Refer to Chapter 13 for more information).

Parks and Gardens
Tokyo has several parks and gardens where residents can escape from the crowds and the hustle and bustle of the city.

Ueno Park in the Ueno area is one of the Tokyo's largest parks and is famous for its breathtaking blooms of cherry blossoms in spring; during this season, people enjoy picnics both day and night in the park. It also offers other attractions such as a zoo (famous for its giant panda) and museums.

Yoyogi Park, located next to the Meiji Shrine in Harajuku, has a nice picnic area and a large field where children can play ball games. It features a jogging track and a bicycling course, and has bicycles for rent. Shinjuku Gyoen Garden and Shinjuku Central Park are two oases found in the midst of the busy Shinjuku area. Hama Rikyu Garden in Shimbashi and Koishikawa Korakuen Garden in Koishikawa are beautiful Japanese-style gardens. Higashi Gyoen in the Imperial Palace consists of a Japanese style garden and a Western style garden filled with beautiful flowers such as irises and azaleas.

Art Museums
The following is a list of some of the most prominent art museums in Tokyo. For descriptions of other types of museums, refer to the

section about museums in Chapter 10.

Bridgestone Museum of Art *(Burijiɗuton Bijutɗukan)*
1-10-1 Kyobashi, Chuo-ku, Tokyo 104-0031
Tel: 03-3563-0241
This small, private museum displays a wonderful collection of Impressionist (Corot, Monet, Degas, Manet, Renoir, Cézanne, etc.) and post-Impressionist (Gauguin, Van Gogh, Matisse, Picasso, etc.) paintings, as well as Western-style paintings by Japanese artists (Saeki Yuzo, Fujita Tsuguharu, etc.)

Isetan Art Museum *(Iɗetan Bijutɗukan)*
3-14-1 Shinjuku, Shinjuku-ku, Tokyo 160-0062
Tel: 03-3352-1111
Conveniently located in the Isetan Department Store in Shinjuku, this museum hosts temporary exhibitions of internationally acclaimed artists.

Museum of Contemporary Art Tokyo *(Tokyo-to Genɗai Bijutɗukan)*
4-1-1 Miyoshi, Koto-ku, Tokyo 135-0022
Tel: 03-5245-4111
This museum specializes in contemporary art works, mainly post-World War II, by both Western and Japanese artists.

National Museum of Modern Art *(Kokuritɗu Kinɗai Bijutɗukan)*
3-1 Kitanomaru Koen, Chiyoda-ku, Tokyo 102-8322
Tel: 03-3214-2561
Reopened in January 2002 after more than two years of renovation, Japan's first national art museum showcases a large collection of modern Japanese art, and also hosts temporary exhibitions of works byWestern artists.

National Museum of Western Art *(Kokuritɗu Seiyo Bijutɗukan)*
7-7 Ueno Koen, Taito-ku, Tokyo 110-0007
Tel: 03-3828-5131

Th only museum in Japan to exclusively display Western art, its permanent collection includes the works of French painters (such as Delacroix, Courbet, Renoir, and Monet) and sculptures by Auguste Rodin. It also holds temporary exhibitions by Western artists from different periods.

ENTERTAINMENT

Television and Radio
(*Refer to* "Television and Radio" *in Chapter 5.*)

Rental Videos
Renting videos is very popular in Japan, with at least one or two rental shops near train stations in almost every neighborhood. You can rent videos and DVDs of Japanese movies as well as of American and European films with Japanese subtitles. The American Club also rents American movies and television shows to members.

Movies
Major movie theaters offer Japanese films as well as American movies subtitled in Japanese. Popular American movies are released in Tokyo at the same time as in the United States; others are shown a few months later. Several smaller theaters specialize in presenting movies from Europe and other parts of the world.

Movie-going in Tokyo is rather expensive – adult admission to most theaters is 1,800 yen, but discounts are often available for students, children, and senior citizens. Every Wednesday is "Ladies' Day" when women can watch movies for 1,000 yen. Also, the first day of every month is "Movie Discount Day", when admission is 1,000 yen for all adults. Advance tickets are also sold at a discount, and these are obtainable at the theater ticket office, network ticket counters, and some convenience stores.

Theaters and Concerts

Tokyo has more than 150 theaters and concert halls showcasing domestic and foreign performing arts, including operas, ballets, modern dance performances, and modern and classical concerts. Large concert halls, such as the Tokyo Dome, Budokan, and Tokyo International Forum, host the big names in popular music. Mid-sized venues (capacity of 1,000 or so), including the Liquid Room in Shinjuku and On Air in Shibuya, entertains domestic and foreign pop or rock acts. Classical concerts, operas, and dance performances are often held at the Orchard Hall, Suntory Hall, Tokyo Opera City, and Ueno Bunka Kaikan.

Jazz is performed at the Blue Note, a branch of the famous jazz club in New York, and at.numerous less expensive jazz clubs around the city, notably the Shinjuku Pit Inn, where one can often hear more cutting-edge jazz and improvised music. Otherwise, there are countless small venues (called "live houses") featuring live music of every type scattered throughout the city, with large concentrations of them in Shimokitazawa and Shinjuku.

News on upcoming concerts and performances are published in English-language newspapers and magazines such as the *Tokyo Metropolis* (**http://www.metropolis.co.jp**) and the *Tokyo Journal* (**http://www.tokyo.to**). However, these listings are relatively brief and generally cover only the biggest attractions. Many people interested in the local music scenes get their upcoming concert information from flyers or posters (called *chirashi*) which are usually distributed at live houses and music stores throughout the city. Tickets for many performances are sold at outlets such as **Ticket Pia** (Tel: 03-5237-9999), **Lawson Ticket** (Tel: 03-5537-9999), and **CN Playguide** (Tel: 03-5802-9999). Unfortunately, most of these outlets offer information in Japanese only over the phone; try visiting their offices instead, some employees may be able to assist non-Japanese speaking patrons.

Karaoke

Karaoke (literally "empty orchestra") began in Japan and has recently become popular in other countries. Groups of friends or colleagues often go to *karaoke* spots after dinner. The experience encourages interaction in a casual atmosphere and allows individuals to express their hidden talents. (People are often surprised to find a quiet colleague transformed into a great singer!)

There are two types of *karaoke* clubs: "*karaoke* boxes" and "*karaoke* bars". The former type are private rooms with *karaoke* equipment that can be reserved by a group of people, and allow friends and colleagues to choose and sing their own songs. *Karaoke* bars are regular bars that have a small stage and *karaoke* equipment; guests go up on the stage to sing. Some smaller karaoke bars often have no stage at all; customers simply pass the microphone around the room and sing from their seats. *Karaoke* boxes are generally more popular, because the prices are reasonable and people are not bothered by poor singers from other groups!

If Japanese colleagues or friends invite you to join them for *karaoke*, try your best to participate even if you cannot sing well. This will make others treat you as "part of the group". Many *karaoke* boxes and *karaoke* bars in Tokyo feature Western as well as Japanese songs.

STAYING ACTIVE

Tokyo offers fitness fans and sports enthusiasts a good variety of sporting options.

Sport Clubs

Apartments and offices in Tokyo generally do not have their own fitness facilities; instead, you have to join a fitness club or a sports club. Popular clubs with locations throughout Tokyo include the Nautilus Club, Tipness, and Do Sports. Most clubs have a gym with exercise machines and conduct classes such as aerobics. Some clubs also have indoor swimming pools.

While guests are sometimes allowed to use the facilities for a fee, it is usually cheaper over the long-run to become a member. Membership fees at a typical club range from 10,000 to 15,000 yen per month. Most clubs also charge a one-time application fee of 20,000 to 50,000 yen.

Many wards have sports facilities that residents can use at a very low cost – check with the ward office nearest your residence.

Jogging

As Tokyo streets are narrow and crowded, avid joggers seek out parks and quiet neighborhoods in which to run. One favorite venue is the promenade surrounding the Imperial Palace. Smack in the center of the business district, it attracts office workers in the early morning and at lunchtime. Another beautiful and peaceful place to jog is the path along the Tama River, on the border between Tokyo and Kanagawa Prefecture.

Golf

Golf has long been popular among Japanese businessmen and is also popular among women and young people. Few people play frequently, however, as few golf courses are located in Tokyo and visiting a course outside the metropolis can take two hours one way. Instead, golfers tend to practice at driving ranges in their neighborhoods. When the economy was good, golfing was very expensive (more than 20,000 yen for non-members) and most people played only when their company footed the bill as business entertainment. Since the economic downturn many golf courses have lowered prices (10,000 to 20,000 yen, with lunch).

Tennis

Tennis is very popular in Japan, especially among younger people.

Many students join school tennis teams when atteding high school or university. However, as there are more enthusiasts than courts in Tokyo, it can be difficult and expensive to reserve a court unless one belongs to a tennis club. As membership can be quite expensive, people often play tennis only when outside of Tokyo.

SPECTATOR SPORTS

Sumo wrestling, baseball, and soccer are the most popular spectator sports in Tokyo.

Sumo

This unique form of wrestling has been around in Japan since ancient times and is the official national sport. *Sumo* is a professional sport and wrestlers fight in tournaments held six times a year. Wrestlers are divided into several ranks, the highest is called *yokozuna,* and are promoted based on their tournament records.

All *sumo* wrestlers are men and, by Japanese standards, extraordinarily large in both height and weight. Most wrestlers are taller than 180 cm (just under six feet) and easily weigh over 100 kilograms (about 220 pounds). Their attire and the rituals followed have not changed much since ancient times. They grow their hair long and tie it into a topknot (*mage*) and wear a belt called *mawashi* when they wrestle; in daily life, they wear *kimono*.

The rules of *sumo* are easy to understand. Wrestlers fight by slapping, pushing, or throwing; a wrestler wins if his opponent steps out of the ring or puts his hand on the floor. A match lasts only one to two minutes, and often only a few seconds!

Sumo wrestlers follow several rituals before and after fighting, and every move has a certain meaning. They repeatedly raise their legs and stamp the ring in a ritual to crush evil spirits that may exist around the floor. They also throw a handful of salt into the wrestling area to cleanse the ring and eliminate bad spirits. These various rituals add to the enjoyment of watching *sumo*.

Sumo tournaments are broadcast on television in English on Channel 1 (NHK) and NHK satellite (for television sets with a bilingual function). For a real thrill, watch a tournament live at the Kokugikan (stadium) in Tokyo where three of the six tournaments take place (the other three are held in other parts of Japan). You can purchase tickets directly at the Kokugikan ticket office, or from ticket agents such as Ticket Pia (Tel: 03-5237-9977) and Lawson Ticket (Tel: 03-5537-9999). The most expensive seats, called *masu-seki*, are those closest to the ring; these tickets can be difficult to obtain because they are usually purchased by companies or patrons of the *sumo* wrestlers. Prices for ringside seats include food and drinks (served at the seats), as well as tournament souvenirs. Friends and colleagues in Tokyo will envy you greatly if you receive an invitation to sit near the ring during a *sumo* match.

Baseball

Imported from the United States, baseball has long been a popular sport in Japan. Professional baseball in Japan is divided into two leagues: the Central and the Pacific. Six teams in each league compete for the league title. League title winners then compete for the Japan series title. The Tokyo-based Yoimuri Giants has produced many star players and is the most popular team in Japan. During baseball season (April to October) games are televised almost every day. You can also catch the games at Tokyo Dome and Jingu Stadium; tickets are sold at the stadiums or from ticket agents such as Ticket Pia (Tel: 03-5237-9977) and CN Play Guide (Tel: 03-5802-9999).

Interest in the American baseball leagues has grown since the export of star Japanese players to the United States – American baseball matches featuring Japanese players are broadcast on Japanese television (mainly on NHK satellite).

High school baseball games are also popular with the Japanese public. Two tournaments are played each year; one in spring

and the other in summer. Winners of regional tournaments represent the prefecture to compete in a national tournament held at Koshien Stadium in Hyogo in western Japan. It is the dream of every high school baseball player to play at Koshien. Games are also broadcast on television.

Soccer

Professional soccer in Japan has a relatively short history. Established in 1993, the J-League currently has more than 10 teams in each division: the J-1 (major) and J-2 (minor), and soccer season stretches from March to November. Several teams are based in Tokyo and the surrounding prefectures, and they occasionally play at Kokuritsu Stadium in Tokyo and at stadiums in Chiba, Kanagawa, and Saitama.

Soccer fans are extremely enthusiastic. Both the players and their passionate fans regularly attract new viewers, especially young people. The recent World Cup 2002 co-hosted by Japan and Korea created a huge upsurge of interest in the sport as well. Tickets are available at each stadium and from ticket outlets.

279

EXPERIENCING JAPANESE CULTURE

Organizations catering to expatriates, such as the American Club (Tel: 03-3224-3687) and the Tokyo Union Church (Tel: 03-3400-0047), host various cultural activities, many of which are open to non-members as well. In addition, many wards and municipal districts sponsor cultural events and classes for foreigners on subjects such as Japanese language, cooking, and dancing.

Kabuki Theater

Kabuki is a famous Japanese traditional theatrical performance in which all the roles, both males and females, are performed by men. The actors' names are hereditary and in order to play major roles, actors must be born into certain families. Boys in Kabuki families are trained from a very young age by their fathers and grandfathers. The female roles have a peculiar charm and eroticism that female actresses might not be able to express; Kabuki actors study every detail of a woman's movements and may be more sensitive to some aspects of female behavior than women themselves are.

Kabuki performances depict stories about ordinary people, members of the court, and *samurai* (warriors) in old Japan. The dialogue is in a form different from that currently used in daily life, and is spoken to dramatic effect. Consequently, it is sometimes difficult even for Japanese people to understand. To help the audience follow the story, theaters rent out headphones and tape players with recordings in Japanese or English summarizing the plot. The colorful, elaborate costumes are also fascinating to watch.

Kabuki is mainly performed at Kabuki-za, a theater used exclusively for kabuki performances. The theater itself is a beautiful, old building conveniently located only a short walk from the Ginza area. Kabuki is also performed at the National Theater (*Kokuritsu Gekijo*). Ticket prices vary greatly, from around 1,000 to 16,000 yen, depending on seat location. Tickets can be purchased at the theaters or from ticket outlets such as Ticket Phone Shochiku (Tel 03-5565-6000), Ticket Pia (Tel 03-5237-9999), and CN Playguide (Tel 03-5802-9999). For people who just want a glimpse, Kabuki-za offers tickets for one act at reasonable rates; seats are on the third floor and offer a relatively good view.

Flower Arrangement (*Ikebana*)

The Japanese style of flower arrangement, known as *ikebana*, was developed in the 16th century and symbolizes harmony between nature and people. Because Japanese society appreciates the four seasons, flowers that best represent each season are used in the arrangements.

Currently, there are about 3,000 different schools of *ikebana*, the most famous are Ikenobo, Ohara, and Sogetsu. Each school has its own arrangement style and is very particular about how stems are cut, the kind of vases used, and the angle of the arrangement. Thus, in class, students are expected to follow the model arranged by the instructor rather than express their own creativity. After students master various styles created by the instructor, who is certified by an *ikebana* school, they are allowed to take that school's certification exam. Students need to pay to receive the certificate – a major source of funding for schools.

Japanese flower arrangement gives you an insight into Japanese culture, which values both patterns and forms. Japanese flower arrangement has gained popularity in the West and some *ikebana* schools have branched successfully overseas. At the same time, Western methods of flower arrangement with its fewer restrictions have become popular in Japan.

Several *ikebana* schools offer classes in English. Each class lasts one to two hours and costs 4,000 to 5,000 yen, including the cost of materials. Contact individual schools for details: Ikenobo (Tel: 03-3292-3071; Ohara (Tel: 03-3499-1200); and Sogetsu(Tel: 03-3408-1151). Tea Ceremony (*Sado*)

Introduced from China around the 12th century, the Japanese version of the tea ceremony was developed in the 16th century. During a tea ceremony, known as *sado*, the host or hostess follows an elaborate, prescribed ritual of pouring hot water over tea powder, stirring it and then offering it to the guest, who then ceremoniously receives the cup, rotates it, and drinks the tea. The essence of the tea ceremony is philosophical; through the rituals, people aim to achieve inner harmony, appreciate the beauty of their surroundings, and show care for others. In order to foster a relaxed inner state, talk is discouraged during the ceremony.

Tea cups and other tea-making equipment, as well as flowers and pictures in the room, must be carefully selected based on the season, occasion, and guest preferences. Tea ceremony hosts must master the rituals and develop an acute ability to show attentiveness to guests' needs. They must also acquire knowledge of and develop a discerning eye for many aspects of Japanese art and culture including flower arrangement, calligraphy, and pottery. Guests are expected to demonstrate understanding and appreciation of the ambience created meticulously by their hosts.

There are several *sado* schools in Japan. One of the most famous, Ura-senke, has been encouraging the practice of *sado* overseas and welcomes foreigners. Information is available in English by calling 075-451-8516 or through the website (**http://www.urasenke.or.jp**). Other famous schools include Omote-senke and Mushanokoji-senke.

Martial Arts (*Budo*)

Many martial arts such as *judo*, *kendo*, *karate*, and *aikido* had their origins in early Japan. Their purpose is not to defeat opponents, but to develop self-discipline that will contribute to mental and physical strength. All forms of martial arts stress highly on following decorum and showing respect for opponents.

Judo, a type of wrestling, is now famous worldwide and

an Olympic sport. *Judo* players are ranked on 10 levels (*dan*) according to their strength; the highest level is 10 *dan* and the lowest one *dan*. Kodokan Judo Hall is the headquarters of the All-Japan Judo Federation (Tel: 03-3818-4172). Here enthusiasts can receive instruction and watch others practice.

Kendo is a form of Japanese fencing using bamboo swords. It was originally a form of training in swordsmanship for *samurai* (warriors), now it is practiced by many schoolboys (and an increasing number of schoolgirls) to enhance their mental and physical strength. Call the Japan Kendo Foundation at 03-3211-5804.

Karate, a form of unarmed self-defense, originated in Okinawa (the southernmost island of Japan); it was developed after Okinawan people were not allowed to bear weapons. Masters of *karate* can break a stone block with only their bare hands. It is now an international sport. The Japan Karate Association (Tel: 03-5800-3291; **http://www.jka.ar.jp**) offers classes.

Aikido was developed in the early 20th century and combines the principles of *judo*, *kendo*, and *karate*. In *aikido*, *ki* (usually translated as "spirit" or "energy") plays an important role; players use *ki* rather than strength to throw opponents. The headquarters of the **International Aikido Federation** is Aikikai (Tel 03-3203-9236; http://www.aikikai.org).

Check the English-language phone directory *NTT TOWNPAGE* for information on private martial arts classes (some of which are taught in English).

Japanese Language Lessons

Living in Tokyo will be a much more rewarding experience if you can communicate in Japanese; it will be easier to find your way around, get information about events and activities, and participate in classes or gatherings. Also, as Japanese people tend to be more comfortable with foreigners who try to speak Japanese, regardless of fluency, it will be easier to develop long-lasting friendships.

Do not be put off by the complexity of the language. Mastering conversational Japanese is not difficulty with constant practice. The writing system can be a challenge, but the emphasis in many language schools is on speaking and listening.

There are several options available for studying Japanese, the most expensive being private lessons conducted by a language school in your home or office. Another option is private or group lessons conducted at a language school; benefits of group lessons are that they are generally cheaper and give you the opportunity to meet and interact with other foreigners.

The following is a short list of Japanese language schools in Tokyo. Additional information is available in English-language publications and the phone directory NTT TOWNPAGE.

Academy of Language Arts
2-16 Agebacho, Shinjuku-ku, Tokyo 162-0824
Tel: 03-3235-0071; **http://www.ala-japan.com**

ARC Academy Japanese Language School
1-9-1 Shibuya-ku, Tokyo 150-0002
Tel: 03-3409-0391; **http://www.arc.ac.jp**

Association for Japanese-Language Training (AJALT)
3-25-2 Toranomon, Minato-ku, Tokyo 105-0001
Tel: 03-3459-9620; **http://www.ajalt.org**

Japan Language Institute (JLI) *(Nichibei Kaiwa Gakuin)*
1-21 Yotsuya, Shinjuku-ku, Tokyo 160-0004
Tel: 03-3359-9600; **http://www.iec-nichibei.or.jp**

Kai Japanese Language School
1-15-18 Okubo, Shinjuku-ku, Tokyo 160-0072
Tel: 03-3205-1356; **http://www.kaij.co.jp**

Sendagaya Japanese Institute *(Sendagaya Nihongo Kyoiku Kenkyujo*
1-31-18 Takadanobaba, Shinjuku-ku, Tokyo 169-0075
Tel: 03-3232-6181; **http://www.jp-sji.org**

A less expensive approach is to attend classes conducted by

many ward or municipal offices for foreigners. Instructors are Japanese volunteers and classes generally meet a few times a week. As the price is low, there is usually a long waiting list. Check with the ward or municipal office nearest your residence for details.

Another inexpensive option is to use language exchange opportunities; many Japanese students and adults are willing to teach foreigners Japanese in exchange for instruction in English. While they might be unqualified as teachers, you will be able to practice conversational Japanese in an informal setting. Such partners are advertised in classified ads in English-language journals or newspapers and on bulletin boards in international supermarkets. At the same time, the English newspaper *Asahi Shimbun* reported that females advertising for language exchange partners or tutors have complained of unwanted sexual propositions and other forms of sexual harassment.

ADULT EDUCATION

Foreigners who want to study Japanese intensively or other subjects, can take classes offered in English at several universities.

Japanese Universities

International Christian University *(ICU/Kokusai Kirisutokyo Daigaku)*

3-10 Osawa, Mitaka-shi, Tokyo 181-0015

Tel: 0422-33-3131; **http://www.icu.ac.jp**

ICU offers a liberal arts education in both Japanese and English, including summer courses on Japanese language and culture. Foreigners are required to take intensive Japanese language classes.

Sophia University *(Jochi Daigaku)*

7-1 Kioi-cho, Chiyoda-ku, Tokyo 102-8554

Tel: 03-3238-3111; **http://www.sophia.ac.jp**

All classes, except Japanese language classes, in Sophia's

Faculty of Comparative Culture are taught in English. Its Japanese Language Institute offers a two-year program for foreigners wishing to master the Japanese language.

National Graduate Institute for Policy Studies (GRIPS/ *Seisaku Kenkyu Daigakuin Daigaku*)
2-2 Wakamatsu-cho, Shinjuku-ku, Tokyo 162-0056
Tel: 03-3341-0489; **http://www.grips.ac.jp**
Courses on areas such as public policy, economics, public finance and leadership are offered in English.

TRAVELING BEYOND TOKYO

Areas outside of Tokyo offer a respite from the busy city life and a different perspective of the country. There are plenty of distinct and interesting places to visit, the most famous of which, for both Japanese people and foreigners, is the historic city of Kyoto. In addition to old cities, Japan also has beaches (Okinawa), summer hideaways (Hokkaido) and winter fun (Nagano, Niigata, etc.),

Photo by Chihoko Tanefusa.

Mount Fuji towers over the quiet hills of Shizuoka Prefecture, a few hours' train trip from Tokyo.

hot springs (*onsen*) and other exciting places.

Traveling outside of Tokyo can be an eye-opening and educational experience: there are fewer signs or information boards in English than in Tokyo; Japanese people outside of Tokyo interact less frequently with foreigners and may be less proficient in English, so they might initially be reluctant to interact with you and may wave their hands in bafflement; and you may also find some people staring openly at you, usually out of a naïve curiosity. Nevertheless, you will probably find that most people are polite and hospitable and willing to offer you assistance.

Travel Seasons

The busiest periods for traveling are: the New Years holidays (end December to early January); Golden Week (end April to early May); and the *Obon* Festival (middle August) when many people return to their hometowns. In addition, people like to take short trips during the period between mid-September and early November when the weather is nice. If you plan to travel during any of these times, to avoid disappointment, make reservations for transportation and accommodations far in advance; tickets sell out quickly and accommodations increase in price. If you are planning to travel by car, keep in mind that major highways will be so congested that you may get stuck in traffic for several hours. (Take along beverages, snacks, toys, and games for children.)

Transportation

The public transportation system is generally well developed throughout the country; most people prefer to take public transport than to endure driving in heavy traffic and high gas prices.

Trains

Trains are by far the most popular mode of transportation for domestic travel. Most long-distance trains are operated by the Japan

Railway (JR) Group. In addition to regular trains, JR operates *shinkansen* (bullet trains), which rank among the fastest trains in the world. *Shinkansen* routes connect most major points in the country. The Tokaido & Sanyo Shinkansen Line covers routes west and south of Tokyo; from Tokyo Station, it runs through Nagoya, Kyoto, Osaka, Okayama, Hiroshima, and on to Hakata and Kagoshima on Kyushu Island. The Tohoku/Yamagata/Akita Shinkansen Line covers the northern parts of Japan; from Tokyo Station, it goes to Fukushima, Zao, Sendai, Morioka, Yamagata and Akita, while its Jyoetsu/Nagano line covers Nagano and Niigata. *Shinkansen* trips can be rather expensive, but to many people the time saved traveling and comfort are worth it.

One pleasure of train travel i the *eki ben*, or boxed lunches sold in the stations. (*Eki ben* literally means "station boxed lunch".) Different stations sell different types of boxed lunches featuring local food. People buy *eki ben* when the train makes a stop, or on the train itself (especially on *shinkansen* or express trains).

Tickets for bullet trains and other local trains can be purchased at Midori no Madoguchi ticket windows operated by JR. As the staff may not speak English, it is a good idea to ask a Japanese friend to assist you with the process, or ask a Japanese friend (or hotel concierge) to write down the details of your journey (date, destination, class of service, number of tickets, etc.) in Japanese and present them to the JR staff. A third option is to write down the details in English, as many Japanese people who do not speak English can read it relatively well. Midori no Madoguchi offices are located in major JR stations in Tokyo (such as Shinjuku, Shibuya, and Tokyo). You can also purchase tickets through travel agencies.

Airplanes

Flights are available to major cities and towns throughout the country. Flying to distant points such as Hokkaido or Kyushu is faster than taking the *shinkansen*, although the cost is usually higher.

However, competition on some routes have led airline companies to offer discount prices that are cheaper than *shinkansen* tickets. Tickets can be bought through airline companies and travel agencies. Domestic flights from Tokyo depart from Haneda Airport as well as from Narita Airport. The major airlines are Japan Airlines (JAL), Japan Air System (JAS) and All Nippon Airways (ANA).

Long-Distance Buses

JR and other railroad companies such as Tokyu, Keio and Odakyu offer long-distance bus services. These used to be limited to night travel but some companies now offer day services. The popular Tokyo to Osaka route takes about eight hours (as opposed to three hours by *shinkansen* and one hour by plane), but the cost is about one third that of the *shinkansen*. The good news for budget-seekers is that the buses have reclining seats and the ride is quite comfortable. Several buses run to ski resorts in northern Japan and are frequently used by young people. Buses leave from major stations such as Tokyo Shinjuku and Ikebukuro, and tickets are available at bus companies or travel agencies.

Rental Cars

(*Refer to* "Renting a Car" *in Chapter 6.*)

Accommodations

Various types of accommodations are available to suit different needs and budget, although the cost is generally quite high in Japan. Beware that prices are usually quoted per person and not per room, not including tax (and sometimes service charges).

You can find Western-style hotels in major tourist destinations; many offer both Western-style and Japanese-style rooms. In Japanese-style rooms, straw mats (*tatami*) cover the floor and guests are supposed to remove their shoes when they enter. Guests sleep on the floor in Japanese-style bedding (generally consisting of a padded mattress, a down cover, and a pillow) stored in the closet during the day. When making reservations, specify whether you want a Western room or a Japanese room. The price per person starts at around 10,000 yen; the nicer hotels often cost more than 30,000 yen. Breakfast is sometimes included in the price.

All the rooms in traditional Japanese inns, called *ryokan*, are Japanese style, and as they generally do not have restaurants, meals are served in the guest rooms. Menus feature typical Japanese food made from local produce. Guests are provided with *yukata* (simple cotton *kimono*) which most people wear as pajamas and when walking around the hotel. You will find *ryokan* mainly located near hot springs (*onsen*). The prices are similar to that of hotels, but the total cost of a night in a *ryokan* may be less because breakfast and dinner are generally included in the price.

For budget accommodations, try *Kokumin Shukusha*, or government-sponsored lodgings located across the country. They are not luxurious, but are quite comfortable. The price is around 5,000 yen per night and usually includes breakfast. Reservations can be made through travel agencies. Youth hostels are yet another budget option. Some require membership in the International Youth Hostel Federation. You can become a member in Tokyo – contact the Tokyo Youth Hostel Federation for membership and reservations (Tel: 03-3261-0191; **http://www.jyh.or.jp**).

You can also save money by staying at *minshuku* (boarding houses) or pensions run by private owners. Staying at a *minshuku* is like staying in the spare room of a Japanese home. Housekeeping service and sometimes meals are not provided, but prices can be as low as 3,000 yen per night. More upscale than *minshuku* are pensions, which are Western-style petite hotels – many offer recreational facilities such as tennis courts, and most serve homemade breakfasts and dinners. The price (including the two meals) ranges from 5,000 to over 10,000 yen, depending on the facilities. Both

290

minshuku and pensions can be booked through travel agencies. For specific information about *minshuku*, contact the Japan Minshuku Center (Tel 03-3216-6556; http://www.koyado.net.

Travel Agencies

Travel agencies offer a variety of packages that include both transportation and accommodations. Tell the travel agent where you want to go and your hotel of choice, and ask if a package deal is available. If not, they can book transportation and accommodations separately. Travel agencies in Japan are very influential and it is often easier to book a popular hotel through an agency than to do so on your own.

JTB (Japan Travel Bureau) and Kinki Nippon Tourists are major Japanese travel agencies with experience in servicing foreigners. Both have many offices in Tokyo.

Japan Travel Bureau (JTB)
Tel: 03-5620-9500
Kinki Nippon Tourist
Tel: 03-3263-5522; http://www.kintetsu.com

In addition, HIS is a relatively new company known for offering discount tickets and packages. Agents may not be fluent in English, but they are still worth a try (Shinjuku Office – Tel: 03-5360-4910; Shibuya Office – Tel: 03-3496-9560).

The **Tourist Information Center (TIC)** (Tel: 03-3201-3331) offers assistance and information to foreign travelers for free. It is affiliated with the Japan National Tourist Organization and their website (http://www.jnto.go.jp) offers many useful travel tips. Travel agencies that serve the foreign community can be found in classified advertisements in English-language media and also in the phone directory NTT TOWNPAGE. (Refer to the "English-language Information Resources" in the Appendices.)

One-Day Trips from Tokyo

In the vicinity of Tokyo are cities and towns with distinctive characteristics and they make wonderful weekends getaways.

Yokohama

The city of Yokohama is located just to the west of Tokyo, less than an hour train ride away. The JR Keihin Tohoku, JR Yokosuka and JR Tokaido Lines, as well as the Tokyu Toyoko and Keihin Kyuko Lines, all run to Yokohama from Tokyo. Many Yokohama residents commute daily to their Tokyo work places.

Yokohama's ambience and culture are very different from that in Tokyo. Facing the Pacific Ocean, Yokohama has been the country's most important port for international trade since the start of the Meiji Period (mid-19th century), when Japan opened its doors to foreigners after more than 200 years of isolation. As such, Yokohama was influenced by the West and at one time hosted a large foreign community. Consequently, the city is more open to other cultures and has a cosmopolitan atmosphere.

A place you should visit is the **Yamate** area, which used to be a settlement for foreign residents – the exotic charm of days gone by still lingers. Several churches and Western-style buildings used by the foreigners still exist, as does a foreigners' cemetery in which more than 4,000 people were buried. **Motomachi Street**, the fashion street that used to serve the foreign community, still has many boutiques carrying imported goods. You will also find several European bakeries and coffee shops in this neighborhood. Another area that contributes to the city's exotic flavor is **Chinatown**. With hundreds of shops and restaurants, this is the largest Chinatown in Japan.

The city continues to evolve. As part of an urban development project called **Minato Mirai 21** (usually translated as "Future of the Port 21"), the city has built new office buildings, hotels, museums, a convention facility, shopping malls and an amusement park, all on reclaimed land. The project is ongoing and the city's goal is to build a multi-faceted, international city of the future for business, culture, and leisure. At the center of the district is Landmark Tower. The tallest building in Japan, it has 70 floors and is occupied by offices, a hotel, conference halls, and shopping areas. From the Sky Garden observatory on the 69th floor, you can enjoy a splendid view of Yokohama, Tokyo, Miura Peninsula, Boso Peninsula, and on a clear day, even Mount Fuji. The nighttime view of the surrounding areas is breathtaking. Other attractions in this area are Yokohama Cosmo World amusement park (Tel: 045-641-6591); the Maritime Museum (Tel: 045-221-0280), and the Yokohama Museum of Art (Tel: 045-221-0300).

The port and waterfront add to the city's lively atmosphere. You can stroll along the waterfront in **Yamashita Park**, watching the sail boats and enjoying the fresh sea breeze. The view of Yokohama Port from the **Bay Bridge** observatory is spectacular. This bridge, modeled after San Francisco's Bay Bridge, is the gateway to Yokohama Port. The observatory is part of a pedestrian walkway spanning the bridge. You can enjoy a view of the Bay Bridge itself from Yamashita Park and from **Harbor View Park** in the Yamate area.

Kamakura

Kamakura is an old city that flourished as the shogun's capital from 1192 to 1333. (See "The Feudal Period" in Chapter 2.) Today, 69 temples and 20 shrines built during that period remain. Kamakura is only an hour train ride from Tokyo on the JR Yokosuka Line. Upon arrival, you may feel that you have transported back in time; Kamakura derives its charm not only from its history but also from nature – mountains on three sides and the sea on one.

The major tourist attraction in Kamakura is the **Great Buddha**. This statue is 13 meters (37 feet) tall and has been in existence for more than 500 years. The face of the statue is very calm and divine, seemingly unaffected by the centuries of human activity.

Near the Great Buddha is the **Hase Temple** housing the 11-faced wooden Kannon (Goddess of Mercy) statue. At about nine meters (30 feet) high, this is the tallest wooden statue in Japan. The temple was built in the eighth century and the statue is believed to have been carved even earlier. The temple is located on a hill and offers a sweeping view of the sea.

After visiting these sites, take a ride on the **Eno-den**, a mini-tram that leaves from Kamakura Station. It runs on a very narrow track and passengers feel as if they are riding a miniature train in an amusement park. It is, however, actively used by local people, and there are many nice coffee shops and restaurants hidden in quiet residential areas along the line.

The **Tsurugaoka Hachiman Shrine** is also popular with tourists. It was built in 1063 by Minamoto Yoritomo, the head of the Minamoto clan that governed one of Japan's earliest shogunates. The path that leads to the main building is called Wakamiya Oji, and was selected as one of the "100 best pathways" in Japan. Cherry trees line this narrow lane, making it a great place to enjoy cherry blossoms in spring. Many shops along the way sell souvenirs and local crafts. One of the most famous souvenirs from Kamakura is *Kamakura-bori*, a style of wood carving used to create items such as trays, boxes and mirror frames.

Nikko

Nikko is located to the northwest and is about a two-hour train ride from Tokyo; take Tobu Line's Limited Express that leaves from Asakusa. The city is famous for the **Toshogu Shrine**, which is the mausoleum of Tokugawa Ieyasu. who unified Japan and founded the Tokugawa Shogunate in 1603 – it reigned for over 250 years. Tokugawa Ieyasu is considered one of the most important people in Japanese history. Tokugawa Iemitsu built Toshogu Shrine in 1636 to deify his grandfather.

Unlike most other shrines, which are simple in design and plain in decor, the Toshogu Shrine features a flamboyant architectural style and elaborate ornamentation. More than 15,000 craftsmen and artists were employed to create the carvings that decorate the shrine, many of which are colorfully painted and gold-leafed. Among the most famous is the "Three Monkeys" on the door of the stable. These monkeys are believed to protect the white horse, considered to be sacred, housed in the stable. One monkey has his hands covering his eyes, another has his hands on his ears, and the third has his hands over his mouth; the carving depicts the old saying "see no evil, hear no evil, speak no evil".

The shrine is located in a grove of ancient Japanese cedars. The cedar-lined road continues for 37 kilometers (about 23 miles) and today, 13,000 of the original trees, planted when the shrine was built in 1636, still stand.

Hakone

Located to the southwest of Tokyo, Hakone is a popular weekend getaway with its many attractions for people of all ages, including hiking, boating, golfing and museums. Above all, many people go to Hakone just to enjoy the clean air and relax in the hot springs.

The most popular way to get to Hakone is to take the Odakyu Express Line, also called the "Romance Car", from Shinjuku – alight at the final station, Hakone Yumoto. You can also take the JR *kodama* bullet train from Tokyo Station and get off at Odawara, then change to the Odakyu regular line and get off at Hakone Yumoto. The whole trip takes about a one-and-a-half hours.

From Hakone Yumoto, take the **Hakone Tozan Railway**, which climbs the hill up to Gora. The journey is about 15 kilometers (about nine miles) long and takes about 50 minutes. The ride through the mountains and forests is quite enjoyable – the view from the train is particularly nice in June when the hydrangeas are in bloom and in fall, when the leaves change colors.

There are a couple of places to visit on the way to Gora. You will find several nice hotels, *ryokan* (traditional inns), and places to eat around the Tonosawa and Miyanoshita stations. If you are interested in the arts, the **Hakone Open Museum**, with about 700 sculptures by Rodin, Moore, Miro and other 20th century artists, is a great place to spend a few hours. In addition, the Picasso Pavilion features more than 200 of the artist's works, and the Picture Gallery has paintings by Miro, Renoir and other artists.

From Gora, the **Hakone Tozan Cable Car** will take you to the top of the mountain known as Sounzan. On the way, you can visit the **Hakone Art Museum,** which features collections of Japanese pottery and ceramics, and a beautifully landscaped Japanese garden that is especially attractive in fall when the maple leaves change colors. A little teahouse in the garden offers Japanese tea and sweets.

To get up close and personal with nature, visit **Owakudani,** (literally, "big boiling valley"), where you can observe volcanic activities first-hand. To get there, take the **Hakone Ropeway** from Sounzan. When getting off the ropeway at Owakudani, you will notice a strong sulfur smell. Follow the short trail through the lava rocks and you will see steam erupting from deep in the ground.

If you have time, go further on the Hakone Ropeway to **Lake Ashi**. If the weather is clear when you descend the nountain on the ropeway, you may get a spectacular view of Mount Fuji. Lake Ashi was created by volcanic activity more than 2,000 years ago, and it has a circumference of approximately 19 kilometers (about 12 miles). Cross the lake on a Hakone Sightseeing Ship, from which the view of Mount Fuji can be magnificent.

Onsen (Hot Springs)

Onsen literally means "hot springs", which are veins of natural spring water that have been warmed by underground volcanic activity. Because Japan still has active volcanoes, thousands of

Photo by Chihoko Tanefusa.

An outdoor onsen (rotenburo) *in Nasu.*

hot springs are found across the country. The water of these springs contains minerals that are good for health; thus, in the past, people drank and soaked in *onsen* waters to cure diseases. Nowadays, people go to *onsen* for relaxation and recreation – there is nothing like soaking in a hot tub at the end of a day in the woods.

For Japanese people, who are accustomed to taking baths every night and love the moment when they dip themselves into hot water (especially during winter), *onsen* resorts and hotels are probably the most popular destination for domestic travel. They are favored not only for the hot mineral water but also for their many other attractions such as golfing, hiking and skiing.

Almost all hotels in *onsen* areas offer large communal baths (separate ones for men and women) filled with hot spring water. When using the communal baths, you have to follow protocol.

Take towels, clean underwear and whatever else you need when you shower. In the common space, take off your clothes and place them and your other belongings in the baskets provided. Next, take a small towel (or washcloth) and enter the bathing room. (Japanese people, especially women, use a small towel to

297

hide their private body parts.) Here, you will find showers and several small stools and wash bowls. Sit on a stool, fill a wash bowl with hot water from the nearest faucet, soak your towel in the bowl, and wash yourself with it or by splashing water from the bowl. Only then can you soak in the large tub. Although you can stay in the tub as long as you like, to avoid getting overcooked, you might want to get out after a few minutes, wash your body and/or shampoo, and then return to the tub. Most communal baths are open from very early in the morning until very late at night. Many people take several baths during the course of a day.

There are also outdoor baths at some *onsen* sites. These are usually hidden from public areas so that bathers do not need to worry about being watched by others. It is a wonderful experience to immerse in an outdoor tub under a starry sky.

In order to enjoy a total Japanese vacation, try staying at a *ryokan* (traditional inn) instead of a Western hotel when you visit an *onsen*. Meals featuring local ingredients will be served in your room, and both men and women wander around all day in *yukata* (simple cotton *kimono*) provided by the hotel. How more relaxing can life be?

There are about 2,800 *onsen* areas in Japan, including several (such as Hakone, Nikko, Atami, Izu, and Shimoda) that are within two to three hours' journey from Tokyo. Be sure to try an *onsen* at least once during your stay in Japan.

✳ ✳ ✳

The best way to reduce the stress of living in a foreign country and feeling homesick is to participate in the numerous exciting activities Tokyo has to offer. There is so much to see and do in Tokyo, that it is rare to hear anyone complain that life in Tokyo is boring! And when you need a short break, take the opportunity to explore the other fabulous cities nearby.

CULTURAL QUIZ

1. You recently moved to Tokyo. At your new apartment one of your Japanese neighbors greets you. He does not speak fluent English, but he seems interested to know you. He says, "My name is Miki". What is the appropriate way to address him?

a) Just call him Miki; it must be his given name if he mentions only one name.
b) Call him Miki-*san*.
c) Ask him whether Miki is his given name or family name, and ask how he wants to be addressed.
d) Call him Mr. Miki.

Japanese people usually address each other by their family (last) name plus "-*san*". They use the given (first) name only among family members and very close friends, and the family name with the suffix "-*san*" or other polite form of address. Thus, when only one name is provided during introductions, it is likely to be the family name. However, Japanese people who are knowledgeable about Western customs, might introduce themselves by their given name. Using the name plus "-*san*" is the safest course of action, as it can be used for both the given and the family name, and for both men and women. At some point, you should clarify whether "Miki" is his first or last name. Even if he asks you to call him "Miki", it is polite to address him as "Miki-*san*"; he will probably also appreciate your knowledge of this Japanese custom.

Answer(s): (b), (c) and (d) are all acceptable but (b) is the best.

2. You and your spouse are renting a house from a Japanese landlord. Since moving in, a couple of appliances have broken down,

and the dishwasher is now on the blink. You like the house but you frustrated that so many things need fixing. Each time a problem arise, you call the landlord who then hires contractors to fix the appliances. As the landlord does not speak English well, you have tried communicating with her in what litttle Japanese you know. This time she has not returned your calls even though you left two messages. What should you do?

a) Stay calm, explain the situation one more time and politely ask for help.
b) Raise your voice to show her you are frustrated and that you want the appliance fixed immediately.
c) Tell the landlord that you will hire a contractor yourself and charge it her later.
d) Ask a Japanese person to speak to her on your behalf; there might be a language problem.

In Japan, dealing with problems calmly and politely, even if you are very frustrated with the person, is the most effective way of solving the problem. Japanese people are put off by a show of anger as such behavior is considered immature and will harm the relationship. Getting a third person, such as a Japanese friend or colleague, to help is better than risking a direct conflict. That person might be able to interpret the situation from a Japanese cultural perspective, or clear the air over possible misunderstanding. There is also the possiblity the landlord has been away and did not received your messages.

Answer(s): (a) is the best response; (d) is an alternative.

3. You have come to know one of your Japanese neighbors quite well. She seems very open and friendly, and you are happy to have a Japanese friend. Your neighbor speaks English fluently

and helps you with your Japanese. One day, on the way to the train station, you see your neighbor with a Japanese person you have never met before. You stop to make small talk with your neighbor, but she does not introduce you to her friend. During the conversation, the other person stands a little behind your neighbor and never looks at you. You feel uncomfortable and wonder why your neighbor did not make introductions.

a) Your neighbor does not consider you as a friend.
b) Your neighbor does not think that you and her friend would meet again, and so does not bother with introductions.
c) Your neighbor's friend cannot speak English, so your neighbor does not want to make her friend uncomfortable.
d) Your neighbor thought that you and her friend would not get along well.

There are several possible explanations. Japanese people usually do not make introductions if they assume that the people involved will have no reason or chance to build a relationship – your neighbor probably assumed that you and her friend would never meet again. In addition, Japanese people tend to separate friends into groups based on factors such as age, background and common interests; thus your neighbor may see her friendship with you as different from that with her friend. Another possible reason is that Japanese people who are not used to interacting with foreigners can be shy and hesitant to communicate, even if the foreigners speak some Japanese. Your neighbor's friend avoided looking at you probably because in Japan, direct eye contact between people who have just met is considered rude (although you may experience people staring at you out of curiosity when you travel outside Tokyo).

Answer(s): Either (b), (c) or both are possible explanations.

4. You and your spouse have invited your Japanese colleagues to your home for drinks and dessert. Not knowing the guests' preferences, you have prepared a variety of both. When you ask your Japanese guests what they would like to drink, they look at each other and do not respond. Then, you tell them what kinds of drinks you have, and ask one of them what he wants. He says, "Anything is fine". When you ask the others, all gave a similar answer. Not knowing what is best, you serve everyone a glass of wine but realize that some are not drinking it. Next you list the desserts available. After a pause, a senior person mentions a preference, then everyone else asks for the same thing. You wonder why this is happening.

a) They all have the same tastes.
b) They do not know what to ask for.
c) The senior person has pressured everyone to request the same thing.
d) They feel that it is not polite to assert their preferences.

Japanese people generally feel that it is not polite to assert to a host their preferences and simply accept whatever is offered. If they must choose, they often select what others have requested because they do not want to trouble the host to serve different kinds of drink or food. Also, the person who chooses first is often the most senior, because Japanese people tend to observe the hierarchy even when away from the office. Hosts who genuinely want guests to state individual preferences should be persistent. In addition, they should offer food or drinks a few times, because Japanese guests tend to decline the first offer out of politeness.

Answer(s): The most likely explanation is (d).

5. Some time ago, you heard from a colleague that he and his wife were looking for an English-language teacher for their daughter, so you introduced the family to one of your friends. A couple of weeks later, you received a gift from the colleague who said, "It is just a little thing". However, when you opened the box you found a gorgeous Japanese doll. You feel uncomfortable about accepting such an expensive gift for such a small favor and are wondering what to do now.

a) Thank your colleague, but return the gift, telling him that you cannot accept such an expensive gift.
b) Thank your colleague, but do not do him any favors again.
c) Thank your colleague, telling him how much you liked the gift.
d) Thank your colleague, and give him something in return on a different occasion.

It is very common for Japanese people to offer gifts in return for favors. If the gift is an expensive one, it may indicate that the person really appreciated your favor. The best option is to accept it, because returning it would seriously hurt the feelings of that person and could damage the relationship. When Japanese people feel that a gift is very expensive, they sometimes give a present in return on a different occasion (for example, a souvenir from holiday).

Answer(s): c) is the best; d) is a possibility.

6. You are the manager of an engineering group at your company's Tokyo subsidiary. One of the Japanese engineers came up with a great idea that has significantly increased the productivity of the group. You want to acknowledge the performance of this young member and wonder what is the best way to do it.

a) Reward the group by taking them out to dinner and commending their increase in productivity.
b) Convey to the engineer through other Japanese members of the group, the message that you are happy with the performance.
c) Call the engineer into your office, and personally acknowledge the exemplary performance.
d) Praise this engineer in front of other group members.

Because Japanese people are group oriented, rewards are usually given to the entire group. Although to you it was the young engineer's idea, some form of teamwork could have taken place giving rise to the engineer the idea. Thus, giving him the reward might not be accepted well by group members. As your employees work for a foreign subsidiary, they might not expect the traditional Japanese management style, and might be willing to accept individual rewards. Even so, praising the engineer in front of the other members of the group would probably make him feel uncomfortable. It would be more culturally appropriate to use an indirect approach such as conveying praise through a third person (probably the senior group member, to show respect for the hierarchy within the group) or praising the engineer in an individual setting.

Answer(s): (a) is the best; (b) and (c) are possibilities.

CALENDAR OF FESTIVALS & HOLIDAYS

New Year's Day	January 1
Coming of Age Day	Second Monday of January
National Foundation Day	February 11
Vernal Equinox Day	March 21
Greenery Day	April 29
Constitution Memorial Day	May 3
People's Day	May 4
Children's Day	May 5
Marine Day	July 20
Respect for the Aged Day	September 15
Autumnal Equinox Day	September 23
Health Sports Day	Second Monday of October
Culture Day	November 3
Labor Thanksgiving Day	November 23
Emperor's Birthday	December 23

If any of these dates falls on a Sunday, the following Monday will be a holiday.

GLOSSARY

Numbers

One	*ichi*
Two	*ni*
Three	*san*
Four	*shi* or *yon*
Five	*go*
Six	*roku*
Seven	*shichi* or *nana*
Eight	*hachi*
Nine	*kyu*
Ten	*ju*

Greetings and Basic Phrases

Good morning.	*Ohayo gozaimasu.*
Good afternoon./Hello.	*Konnichiwa.*
Good evening.	*Konbanwa.*
Goodbye.	*Sayonara.*

See you later.	*Dewa mata.*
How are you?	*Ogenki desuka?*
Fine, thank you.	*Okagesamade genki desu.* (Literally it means "Owing to you, I am fine".)
How do you do?	*Hajimemashite.*
Pleased to meet you.	*Dozo yoroshiku onegai shimasu.* (Literally it means "Please take care of me".)
What is your name?	*(Anatano)* o-*namae wa nan desu ka?*
My name is _____.	*Watashi (no namae) wa* _____ *desu.*
Thank you.	*Arigato gozaimasu.*
You are welcome.	*Dohitashimashite.*
Excuse me./Sorry.	*Sumimasen.*
Do you speak English?	*Eigo wa hanashimasu ka?*
Yes.	*Hai.*
No.	*Iie.*
I do not understand Japanese.	*Nihongo wa wakarimasen.*
Please.	*Dozo.* (as in "Go ahead." or "Have some.")
Please.	*Onegai shimasu.* (when asking for something)
Please give me _____.	_____ *o kudasai.*

Getting Around

Train	*densha*
Subway	*chikatetsu*
Station	*eki*
Ticket	*kippu*
Bus	*basu*
Bus stop	*basu noriba*

Taxi	*takushi*
Right	*migi*
Left	*hidari*
Straight	*massugu*
Behind	*ushiro*
To _____, please.	_____ *made onegai shimasu.* (said to a taxi driver)
Where is _____?	_____ *wa doko desu ka?*
How can I get to _____?	_____ *e wa doh ikeba ii desu ka?*
How much is it to _____?	_____ *made ikura desu ka?*
How long does it take?	*Jikan wa donokurai kakari masu ka?*

Shopping

Vegetable shop	*yaoya*
Fruit shop	*kudamonoya*
Meat shop (butcher)	*nikuya*
Fish store	*sakanaya*
Bakery	*panya*
Bookstore	*honya*
Supermarket	*suhpah*
Department store	*depahto*
Convenience store	*konbini*
Cash	*genkin*
Change	*otsuri*
Credit card	*kurejitto kahdo*
How much is that (this)?	*Sore (kore) wa ikura desu ka?*
Please give me that (this) one.	*Sore (kore) o kudasai.*
Do you have _____ ?	_____ *wa arimasu ka?*
Do you have a smaller (larger) size?	*Motto chiisana (ohkina) saizu wa arimasu ka?*

Eating Out

Restaurant	*resutoran*
Menu	*menyuh*
Do you have a menu in English?	*Eigo no menyuh wa arimasu ka?*
_____, please.	*_____ o kudasai.*
What is that?	*Are wa nan desu ka?*
Do you have _____?	*_____wa arimasu ka?*
I cannot eat _____.	*_____wa taberaremasen.*
It is delicious.	*Kore wa oishii desu.*
Cheers!	*Kanpai!* (before drinking)
I humbly receive the meal.	*Itadakimasu.* (before (eating)
Thank you very much for the meal.	*Gochisoh sama deshita.* (after eating)
The bill, please.	*O-kanjoh-o onegai shimasu.*

Health Problems

Doctor	*isha* (Use *sensei*, when addressing the doctor.)
Hospital	*byohin*
Ambulance	*kyuhkyuhsha*
Pharmacy	*yakkyoku*
Medicine	*kusuri*
Pain killer	*itamidome no kusuri*
I have been injured.	*Kega o shimashita.*
I am bleeding.	*Shukketsu shiteimasu.*
I am feeling sick.	*Kibun ga warui desu.*
I have a fever.	*Netsu ga arimasu.*
It hurts.	*Itai desu.*

RESOURCE GUIDE

MEASUREMENT CONVERSION

Following are some conversions for the metric system, which is widely used in Japan.

Metric System		Other System
1 centimeter	=	0.39 inches
1 meter	=	3.3 feet/1.09 yards
1 kilometer	=	0.62 miles
100 grams	=	3.5 ounces
1 kilogram	=	2.2 pounds (lb)
1 liter	=	0.88 Imperial quarts/ 1.06 U.S. quarts

Other System		Metric System
1 inch	=	2.5 centimeters
1 feet	=	30 centimeters
1 yard	=	0.9 meters
1 mile	=	1.6 kilometers
1 ounce	=	28 grams
1 pound (lb)	=	450 grams
1 Imperial quart	=	1.14 liters
1 U.S. quart	=	0.95 liters

Centigrade/ Fahrenheit

~To convert degrees in Centigrade (the scale used in Japan) into Fahrenheit, multiply the Centigrade degree by 1.8 and add 32.
~To convert degrees in Fahrenheit into Centigrade, subtract 32 from the Fahrenheit degree and divide by 1.8.

INTERNATIONAL ORGANIZATIONS IN TOKYO

Following are the telephone numbers and website addresses of some international organizations in Tokyo.

Culture-Specific Organizations

Indian Community Activities Tokyo
03-3727-4419 (Fax)
http://www.manicat.org

Japan British Society
03-3211-8027

Jewish Community of Japan
03-3400-2559
http://www.jccjapan.or.jp

Philippine Women's League of Japan
03-3491-2408

Singapore Association in Japan (SAIJ)
03-3584-6032
(This is the number of the Embassy of the Republic Singapore. Ask for the telephone number of the current president of the SAIJ.)
http://groups.yahoo.com/group/saij

Tokyo American Club
03-3224-3687
http://www.tokyoamericanclub.org

Tokyo Canadian Club
03-5401-2454
http://www.tokyocanadianclub.com

Tokyo Japan Australia New Zealand Society	03-3590-8581

Professional Organizations

Foreign Correspondents' Club of Japan	03-3211-3161 http://www.fccj.or.jp
Foreign Executive Women	090-7216-5171 http://www.few.gol.com
Foreign Nurses Association in Japan	03-5469-0966

ENGLISH-LANGUAGE INFORMATION RESOURCES

English language resources available in Tokyo include directories, magazines, websites, and telephone counseling. Several are listed below.

Directories
NTT TOWNPAGE
This telephone directory in English is available for free at any NTT office or by calling (03) 3459-7511. The directory service is also available on the Internet at http://english.itp.ne.jp.
TELL Calendar
Published by Tokyo English Life Line, this calendar contains many useful contact numbers. To order call 03-3498-0261.
English-Language Magazines
The following are examples of magazines in English published in Tokyo; they are sold at major bookstores that offer foreign book sections. (Please refer to Chapter 13 for a list of bookstores.) Contents of these magazines include information about Japanese so-

ciety, current events, interviews with people, restaurant recommendations, and classified ads. The magazine websites also contain information on a wide variety of topics about life in Tokyo and Japan in general.

- **EL Magazine**
- *Hiragana Times* (http://www.hiraganatimes.com)
- *Japan Select Magazine* (http://www.jselect.net)
- *Metropolis* (http://www.metropolis.co.jp)
- *Tokyo Journal* (http://www.tokyo.to)
- *Tokyo Weekender* (http://www.weekender.co.jp) (free of charge)

Websites
Homepage of Tokyo Metropolitan Government:
   http://www.metro.tokyo.jp/index.htm
Comprehensive advice for general living matters in Tokyo is offered on this official website.
Japan Information Network: http://jin.jcic.or.jp
This website offers various useful resources such as maps, Japanese arts, statistics, and contact information, as well as a bulletin board.
Asia Xpat: http://Tokyo.asiaxpat.com
Information on a variety of topics for
expatriates living in Tokyo is provided.
Tokyo with Kids: http://www.tokyowithkids.com
Offers various types of information regarding child-care and children's education in Tokyo, along with discussion forum.

Telephone Counseling
Tokyo English Life Line (TELL):   Tel 03-5774-0992;
   http://www.telljp.com
Provides information and counseling on a variety of topics that

313

foreigners might encounter while living in Tokyo. Services are free of charge.

Japan Helpline: Tel 0990-53-8127; http://www.jhelp.com

Provides 24-hour counseling and advice over the telephone on topics ranging from simple questions to emergency situations. Their website also contains useful information and links to other websites.

Japan Hotline: Tel 03-3586-0110

Provides English-language counseling over the telephone concerning various aspects of life in Japan.

Foreign Residents' Advisory Center (Tokyo Metropolitan Government): Tel 03-5320-7744

Offers telephone or in-person appointments to provide information on a wide range of topics including daily life, traffic accidents, education and Japanese customs.

Photo by Chihoko Tanefusa.

Capsule hotels, a uniquely Japanese concept, rent out 'capsules' only to men at about 5,000 yen a night.

FURTHER READING

Daily Life

A Look Into Tokyo. (JTB's Illustrated Book Series Vol. 7). Tokyo: Japan Travel Bureau, 2001.

Being A Broad: Everything a Western Woman Needs to Survive and Thrive. Pover, Caroline. Tokyo: Alexandar Press, 2001.

Eating in Japan. (JTB's Illustrated Book Series Vol. 3). Tokyo: Japan Travel Bureau, 1987.

Japan for Kids: The Ultimate Guide for Parents and Their Children. Wiltshire, Diana and Huey, Jeanne. Tokyo: Kodansha International, 2000.

Japan Health Handbook. Maruyama, Meredith E.; Shimizu, Louise P., and Tsurumaki, Nancy S. Tokyo: Kodansha International, 1998.

Kid's Trips in Tokyo: A Family Guide to One-Day Outings. Maeda, Ivy; Kobe, Kitty; Ozeki, Cynthia; and Sato, Lyn. Tokyo: Kodansha International, 1998.

Little Adventures in Tokyo: 39 Thrills for the Urban Explorer. Kennedy, Rick. Berkeley, California, USA: Stone Bridge Press, 1998.

Living in Japan: Getting Closer to Japan. Para, Andy D. Tokyo: ASK, 2001.

Living in Japan. Tokyo: The American Chamber of Commerce in Japan, 2002.

Living Japanese Style. (JTB's Illustrated Book Series Vol. 2). Tokyo: Japan Travel Bureau, 1991.

Tokyo Finder: How to Live, Work and Play in the 21st Century. Sasaki, Rie; Ng, Tzyh; and Tsuchiya, Takemi, eds. New York: Y's Publishing, 2001.

Tokyo for Free. Pompian, Susan. Tokyo: Kodansha International, 1998.

Tokyo Living Guide. SOA Communications, ed. Tokyo: Yohan Publications, 1996.

Japanese Culture

A Look Into Japan. (JTB's Illustrated Book Series Vol. 1).Tokyo: Japan Travel Bureau, 1998.

Behind the Japanese Bow: An In-Depth Guide to Understanding and Predicting Japanese Behavior. De Mente, Boye L. Lincolnwood, Illinois, USA: Passport Books, 1995.

Discovering Cultural Japan: A Guide to Appreciating and Experiencing the Real Japan. De Mente, Boye L. Lincolnwood, Illinois, USA: Passport Books, 1995.

Festivals of Japan. (JTB's Illustrated Book Series Vol. 4). Tokyo: Japan Travel Bureau, 1987.

Japan As It Is. Tokyo: Gakken, 2001.

NTC's Dictionary of Japan's Cultural Code Words. De Mente, Boye L. Lincolnwood, Illinois, USA: NTC Publishing, 1997.

The New Japan: Debunking Seven Cultural Stereotypes. Matsumoto, David. Yarmouth, Maine, USA: Intercultural Press, 2002.

Who's Who of Japan. (JTB's Illustrated Book Series Vol. 9). Tokyo: Japan Travel Bureau, 1987.

Business

Doing Business with Japanese Men: A Women's Handbook. Brannen, Christalyn and Wilen, Tracy. Berkeley, California, USA: Stone Bridge Press, 1993.

Doing Business with the Japanese. Goldman, Alan. New York: State University of New York Press, 1994.

Doing Business with the New Japan. Hoggins, James D; Sano, Yoshihiro; Graham, John L.; Hodgson, James. Lanham, Maryland, USA: Rowman & Littlefield, 2000.

Going to Japan on Business: Protocol, Strategies, and Language for Corporate Traveler. Brannen, Christalyn. Berkeley, California, USA: Stone Bridge Press, 1997.

Hidden Differences: Doing Business with the Japanese. Hall, Edward T. and Hall, Mildred R. Garden City, New York, USA: Anchor Press/Doubleday, 1987.

How to Do Business with the Japanese: A Complete Guide to Japanese Customs and Business Practices. De Mente, Boye L. Lincolnwood, Illinois, USA: NTC Business Books, 1994.

On Track with the Japanese: A Case-by-Case Approach to Building Successful Relationships. Gercik, Patricia. New York: Kodansha America, 1996.

"Salaryman" in Japan. (JTB's Illustrated Book Series Vol. 8). Tokyo: Japan Travel Bureau, 1987.

The Japanese Negotiator: Subtlety and Strategy Beyond Western Logic. March, Robert M. Tokyo: Kodansha International, 1990.

Working For a Japanese Company: Insights into the Multicultural Workplace. March, Robert M. Tokyo: Kodansha International, 1996.

History

Japan: A Modern History. McClain, James L. New York: W.W. Norton & Company, 2001.

Japan: The Story of a Nation. Reischauer, Edwin O. Boston: WCB/McGraw-Hill, 1989.

The Japanese Experience: A Short History of Japan. Beasley, W.G. Berkeley, California, USA: University of California Press, 1999.

The Japanese Today: Change and Continuity. Reischauer, Edwin O. and Jansen, Marius B. Cambridge, Massachusetts, USA: Harvard University Press, 1995.

The Rise of Modern Japan. Beasley, W.G. New York: St. Martin's Press, 2000.

THE AUTHOR

 Yuko Morimoto-Yoshida is an intercultural business consultant and trainer. Born and raised in Tokyo, as a child she lived in Europe and Mexico with her family for a couple of years. Currently she resides in California and frequently goes back to Tokyo for work and to visit her family and friends.

While living in Tokyo, Ms. Morimoto-Yoshida worked in an international bank for more than ten years and interacted frequently with expatriates. This experience exposed her to the issues of cultural differences between foreigners and Japanese people and led her to pursue a career as an intercultural business consultant. Now living in the U.S., she enjoys the opportunity of observing the cultural differences from yet another perspective.

Ms. Morimoto-Yoshida holds a Masters' Degree in Speech and Communication from San Francisco State University. In addition to her native Japanese, she is fluent in English, and conversational in Spanish. She loves to travel and try cuisines from different parts of the world.

Her e-mail address is yukomor@earthlink.net.

INDEX